High Horse

High Horse

Contemporary Writing by the MFA Faculty
of Spalding University

Fleur-de-Lis Press ~ Louisville, Kentucky

Printed in the United States of America

First Printing

Library of Congress Cataloging-in Publication Data

Naslund, Sena Jeter and Driskell, Kathleen
High Horse: Contemporary Writing by the MFA Faculty of Spalding University
1. Title
Library of Congress Control Number: 2005921700

ISBN: 0-9652520-2-7

Cover design, interior design, and composition by Jonathan Weinert
Printing by Thomson-Shore of Michigan

Fleur-de-Lis Press of The Louisville Review Corp.
Spalding University
851 S. Fourth St.
Louisville, KY 40203
502.585.9911, ext. 2777

louisvillereview@spalding.edu www.louisvillereview.org

Contents

Poetry

Greg Pape

Fog 3

Some Guardian Spirit 3

Elegy for the Duke of Earl 4

Molly Peacock

Celtic Lady Sex Gargolye on Medieval Lintel 11

Of Night 12

Artichoke Heart 12

The Flaw 13

Jeanie Thompson

How to Enter the River 14

The Lyrical Trees 15

True Course 15

Poem at Fifty 16

Woman, This Body— 18

Richard Cecil

Twenty First Century Blues 19

Job's Advice 21
Lament for the Makers 23

KATHLEEN DRISKELL

Nativity 26
Leaving the Argument 27
Why I Mother You the Way I Do 28
To the Outdoor Wedding 29

DEBRA KANG DEAN

Lights, Please 30
Peeling an Onion 34
Beads 35

MAUREEN MOREHEAD

Fire 36
What Makes Things Move 37
The Window 38
The Interview 39

FICTION

SENA JETER NASLUND

from *Four Spirits, a Novel*
Helicon, September 15, 1963 45

MELISSA PRITCHARD

Port de Bras 50

ROBIN LIPPINCOTT

The 'I' Rejected 74

LOUELLA BRYANT

Uncharted Territory 81

ROY HOFFMAN

from *Chicken Dreaming Corn*
The Land of Cotton 92

JULIE BRICKMAN

from *An Empty Quarter*
Message from Aysha 106

LUKE WALLIN

Collecting Butterfish 111

MARY CLYDE

Krista Had a Treble Clef Rose 123

CONNIE MAY FOWLER

from *The Problem with Murmur Lee*
Charleston Rowena Mudd 137

BRAD WATSON

Bill 144

Neela Vaswani

The Pelvis Series 150

Kirby Gann

Disasters of the Catastrophic Kind 161

Mary Yukari Waters

The Way Love Works 182

Crystal Wilkinson

The Fight 197

Silas House

Saints 210

Creative Nonfiction

Dianne Aprile

from *The Eye Is Not Enough*
The Y of a Tree 223

Roy Hoffman

Witness to Change: Charles Moore, Photographer
of the Civil Rights Movement 226

Luke Wallin

River of Silence 236

Charles Gaines

Wendell Berry Profile and Interview 245

Molly Peacock

from *Paradise, Piece by Piece*
Two Short Excerpts 258

Robert Finch

Sometimes I Live in Town 260

Richard Goodman

Wings of Maine 275

Elaine Neil Orr

from *Gods of Noonday: A White Girl's African Life*
Green Like the Green Mamba 282

Writing for Children

Louella Bryant

ages 4-8
Great Gobs of Goose Grease 297

Luke Wallin

from *Ceremony of the Panther*
Grandfather Rattlesnake 298

SUSAN CAMPBELL BARTOLETTI

No Man's Land, Chapter One 307

PLAYWRITING & SCREENWRITING

SAM ZALUTSKY

SuperStore 315

CLAUDIA JOHNSON

Propinquity 334

FACULTY CONTRIBUTORS 349

PERMISSIONS 371

Editors' Notes

"Come down off your high horse," my mother used to tell me sometimes, in a smiling, teasing way. What did she mean? Perhaps that I felt just a little too good, too strong, too jaunty, too assertive, too full of myself. But still she seemed proud and pleased that I was up there.

We at the Spalding University brief-residency MFA in Writing Program often feel that we're riding high. Counting all the students, faculty, and staff, we had 167 people on campus at our most recent residency in late October 2004 to begin our biggest semester yet.

From all over the United States and several foreign countries, both students and faculty come here to study the writing of poetry, fiction, creative nonfiction, writing for children, and playwriting/screenwriting. We believe in writers focusing on an area of concentration but also reading and experimenting in other areas, too. We believe in studying writing in the context of the sister arts. This past October we all went to Actors Theatre to see *The Glass Menagerie* together; last semester we went to the Speed Art Museum here in Louisville, and soon we'll go to The Jazz Factory.

Even more important than our enriching outings, we as a faculty intend to nurture every individual talent by being both intellectually stimulating and emotionally supportive. We create a friendly, noncompetitive atmosphere.

If you look at the beast on the cover (we added the toenail polish), you'll see a horse reaching up with an albatross wing and pushing off with a mermaid tail, and a broad, strong back in between. She's rising up from the water and headed toward the sky. In one of his poems, W. B. Yeats suggests a question that I like to paraphrase this way: "And shall poetry, that high horse, go riderless?" In this utterance, poetry refers to all the literary arts. And the answer to the question is No! There's enough room on that broad back for all of us to ride sky high.

We invite you to enjoy the work of our faculty presented in these pages and to come visit our unique MFA program at our web site, www.spalding.edu/mfa, or in person. And if you should come here to study writing, Kathleen and I will be asking all of you to enhance your own writing through the editorial experience of reading submissions for *The Louisville Review*. With this book, we celebrate and showcase our faculty, we thank our wonderful students, and we express the hope that some of you will come write with us.

SENA JETER NASLUND

Sena and I thank Spalding University for the support it offers The Louisville Review Corporation. We also thank our MFA Faculty for the strong creative writing they contributed to this anthology. We could not have finished this book without the help of Karen Mann or Katy Yocom, our colleagues in the MFA Program. Likewise, this anthology would not be possible without the help of our editorial assistants, Jan Mattingly-Weintraub and Liz Nethery. We are grateful to the student editors of Fleur-de-Lis Press who helped copyedit and proofread *High Horse*. And finally, I am particularly indebted to Jonathan Weinert for his talent, knowledge, and patience while designing this book, both inside and out.

KATHLEEN DRISKELL

⚜ Poetry

Greg Pape

Fog

My son has built a tent-cabin
in the front room and invited in the dog.

He has constructed an imaginary machine,
with an invisible lever, for catching the fog.

Fallen clouds drifting through the valley
along the river-bottom, up and over the lines

and folds and contours of the hills, coulees
and benches, combed by cottonwoods and pines,

breaking softly against the windows
like thought or breath, then passing on,

flowing, opaque body of air, and we are both
caught up in this elemental conversation

of house and fog. The fog got in the house,
he says. I am catching it with this.

Some Guardian Spirit

Freezing fog, visibility maybe a hundred yards.
Frost builds up on the pine needles,
the yellow grass, the leafless cottonwoods
and apple trees. Voices of carpenters
and the sound of hammers, saws,

a compressor kicking on and off
in that other world somewhere across
the pasture. Not a bird or a squirrel or a horse
in sight. A rooster and a lone dog
send their voices out into the fog that seems
to be closing in, growing denser, a cloud
barge drifting down the valley spiriting us away.

Sometimes the smaller the world the better.
This window sill is a true horizon.
In one of the rooms down this cloud hall
someone may be waiting for someone
to listen to a story that needs to be told.
Right here, in the wavy lines of the woodgrain
there's a kind of far off water sound,
a hush of low tide, salt scent, footprints
in the sand, someone walking in the fog,
her black shoes in her hand, a little worn out
from all the worrying, the dull hours of work,
the gossip, the waiting, the news, the grief,
the anger, all of it, lulled now by the waves, coming
slowly back to herself, grateful for what she
can't hear or see, feeling close to something
she won't try to name, some guardian spirit
maybe, content just to be walking with her
in the fog like this.

Elegy for the Duke of Earl

Prologue: Monstrous Families

"I spoke of [The Duke of Earl] and others
as well, but failed to realize that I had allowed

their names to function ambiguously. This proved
an embarrassment to me in that my oversight
has served to raise two pertinent objections.

It was argued that I had not properly
described [The Duke of Earl] or his work
and that my handling of [same] was pitifully
inadequate in terms of the totality of his thought.

It was argued that I had created monstrous
families by bringing together [The Duke of Earl]
and Linnaeus or in placing [The Duke of Earl]
next to Darwin in defiance of the most readily
observable family resemblances and natural ties."

"When we say [The Duke of Earl] we are using
a name that means one or a series—"

Duke Duke Duke Duke of Earl
Duke Duke Duke of Earl Duke Duke
Duke of Earl Duke Duke

I. THE FLYING RED HORSE

It was a nice old two story house
four or five of us rented
for seventy-five dollars a month.
The neighborhood was condemned
to make room for a new freeway.
We were a free-flowing family of transients,
soldiers back from the war, musicians,
students, dogs. We were known
for our parties. We took in strays.
We bought rice in fifty pound sacks,
beer by the case. We had a male

basset hound named Crash. And once
when our neighbor's poodle, across the street,
came into heat, we put Crash in an upstairs
bedroom, closed the door, but left the windows
open. A few of us were leaning on someone's car

in the street when Crash came out the window,
sniffed the air, whined, and began to pace
back and forth along the roof above the porch.
Before anyone could get to him,
he leapt from the roof.
I can still see him in the air
like the flying red horse above the Mobil
station, his deep chest, short legs, long ears
straight up, and the wild look in his eye.
He came down right on the points
of the picket fence, took out two boards,
gashed his belly, let out a howl,
stood up, shook himself, and headed across
the street, oblivious to his bleeding.
We all laughed. That was how we lived then.

II. Whatever Happened to J. C.?

I asked my brother, whatever happened to J. C.?
He said the last he heard J. C. was working
on a road crew somewhere down south.

Jesus Contreras, citizen of the United States,
friend, part Mexican part Mescalero Apache
part philosopher part coyote stood five four

in his court shoes and weighed about as much
as your best bad dream, or a skin bag
full of peyote buttons. He left California

dragging his history behind him in the dust
like a broken chain. When my brother
introduced us I saw the chain and shook his hand

that bore a blue tattoo of the cross
with blue lines suggesting radiance.
I hugged my brother who I hadn't seen in years

and welcomed them into the house.
We broke out beers and stories around the kitchen
table, and rode those horses late into night.

By dawn we were all brothers. We went out
into the desert to be part of the sunrise.
We picked the hard beans of jojoba

to sell to a dealer in town, who trucked them
to California to be rendered into essential oils
for cosmetics, soap, and shampoo.

We picked our way to a delicate delirium
under a blaring sun. We sang and danced
and roughed around in creosote, sat down

in ironwood and palo verde shade
to shelter with scorpions and tarantulas.
We did the snake, the owl, the wren.

We gave each other nick-names: I was Hunger,
my brother, Thirst. J. C., depending on the mood,
was Blood or Skin or Bait. Bait

for his uncanny knack of attracting
agents of the law, when all he wanted
was a little slack, all he needed was a little

respect, and one clear vision to free him
from his name, one clear vision
to give him his true name. Last time

I saw him he was standing at one of the old
crossroads with his thumb in the air
smiling, saying, see you on the news.

III. EVENING NEWS

He comes home from work, tired,
his mind braking and accelerating,
weaving through the day's traffic
of acts and images—the slim hooker
in yellow heels strolling the shoulder
of Biscayne Boulevard, Tina Turner's voice
sweating, the astronauts flaming out
like meteorites over the Atlantic,
a rusted shopping cart tipped over
a curb, its burden lifted, its ghost fled.

He puts the key in the door.
The small green lizard on the wall
above the mailbox cocks its head
and holds still as if listening.
I'm home, he says, and opens
the door, steps into the familiar room,
into the quietest moment of the day.

He turns on the news. He sips his beer.
They are showing a poorly focused
unsteady video segment taken by a bystander
of a shirtless man stabbing another man
on a canal overpass in Miami Beach
just blocks away. Jesus, he says,
what am I supposed to do?
The news anchor says it began apparently
as an argument over money.
The men were friends. One
owed the other ten dollars.

He turns off the news. He runs the video
backwards in his mind. The shirtless man
rises from the railing, his friend
bursts up from the bloody water,
flips over the railing, lands on his feet,
grabs the bare shoulders of his friend
who pulls the knife from his chest,
steps back quickly, swallowing his curses,
hiding the knife, moving back across
the line into a life of debt and anger,
friendship and choice, a life, now his,
he must invent the next move for.

He goes to the back window, stares
at the uncut grass. From somewhere
a bird, a painted bunting, alights
with a claim from the offices of air—
chartreuse, flame red, indigo blue.
The bird says, this is for you.

IV. SONG: THE DAY THE DUKE OF EARL DIED

It was a day like spring in Babylon.
The mothers of the streets
were waiting for birth.
In the earth of their bodies
earth was busy.
The youths were confused,
their eyes seemed to run.
Funerals of the murdered
went on and on. More were murdered
and the sky yawned,
the day the Duke of Earl died.

The day the Duke of Earl died
was like a song one heard
at the end of a list—
said do this and this and this.
And this was a day like spring in Babylon.
The fathers of the streets
were waiting and waiting.
In the earth of their bodies
earth was busy
the day the Duke of Earl died.

When they looked in the coffin
and saw inside
everyone knew, but only a few cried.
It seemed like everyone
but no one was there,
including the Duke and the dogs of his hair
gone gray and wild
this day like spring in Babylon.

EPILOGUE: MORE OF THE SAME

"Storytellers continued their narratives
late into the night to forestall death
and delay the inevitable moment
when everyone must fall silent."

"[The Duke of Earl's] story is a desperate
inversion of murder; it is the effort,
throughout all those nights, to exclude death
from the circle . . ."

Duke Duke Duke Duke of Earl
Duke Duke Duke of Earl Duke Duke
Duke of Earl Duke Duke

Molly Peacock

CELTIC LADY SEX GARGOYLE ON MEDIEVAL LINTEL

Shelagh na gig, lady on her haunches,
squats with arms down, pulling her pudenda
away from her clitoris which launches
out of her stone sculpted body's end a
prow that even when wind and hail blast a-
way her dugs and ribs and ears and bald head
snorks past any dilemma
of what it is: sex flung wide above a
church door, a masturbating gargoyle wed

to worship, her bulging eyes popping in
an orgasm, or death, or warning, or in
the puckered surprise of the release of
her god inside—old, old among the folds. Of
the wisdom of the wenches this: self-love.

OF NIGHT

A city mouse darts from the paws of night.
A body drops from the jaws of night.
A woman denies the laws of night,
Awake and trapped in the was of night.
A young man turns in the gauze of night,
Unraveling the cause of night:
That days extend their claws at night
To re-enact old wars at night,
Though dreams can heal old sores at night
And Spring begins its thaw at night,
While worry bones are gnawed at night.
He sips her through a straw at night.
Verbs whisper in the clause of night.
A finger to her lips,
the pause of night.

ARTICHOKE HEART

Every time I cook an artichoke I
think of you—you taught me. Every time I
pay too much for a plump cutlet I hear
your praise-in-disapproval: you'd steer

toward something with the bone in. Now pastry:
there's two sexes of Sicilian pastry,
penises (you'd point at a baba), or
female (pointing to that crusted butterfly d'or
next to it). That was certainly true of
us. Every minute we were aware of
the biology of our lovers differences.
Our kind of break-up doesn't mend fences,
so I have not called you up the hundreds
of dinner times I've thought of you. Instead,
I've prepared an artichoke head.

The Flaw

The best thing about a handmade pattern
is the flaw.
Sooner or later in your hand-loomed rug
among the squares and flattened triangles,
a little red nub will soar above the blue field
or a purple cross will sneak up among
the neat ochre teeth of the border.
The flaw we live by, the wrong bit of floss
that wreathes among the uniform strands and,
because it does not match, becomes a gem,
will make a red bird fly,
turning a blue field into a sky.
It is almost, after long silence, a word
spoken aloud, a hand saying through the flaw,
I'm alive, discovered by your eye.

Jeanie Thompson

How to Enter the River

for Mickey Landry

Now the singing of the river is his.
He has opened his eyes and each tree
in its green integrity
bows as he moves past.
Beneath him, around him
the water is a muscle,
a heart of jewels spilled over rock.
He's forgotten his hand on the paddle,
his arm dips and pulls, guides the boat
to enter the river, unnoticed.

He keeps his back turned
as his children pry effortlessly
through the rapids,
sure of their skill, that they feel
where the boat must go.
Still, there is a sadness
in his straight, impassive back,
as if by turning from them,
he insures they will go on
paddling forever, forever his,
here among lighted waters,
flexing, opening around him
in song.

The Lyrical Trees

It's winter and we've turned once again
to the landscape for some scrap of truth
to confound us, to show us who we are.
But the land is cold, burrowed deep into itself this winter.
A brown furze covers the pastures where cattle
huddle against one another in the bitter, afternoon light.
Across the ground, around the deserted house,
over the trees, the vines of summer make a ghost network
holding fast for spring. It's all set
to pull us down, into its slow metabolism, all but these three,
rising in twists that dancers dream to imitate,
in love with this season
when their beautiful bare limbs, their smooth bark
can sing and move upward in the shattering air.

True Course

This morning, I set out my little ship
into a sea of fern—feathery and almost flowering
as the fiddleheads reach into the morning air.

Transplanting these, I must dig parallel
to the rhizome, knowing I will sever the tiny
root hairs no matter how carefully

I lift, no matter the black dirt that travels
with them. Parting these ferns that are delicious
as new lettuce, I know to trace the root

to an acceptable parting, then spear
the trowel sharply. My helper digs a trench
and I place the shocked plants. His strong fingers

filter back the dirt dispassionately.
Thickened by rain all spring, these ferns—
so profuse, so heartbreaking—have

called me into the garden again.
Though I am tempted, I do not recall
other gardens but set my face squarely to this one.

I have said before, *If I am anything, I am . . .*
but today I do not want to say, *if*. I say, *I am*
alive in the cool breath of this morning

where ferns planted by hands I've never seen
return, tokens of the world's true course,
Mute partners billowing greenly in their sails of light.

POEM AT FIFTY

for Haley

Coming awake
    in the predawn bedroom
        to the scratch of your nails
    on hardwood, I remember
that past all pain, desire to be abed

I must rise, search for shoes,
    and will you not to mess
        before I lumber, you bounce
    to the door.
On the top deck step, I perch
    like a small ruffled city bird
        as you merge

into the opening morning—
of fifty years how many dawns can I claim?

The shimmer as mocking bird, towhee,
cedar waxwing, cardinal
wake, their songs like buckshot
rattling in my head—

or a shaken silver bracelet, charming
me awake.
By now, the blood
has made some courses through my brain
so I can start to see

dawn lift her skirt,
flatfoot it in the dew.
A puppy nips her ankle.
Every leaf is moving in a dance
or is a 1,000 volts of life?

Where have I been
when all this ecstasy took place?
Through the slow focus
my neighbor's oak rises, stalwart tree,
trunk straight, limbs reaching symmetrically,

the sentry of her yard.
Why have I
never noticed her? In the stillness
just after dawn has crowned,
cacophony like birth pains

or the knife of love,
just memory receding.

I'm drawn to you,
oak with a purpose, wisdom
shaping itself like a green flame,

bouquet, a bower of sense.
Time to chase the ball, watch a puppy
from the terror of the street,
keep holding the scherzo of birdsong
long enough to translate

dawn to day.

WOMAN, THIS BODY—

let it be as fine as the salt
he found on your neck
like a bird glancing a branch
in high summer:

let it be as full as the palm he cupped
across your breast
in the morning when sleep unbound
you to him: Woman, let this body

be wind blowing leaves before rain,
salutation's entry
and outcry, the temple
catching fire: Woman, this body,

the one vessel from which you pour
your life, the rich flower of your heart,
spilling every leaf, petal, branch
of your exquisite tree where birds light

or fly from: to which the wind
speaks in late evening
when you are, Woman,
simply this lightened, lonely, lovely body

Richard Cecil

Twenty First Century Blues

Why should I live now? I wondered,
when Carol Anne announced to us
her father had been transferred South,
which wrecked my plans to marry her
in fifteen years and buy a row house
exactly like the ones we lived in
and raise a couple of kids like us.
Suppressing sobs, I asked my playmates,
"what's your favorite century?"
For why not live some other time
beginning with the dinosaurs
and ending with the Last Judgment
raining fire on all our houses,
burning up our dogs and cats
who wouldn't get to go to Heaven.
Already I'd reached double figures,
ten years old and broken hearted,
failing Penmanship and Conduct.
I might not ever get promoted

to fourth grade books with smaller print
and characters with darker thoughts
than Dick and Jane and Puff and Spot.
I'd have to waste my whole existence
rounding out my big G's loops
and learning to keep my mouth shut.
But even if my third grade teacher
got rid of me with a gift C-,
my future looked too desolate
with Carol Anne ripped out of it.
I wished that I could travel back
before my misery was born.
Since history wasn't my best subject—
the only era I knew well
was "yesteryear" when The Lone Ranger
roamed the plains with his friend Tonto—
I turned to my friends Cal and Jack,
both experts on the pre-cowboy past.
"I'd like to wear the lace and velvet
of Louis XIV's court at Versailles,"
said Jack, who was into fabrics
so deep he helped his older sister
cut patterns for her dresses out.
"Give me Nero's Rome," said Cal,
fond of pulling legs off bugs,
who'd seen *Quo Vadis* three times
and said he rooted for the lions
when Caesar flung the Christians to them
in the first Olympic games.
But Carol Anne, whose blue eyes stared
like x-rays through me and my friends,

looked as if she'd moved already
to a future that excluded us.
At last she tossed her curls and said,
"What does it matter when we live?
By 2000 we'll be fifty
and you'll have all forgotten me."
Then she stood tip-toe on saddle shoes,
pirouetted, marched away
down Argonne Drive, out of my life,
but not out of my memory
for the remnant of our century
or the small piece of the next one
left before I have to die.

Job's Advice

Sooner or later something terrible is going to happen to you,
and you're going to write a poem about it.

— Joe Schmidt

"Curse God and die." That's beautiful advice,
but what if my luck suddenly reversed?
Hope messes up my urge to hang myself.

"Then why not take up dancing?" Great idea,
but with my children dead and my crops blighted,
I don't much feel like kicking up my heels.

"Try sin." I would, but virtue's such a habit
I automatically stare down at my shoes
when scented women pass me in the street.

"Well, throw yourself into hard work." I did,
but once I'd buried my plague stricken dead,
I threw away my splintery pick and shovel.

"Try exercise and diet." I'm starving now
and walking everywhere instead of riding,
but weariness and hunger just depress me.

"Prayer?" "Ineffective!" "Meditation?"
Every time I concentrate on nothing,
bitter memories keep seeping through.

"People say that drinking helps." You bet!
But, next morning, when the wine's worn off,
I wake up sadder with an awful headache.

"Time will cure you—just you wait." You're right,
I'm growing used to pain. But what's the point
of learning how to live in misery?

"No wonder God hates you—you whine too much."
Back when I was happy, my rejoicing
seemed to make Him hate me even worse.

"Think of those who suffer more than you."
I try to but when I imagine victims
of man-made and of natural disasters—

of mutilated genocide survivors,
of raped and tortured, imprisoned and enslaved,
burnt out, flooded, drought stricken multitudes—

I feel worse, not better. "Then think positive."
But when I call to mind my happy past,
my darlings dead, my property destroyed . . .

"I see your point. Your case is hopeless." Yes,
but so is everybody else's, right?
You're going to lose all that you value, too.

"I hadn't thought of that." Orphaned, widowed,
sickened unto death—it's going to happen
eventually and poison your whole life.

You're being herded toward the slaughterhouse—
if you listen you can hear the distant screams—
toward pain and loss as hideous as mine.

"There's nothing I can do about it?" Nope.
But when your turn to suffer like me comes,
what I'd suggest you do is write a poem.

LAMENT FOR THE MAKERS

Thank god the twentieth century is over.
It started great, with Yeats and Robert Frost
abandoning the artificial diction
of nineteenth century poetry and writing
lines that thoughtful people might have spoken
after they'd keep silent for a long time.
Then World War I wrung great poems from
doomed soldiers at the front, like Wilfred Owen,
and transformed T. S. Eliot's "The Waste-Land"
from an obscurely personal lament
for pyscho-sexual failure and neurosis
into a moving dirge for pre-war Europe's
disintegration into twenties chaos.
But Europe in the thirties could inspire

no poetry as eloquent as cries
of anguish by the victims of the Nazis,
so modernists like Stevens plugged their ears
and turned for inspiration to Ideas
which they worked into satisfying Texts
suitable as subjects for a Thesis.
They left the second war to novelists,
young soldiers like James Jones and Norman Mailer,
whose minor masterpieces sold to the Movies,
which turned their tragic views of History
into star vehicles for Donna Reed.
Meanwhile soldier poets wrote odes and sapphics
based on dead forms borrowed from the Greeks
while laying plans to translate the Aeneid.
Jarrell's "The Death of the Ball Turret Gunner"—
five lines of iambic pentameter—
is World War II's only major poem.
But in the forties greatness wasn't dead.
Robert Lowell, if he hadn't failed
the Navy's eye test when he volunteered,
would've been the Wilfred Owen of his war
instead of the celebrity protester
who burned his 4-F draft card after Dresden's
incineration by the Allies fire-bombs.
Instead of getting drowned or Kamikazeed
assaulting some bleak atoll near Japan,
he thrived in jail, and afterwards discovered
that his authentic muse was Mania,
his Yaddo an asylum called McClean's.
He founded, without meaning to, the school
of Confessionals, who, in the 60s, raced

like rich Twits in the Monty Python Skit
toward the finish line, their suicides,
which fixed their place in literary history
and guaranteed space in anthologies.
Their flashy deaths obscured much finer work
by Robert Hayden, buried in the South
beneath a four course load at a black college,
whose Elegies for friends and foster parents
trapped in his childhood ghetto in Detroit
turned Lowell's sour rich kid memoirs inside out,
and by Lowell's great friend Bishop, who holed up
for decades with her girlfriend in Brazil
writing formal narratives and lyrics,
ignoring world and literary politics
while Lowell cranked out his "Notebook" free verse sonnets
chronicling his Viet Nam war protests,
his infidelities and second divorce.
Then one by one, these three great poets died
twenty years before the century ended
leaving only Larkin, almost silent,
grinding out his mordant, funny lyrics
at the rate of two or three a year
on the other side of the Atlantic.
Then he died and left the pages blank
for us to fill in—for if you're reading this,
statistics say that you must be a poet,
one of the many thousands who apply
for NEA's bi-annually and are denied.
Or have you been awarded one or two?
Well, then, maybe you're the major poet
whose works will light the 1990s up

as soon as jealous rivals like me die
and critics gain the necessary distance.
Or maybe I'm the secretly great voice
almost drowned out by all that background noise,
twenty thousand singers tuning up,
almost all of them way out of key.
But sister, brother, our bones will turn to dust
long before the new anthologies
replace crap written by X and Y and Z
with the major works of you and me,
so I'm leaving blank the end of this lament
for you to fill with your own elegies:

Kathleen Driskell

Nativity

It was the first and only time I had seen it, the way
the eyes lose everything, become unholy,
become things. My dog, beloved, had traded
the exotic green sweetness of some neighbor's
discarded anti-freeze, unknowingly, for her life.
For a week, the young vet placated me,
keeping her hooked to an IV, telling
me maybe, maybe, though he knew
there was no chance, but just pregnant
with our first son, I ordered the clear fluid
to continue pumping through her body because

I would have nothing of anything but life.
Now pregnant with our second child,
it is what I think of when I wake at night,
wondering how much the tests will reveal,
worried about again risking it all,
risking our three lives on this new life.
I remember the IV's final feeding:
I held her, good dog, watched her eyes,
not realizing how ready she was
to go, how readily she would go.
When we announced this second pregnancy,
friends and family offered not one wary word.
No one said consider what you already have,
what you are risking. As if there is only
one heart for all of us, now strong enough, rugged
enough to make room for
any sort of letting go.

Leaving the Argument

After you have gone again, angrily,
I remember that morning we had wandered
onto the pier, the scaffold's complaint
against the ocean; the whip of the sea
wind tugged at the fisherman's jacket.
We watched as he cast line far out into
the black air, reeled line through the shimmer
of water that I said was glamorous
as a beaded evening gown.
You laughed for we were three days married and

sure everything, everyone,
that man alone at the end of the pier, drunk
on whiskey, was sent and set before us
only to please.
All hands in hands, legs tangled,
we could not contort ourselves together
tightly enough and in the background, then,
we cared nothing that the man had pulled in
a shark, gray-blue, radiant, small as a foot.
It swung wildly through the air while
the man slashed at it with his filet knife,
finally separating its clubbed head
from the twisting.

WHY I MOTHER YOU THE WAY I DO

That afternoon, I have to admit, there were no thoughts
of you. I was in high school—making my way past
the buses to a waiting car—a boy who would not be
your father—when the line of traffic stopped. The girls,
classmates, sisters, had darted between buses
and into the highway, trying to cross the field to their home.
They both lay twisted in the road. My science teacher,
Mr. Desaro, took off his suit coat and laid it over Susan's
face. He was crying because he only had one coat.

By the time they let us pass, Eve had been covered with a white
sheet. The ambulances had come. Red lights flashed, but
their mother was still pushing her silver cart
through the grocery. The sheriff was walking up behind
her. As she reached for a gallon of milk, he moved
to touch her arm.

To the Outdoor Wedding

All come, forgive, and bless the dogmatic over-ripe bride
who insists she *will* be married in the garden
of her dead mother, though the guests and wedding party
hiss and shiver as the light rain turns unrepentantly
to pelting ice. All rise, and love the narrow bridesmaids,
numb and under-dressed in lavender slivers of spaghetti strap,
and listen to their teeth shatter as they scurry down
the aisle, drawn to the collective body heat
of the groomsmen and minister shifting from foot
to foot under the wavering trellis of altar. Praise
the wind picking up mightily, and the groom, unsteady
and sallow, who does not beam when she appears
in blown splendor on her father's arm—and the guests
who are wet-faced, their heads bowed down
to keep the sleet from stinging. It is the bride, prayer-
ful and confident in her white faith, we have to thank
when a gust picks up and wraps her long veil three times
around her father's head, shrouding him from the booming
garden tent about to unpluck itself from the soggy ground.
Who else but her to be thankful to when instead of the tent,
her veil snaps free from the father's flailing and lifts high,
then thrashes away over the Indiana cornfields, just now
brilliant in their new spring greening—the green shine,
the sumptuous periwinkle sky, the brilliant white strata
folding into itself, and dropping its knot—*but wait!* Again
the wind sends it sailing and the guests, heads up now,
mouths open in collected prayer of *ah* and *ah* as the veil
transforms into a bucking Chinese dragon, taking away
all that is old, folding, dancing off and far. The guests

gather themselves and offer the warm utterance
ooh when from the thawing and newly planted fields
a thousand black starlings lift in alarm.

Debra Kang Dean

LIGHTS, PLEASE

Late at night, under an incandescent light,
you sit at the kitchen table.
Steam rises from your coffee cup.

Those hands, folded as if in prayer
and propping your chin up,
bear the day's weight. For several nights,

after the other lights on the block have gone out,
your knowledge of darkness
has grown increasingly intimate.

You used to believe that small circle
of light could be a simple oasis in darkness.
You've found yourself somewhere outside it.

The house settles. Creaks
and groans rise from the cellar.
Tonight, when sound is magnified,

you are drawn to the cellar door.
Cellar door. Poe said he loved those words
for their beauty, liquids extending

the vowels' descent from high
to low, tongue stopping the breath
like a door swung closed then open.

But how trust a man whose ideal
beauty was a dead woman?
Stasis and darkness, the idea of

life moving in death, was what
he loved, the dark cellar,
primitive fridge, keeping things

cool. Unlovely and poor, Poe
died alone in a gutter, housed
in the dark to which he surrendered.

And Plath, hearing her head thump
in the crawlspace where, self-drugged,
she hid, loved the idea too. What was death

to her but an anaesthetic,
an expedient on her way elsewhere.
It must be so for one intent on arrival.

A child willingly lies down, thinking
of cookies and milk, and, in spite of herself,
falls asleep. Plath, beset by fevers, set out

cookies and milk then
bowed to the oven. In one poem,
she spoke as a Jew in a cattle car:

"How far is it? How far is it now?"
Plath thought death would make her
godly. And why not? The disciples of Christ

insist it true of him. Still it's hard to believe
this life is a skin bruised then shed.
Think of Pound. During the war,

he saw himself a sacred bell
destined to toll the time at hand:
Radix malorum est cupiditas;

time to pay, Usurer. But the world
did not repent. After the war,
after being caged like a kept hen,

after thirteen years in the senile ward
at St. Elizabeths, Pound's release
was a kind of re-incarnation. You might say

bad karma caught up with him in this life.
He died and lived but wouldn't tell it.
Mastering himself, he chose exile

in the dank cell of the self,
slammed the door shut.
We know only the figure he cut.

So that, in the end, his life, unmediated,
became the poem he dreamed, punctuated
by the beat of his walking stick.

These are the lives of poets
you've discovered on your own.
In your own. Afraid of what

you'll find, you go outside. Circle
and circle the block long past midnight.
What are its terrors to the night sweats

and fevers of the dark inside the dark?
An audience of one unable to leave,
unable to stopper both eyes and ears,

unable to stop the succession of images
on the screen, all you can think to say is
"Lights, please." The air is chilled.

You're thinking, if matter is evil, you are of it.
But how can you know what you are
when what is known is always half imagined?

Your heels click against the pavement
till the first inkling of light. Go on.
You've reached the threshold

that must be crossed. Poe stopped short.
Go on. Open the cellar door.
Blow on the bare bulb lighting

the stairs. Its threaded root
is a metal wick. Your pupils will widen
in search of light that is not there.

The sole of your left shoe
is tuned to touch. It will find
the first stair; all you need do is

let it. Go on. Take another step.
Under your right hand
the rail will be smooth as a slide.

Each descent has a rhythm; open
hand sweeping the rail,
your body will light, if you let it.

There's wine, fruit
in the cellar. They wait to be borne
up to the light. Go on.

Pick up the pen.

PEELING AN ONION

Earlier I sliced off the ends
of a yellow onion, root and stalk.
The bulb's cut ends oozed sap
that stickied my hands. Even now
I can smell it. Of course
my mother taught me to freeze
an onion first, and cut it last.
And, of course, I forget
so often onion and I weep.
Away I peeled a thin dark layer
that crinkled like cellophane;
then two layers of bruised flesh
and the thin membrane between them.
Though shrunken, the onion was flawless.
My mother's cuts were exacting—
an onion the size of her heart
diced into nearly perfect squares—
a concrete example of calculus,
curves divided to straighten them,
the pieces so uniform, so beautifully
removed from the onion itself.
A scrape of the blade, and they're
in the pot. I know how to do all that.

But when the damage is more than superficial,
I sometimes find myself
peeling an onion as if it were
an orange, as if I might find something
like the hard core of a golf ball
I unstrung a mile of elastic from
to get to. Layer by layer
I peel the onion until
nothing is left.

BEADS

All through that summer she lingered, dreaming of rain,
Tracing the rim of a chilled glass beaded with rain.

The wind picked up, lifting and crumpling news-
papers, skirts, and dead leaves annealed by the rain.

The gray sky thickened as Cain walked away;
Blood darkened the soil in the field, like rain.

You called on the waiter to bring wine for the house.
Mercifully blurry, the world seen through rain.

"No more," said Li Po, longing for home. And
"No. *More*," as under a waxing moon cool rain fell.

Maureen Morehead

FIRE

For ten years she'd been thinking
I'll go to Sears this weekend, buy the house
a rope ladder, for no breath even the size of a wolf's
will save it, or them, if the fire is in the walls,
sneaking up the stairwell. Their son's room
is up three stories. Its walls are green. He looks
down on cedars and out at oaks, gray sky
through empty branches. Let me in, little one,
or I'll blow your house down. Snow falls.
Wind rattles in the wolf's throat, shaking even
storm resistant windows. Ten years ago
she said I need to go to Sears, buy a rope ladder
in case of fire. That summer, they'd seen a wolf
in Yellowstone and a station wagon overturned,
its contents on the highway. I'll huff and I'll puff.
I'll come at you like a geyser. She'd checked
the fire alarm in each motel, noted the nearest
Exit. But then at home green apples and red grapes
sat fixed in a bowl upon the kitchen table,
and they'd bricked every outside wall to begin with,
never even considered straw or kindling:
so unabashedly flammable are they.

WHAT MAKES THINGS MOVE

A man and a child.
A man and a child two fields over,
and you watch them from the house.
A man and a child, and the man
is holding the child's wrist
because walking over what's left of corn
is difficult, and it takes a long time
for a long-legged man
carrying a rifle against his shoulder
to cross a cornfield when he's with a child.
Small, a white dog circles the two,
runs ahead and back again.
A single cloud casts a shadow
upon the three of them.
Two children,
two fair-haired children.
Each is the color of the cornfield,
the shocks that are missed
undarkened as yet by winter. Child,
do you see it, do you see the quail scatter,
flushed from the fence row,
the gun, the kill, your father,
his walls and storms and wells?
My imagining?
A man and a child
walking together upon the crest of hill.
You cannot distinguish them now from air.
It is the glint of the sun from the metal on the rifle
that says they're there.

THE WINDOW

on Andrew Wyeth's "Groundhog Day"

When he is finished, he will come in.
Why he left before breakfast,
he didn't say. I was in the bed,
but I was awake. He didn't look at me,
just dressed, and left. I saw the back
of his brown jacket, and the back
of his head, then the empty doorway—
I prefer to think he thought me sleeping.
I expect he'll be home for dinner,
but if John happens to be walking
his field adjacent to ours,
and the two of them get to talking,
he won't. He won't.
Just now the winter sun
leaves a trapezoid of light
upon Dan's mother's tablecloth.
I am partial to linen, white,
and the pretty stenciled flower baskets
upon her yellow wallpaper. A few things
in this house are mine. If I'd had children,
this house would have been theirs
one day. Would they have left as certainly
as has their father? I'll set his cup and plate
and knife upon the dining table. Always
he has wood to chop, one fence to mend.
I'll see him, though, from where I am,
come up from the woods, and through the dry,
  white grass, behind us.

The Interview

1
Hester Prynne.

2
I was nineteen, and I was vanishing.
He was the smartest man I'd ever met,
and I loved the way his argument
swirled inside my ears.

3
He made his need a mirror;
it captured me.

4
No, a lullaby is sweeter.

5
Because I had a map inside my head
with a forest of cypress and cedar
and a sycamore
hovering over an unnamed creek.

6
Perhaps God placed it there.

7
It means adultery.
It means I did not wait for my husband
to arrive in Massachusetts to care for me.

8
Perhaps forgiveness,
but never shall I, even in death,
reconcile with him.

9
Pearl is circumspect as her name.
She is my favorite book.
She has always been the heart of me.

10
Because he was beautiful:
a beacon, a windless night,
and what darkness I found in him
made perfect sense to me.

11
I think God played a trick on us.

12
I do not think my story
is a treatise on women's liberation.
The sun comes up, goes down.
It leaves no sign upon the water.

13
I tell them if you like to talk,
find a man who will talk with you.
If silence is what you long for,
perhaps marriage is not the path for you.

14
Our passion was neither scaffold nor rose.
It warned us it knew no boundaries.

15
It was not just one time.

16
It was everywhere.

⚜ Fiction

Sena Jeter Naslund

from *Four Spirits*, a novel

HELICON, SEPTEMBER 15, 1963

In Helicon, Alabama, old Aunt Charlotte told her aged children Christopher Columbus Jones and Queen Victoria Jones, "He'p me up to the Methodist church. I want to sit there."

"Let me get you a fresh head rag," Victoria said.

Chris pulled a quilt off his mother's bed to line the wheelbarrow.

The barrow lay upside down to keep out the rain, right beside the worn steps. With difficulty, Chris righted it, but he had to take his time.

"Let me walk," his mother was saying as she hesitated at the top of the three stairs. She wore a clean, faded apron, and the clean head rag was a matching strip of fabric printed with now-faded red circles.

She over a hundred years old. She don't look it, Chris thought. Dressed up, matching clothes. *I look older than my own mama.*

"Church folks done be gone," Victoria said, "time we get there 'less you let Chris push you."

"They already gone," Charlotte mumbled too low for even Victoria (standing right beside her on the threshold with her hand under Charlotte's elbow) to hear. Charlotte had felt their passing. Good children. Good girls. *We come to say good-bye*, one of the spirits had whispered. With utmost respect, *because you the oldest living.*

'Cause you seen so much, another girl-voice said. Words like distant cowbells.

We be waiting for you, when you come. The third girl had a low, patient voice, like creek-flow.

Number four child said, *Grannie, would you tie my sash a little better?*

They'd wakened her from her doze with their wispy young voices. Four spirits passing. They troubled the air over where she lay snoozing in bed. No more than breath, they wafted past, talking among themselves. Detouring. Little city girls, *leaving Birmingham.* They sang a hymn, so high up in the air, each with her own note but all together. They sang so high as they disappeared, grew small as four specks, into infinity.

They sang like they were already angels. Voices like chimes.

Well, Charlotte would know what had happened up in Birmingham when she saw the white folks leaving their church. She'd see the fact of it.

"You come ride in the barrow, Mama," Chris said. "I have you there in no time."

"I scared you spill me, Chris."

"No, I'll just walk. Not but a mile. They church not even started yet. Y'all come get on each side."

Chris felt his neck creak, his head bend a little lower—oh, just a tiny fraction of an inch closer to despair. When his chin touched his chest, he'd likely die. But not till then. Till then, his mama was the boss.

Slowly Charlotte crept down the steps. Victoria plucked the quilt from the barrow in case her mother needed to lie down beside the path and rest.

Tentatively, Charlotte sent one foot sliding forward through the raked red dust. Her shoe sole grated over the little stones under the dust. Then the other foot followed, sliding and scuffling.

"See," Charlotte said proudly. "That's how walking's done. One foot at a time."

"We'll get there," Victoria said. Her voice was as strong as a steel spring in a mousetrap.

"Reckon I'll stay home," Chris muttered.

His mother look back at him and slowly smiled. "No, you come on, too, honey. Mama needs you to help her."

So the three of them slowly progressed to the edge of the yard.

Today was a good day at Helicon in September, still warm enough for the pine trees to give out their piney smell. Their fallen needles, long and brown, were soft underfoot, but they could be slippery, and it was best to hold to somebody.

I wish you Birmingham gals could all just stay here with me, Charlotte thought. Where had those specks gone? *Enjoy this Alabama sunshine. These good smells.* This soft path. She breathed it all in, could feel her nostrils spread. *Reckon y'alls feet don't need no earthly path.* She had her faith, but it was a sad thought. *Y'all mighty sweet. Coming by my bed like that, tell old Grannie good-bye.*

Then Charlotte took such a mighty breath—life, life—it resounded like a snore, and Victoria said, "You all right, Mama?"

"Sure am," Charlotte answered and quickened her steps. *They've flown on.* Hardly stayed a second, just long enough for Charlotte to get her eyes open, see the place where they'd hovered in the empty air.

She glanced to her left, saw the pond below the spring all covered with green. She wished Victoria and Chris wouldn't let the water scum up that way. She swung her gaze to the right. Yes, there was her big rock. Even in the winter, when she sat down there, her boulder had stored-up sunshine to offer. She'd rather be buried under that rock than anywhere else on earth. Lie close to home. But that was a wish *she*'d never tell; she knew it was her duty to go into the church graveyard—colored side—when her time come.

Oh, she remembered now: she'd decided against dying. She was staying here. *Y'all come back to visit.* She sent the message out to all who had gone before. *Anytime.*

To her own children, she thought, *Now if you waiting for me to die fore you light out for the city, you barking up the wrong tree. You be here forever, you waiting for that event. I ain't making you leave, but I was you, I'd go while I still had some gumption.*

Here was the patch of oak trees to pass. Acorns still clung in clusters up among the green leaves. Charlotte thought an oak leaf was the prettiest shape in the world—the kind with lobes, not the red oak leaf. Too pointy. When she was just a girl, long long ago, she'd seen a woman with an oak leaf branded into her cheek.

And there was a dogwood with one red leaf on it already. Always the first sign of earliest fall when the dogwood started to turn red. Now they were onto the road leading to the church.

"One foot in front of the other," she encouraged her children. *Y'all ought to just keep walking. I want you to be free.*

She heard a cardinal sing, and she sang back to it out loud, "Pretty bird, pretty bird." Birds always sang prettiest on a Sunday morning. "I love to hear the bird choir," Charlotte said.

"Yes, ma'am," Victoria said with a snap in that spring steel voice.

"I do too, Mama," Chris said, muted, and his mother pinched his arm a little so as he would know her thought: *You such a good boy.*

One foot in front of the other. Charlotte wished folks pent up in the cities could look down on them from one of their high buildings, see how peaceful and good things were here in the woods. Here everything just grew as it would, no matter who lived here or who didn't. They had the prettiest woods in the world. She saw goldenrod beside the road.

In the country, they didn't have much, but they didn't need much.

In the country, folks got along with one another. Acted right.

She wondered sadly about the four girls and why they'd passed on so young. Good girls. Dressed so nice. They needed to be here.

Ought to have been with her, in the country. They ought to have been four real girls come to visit their grannie in the country for the summer. Well, she guessed this was autumn coming on. She remembered the dark red leaf on the dogwood. School time.

The girls needed to be here, whenever it was, enjoying the birds and the green trees.

By the time Charlotte and Victoria and Chris reached the church, those inside were saying the benediction, in unison: "The Lord bless you and keep you; the Lord make his face to shine upon you. And give you peace. Amen." It was as though the building itself had a voice.

The sun glinted on the chrome of the cars parked all around the church. The cars were like a herd of little piglets snouting up to a sow.

"Quick, quick," Charlotte told her children. "Let me sit here on the stump. I got to see'em come out. You all hurry on, then come back and get me. Hide now."

Charlotte settled herself on the stump. Yes, they were coming out now, first a few men—Charlotte eagerly looked at their faces, their arms—then the women—Charlotte held her breath, appalled—then couples emerged from the door under the steeple. Every white face, their hands and arms were marked.

Covered with blood, they were. Every one of them. Stained with guilt. She could see.

Smiling and pleasant, as though nothing had happened.

No, to them nothing bad had happened for the last hundred years.

Melissa Pritchard

PORT DE BRAS

> *Ballerina is a magic word. Any girl who hears it pictures in her mind a beautiful dancer in a sparkling costume, skimming along on the tips of her toes, seeming to fly like a bird. Of course, the dancer in the girl's imagination usually turns out to be herself.*
>
> — MAE BLACKER FREEMAN,
> *FUN WITH BALLET, A BEGINNER'S BOOK FOR FUTURE BALLERINAS*

I first met Donna Rae Earps while suspended upside down by my knees. She hung beside me, the new girl from Livermore, not caring if her white tulle petticoat rocked over her head like a motel lampshade or that the elastic waistband on her panties was shot six ways to Sunday, as my mother would surely have said. With her single braid like a flat gold belt snapping the dirt, her narrow, piquant face going redder by the second, nothing was more obvious to me than our destined friendship and nothing less clear than its surprising end.

There had been, during our sixth grade's last two weeks of school, a spotty epidemic of witless but irresistible Chinaman jokes. So when, with some small difficulty due to my weight, I spun off the steel bar and landed upright in the school yard, I showed the new girl what Kristine Leipzig had pointed out to me that morning: a Chinaman's face staring straight up from my left kneecap. When she asked, I examined Donna Rae's kneecaps—they were smooth and white, unblemished—but didn't see anybody.

"Who'd you put there if you could?" I was panting, another excuse my mother had for enrolling me in Miss Gita's Academy of Ballet.

Besides "acquiring a feminine carriage," I was supposed to get "toned."

"My baby brother." Her face, still radishy, looked tragic and closed. "Or my mother. She's dead, too."

I told myself, by way of both consolation and awe, that Donna Rae Earps was pageant-beautiful. At twelve, she was a thoroughbred of physicality, lily amid the weeds, jewel among rough stones. Whereas I, Eleanor Stoddard, the most worried person I knew, seemed cut out to be a politician, a circuit court judge or an FBI detective like Fred Borcher's brother-in-law. Fred Borcher owned the local butcher shop, and my mother bought meat from him, my father liked to tease, just so they could chew the fat, sling dirt on people they had both known too long, since high school in fact. As for me, whatever demanded a qualmish and squinted view of the world, that's what I seemed headed for. (Though who I yearned to be, since Miss Lassiter made us read her diary, was Anne Frank. A heroine, suffering tedious roommates and vicious enemies, smarter and quicker than the adults around her. I learned enough, that summer of 1960, to respect my worry and to understand there were legitimate reasons to fret. I read and reread *The Diary of Anne Frank*, lay awake plotting the circumstances that would empty me out.)

So while Donna Rae was all sinewy catlike grace, I was inclined to sit and be one of two things, a staring or a reading lump. Which is how we wound up at the *barre* together in Miss Gita's Academy of Ballet, I to be toned, blah, blah, and Donna Rae to *plié* (plee-AY), *demi-plié* (d'mee plee-AY), *pas de chat* (pas d'SHAH) and tuck in her spoon-sized *derrière* (dare ee AIR) with cool aplomb.

From her first lesson, Donna Rae took to the ballerina regime as impeccably as I managed to insult it. Her bedroom became her studio, and while she *relevéd* (re-levAYED) on pink satin toe shoes she wasn't even supposed to have yet, but that she'd talked Mr. Earps, who didn't know a thing about ballet except what she told him, into buying, I'd flop across her pink canopy bed, asking myself whether I would have had Anne's courage, locked in a secret annex in Amsterdam. Moreover, how would I know unless I devised trials of character, secret hurdles of courage—a virtue, I decided, that could only be incrementally acquired. I fasted, stuck bits of colored fish-gravel in my shoes, held my breath until my lungs burned, pierced the skin of each of my fingertips with sterilized needles. I kept a secret list of these things, for what I wanted, eventually, was to shine in moral crisis. I even chopped my hair, that hateful bramble of dust, to look more like Anne's. One afternoon, Donna Rae, who knew nothing of my list or my ambition, thumbtacked white bedsheets over her curtainless windows, switched off the overhead light, lit a circle of twelve white candles, and danced inside her arena of flames. She insisted I take the boy's part, catching her as she *jetéd* (jeh-TAYED) off a small yellow kitchen chair. Later, I helped her write ballet definitions and pronunciations on pieces of paper that she taped to her walls. *Arabesque* (ar a BESK), *barre* (bar), *battement tendu* (baht MAW tawn DU), *frappé* (frah PAY), *pas de boureé* (pah d'borr AY), *sur les pointes* (soor lay pawnt), on and on; they would make dry, fluttering sounds as she leapt and *pirouetted* (peer-oh-WETTED) around her room.

Some part of her grace came from having to dance noiselessly so as not to wake her father, asleep in the next room. I had seen Ray Earps once, standing in front of an open refrigerator, and he had looked like an Everly Brother whom fame had not yet reached, or worse, had bypassed. He worked at the same place my father did, Stanford Research Institute; Ray worked nights cleaning and maintaining the computers my dad designed. "Fried-egg sandwich," he'd grinned, saluting me with a blackened spatula, an egg hanging lifelessly over its sides. He'd worn a blue shirt with a pack of cigarettes shoved into each rolled-up sleeve. His hair was a darker blond than Donna Rae's, and it languished in a wide, sensuous curl down his forehead and feathered into a ducktail at the back. I knew his wife had been the drama instructor at Livermore High before she'd died in the same car wreck as the baby brother. Donna Rae showed me the photograph she kept beneath her pillow.

"You don't have a picture of him, too?" I felt inexplicably jealous.

"That's his fire truck." She gestured airily to a toy engine high on an otherwise empty shelf. "I'm never supposed to touch it."

So, I decided, the tragic deaths of his wife and son accounted for the overstuffed pale blue wing chair on the front porch, the granulated hill of silver beer cans, the sampler-sized whiskey bottles stubbed like wet fruit into the leafless hedge beneath the picture window. Ornaments of sorrow. I listened for Ray Earps sleeping on the other side of the wall. I made no noise as I lay on the canopy bed, listening to Donna Rae hum what sounded like Ferrante and Teicher's "Theme from *Exodus*" while she worked her way through *demi-pliés* and *arabesques* with a joy in her own movement that struck me as foreign and nearly unbearable.

The one time I got to invite Donna Rae over for dinner, my mother said afterward that she didn't trust her. That was the word she used, "trust." She said her clothes looked cheap and badly laundered, her table manners were poor . . . *(The Goops they lick their fingers, and the Goops they lick their knives; They spill their broth on the tablecloth, oh, they lead disgusting lives!)* . . , her father was obviously a blue-collar type, and even if he was working to put food on the table, it wouldn't do, leaving a twelve year old alone at night. Donna Rae seemed to know my mother didn't like her, seemed used to being distrusted, and never again asked to come to my house. So late Wednesday afternoons, we'd meet at the corner of Cortez and Balboa—the streets in our neighborhood were all named for Spanish explorers—and swinging our round plastic ballet cases, we'd walk the six blocks to Miss Gita's Academy. The ballet school was inside a Spanish-style bungalow, a house converted to office space, and was protected by a yellowish-green fortress of stately, peeling eucalyptus trees. Sometimes, when the piano music stopped, we would hear typing coming through one of the walls or a telephone shrilling in the real estate office next door.

Miss Florence Gita's constant companion and authority was a slender black stick she struck against the floor or whacked dryly against her long, flat palm as we rallied to keep time. Each week she appeared in a royal-blue, long-sleeved leotard, her wandlike legs in snowy tights, her narrow feet encased in glossy, black slippers that reminded me of giant éclairs. A short white chiffon skirt was bolted to her waist, and her strangely marbled blond-and-gray hair—shaped into the most extraordinary bun, large as a second head—hung like some awful, wilting flower from the nape of her rigidly fluted neck. Her *derrière* was flat as a shirt box, her hips winged out like a cow's; her whole image was shocking to me, and I cannot say why.

Miss Gita detested me, and—stung by the unfairness—I detested her back. To her I must have been a living war on beauty, there by way of my mother's dream of rehabilitation: a sullen, wild-haired lummox in twisted, linty black tights, with a *derrière* like a brick. I also had insanely high arches. At least once a class, I would drop to the floor in the midst of an ensemble exercise, whinnying with pain, gripping whichever arch had collapsed this time, my pear shape mocked in three sets of wall mirrors. I was only partially absolved by being Donna Rae's friend, and tried to hide behind her gamine shape and passionate clean attention. A dozen times during class, Miss Gita would single her out: "Open your eyes girls, the classic *pas de chat*," "the perfect *glissade*," on and on. Donna Rae made us all look stilty and bad, an especially embittering experience for Hayley Schmadabeck, once the Mosquito's pet, now demoted to a second-rate resin-collector like the rest of us.

I couldn't exactly ask did they die right away, so I said, "What was his name? Your brother's?"

We were playing Ping-Pong under the walnut tree in my backyard, a game I played with torpid motions of the wrist and slothful extensions of the arm, my strategy to make the ball come to me, the single, stolid force it could not avoid. Tapping the hollow white sphere, I repeated my question. Donna Rae, her hair stacked up in a "Grace Kelly coronet" (exactly what she called it), answered as she clipped the ball back, and I missed it.

"Roland Arnold Earps. His initials turn into the same name as me and my dad."

I was now prowling in the long grass beneath the table, hoping not to be bitten by earwigs. Her voice filtered dreamily down.

"Roland died on the morning of his fourth birthday. He and my mom were driving his birthday cake back to the bakery my aunt owned—we always got our cakes for free. The design on top was supposed to be a fire engine, but when we opened the box it was a cowboy-shaped cake with the name Billy Swan and the number eight written like a lasso."

I reemerged to spank the ball off the table's left edge, my one trick.

"They got killed because somebody at Aunt Dora's bakery got two boys' cakes confused. My dad'll never get over it. Oh, cripes . . . " Donna Rae had just lofted the ball, like some light blown egg, over our new fence and into the Murphy's yard. At my mother's insistence, my father had recently erected the woven redwood fence, to better seal the Murphys' lives off from ours.

"Our entire dining room was decorated with little yellow ladders and red fire helmets. The ceiling was hung with red and yellow streamers with a fan blowing up to look like flames. My dad refused to let anyone touch any of it. How do we get the ball back?"

Her skipping from one thing to another like that seemed shallow, still, no one I knew besides Doc Hargreaves had died, so what, really, did I know? Since I was born, Doc had been our neighbor—a bald, avuncular, onion-headed man who wore, year-round, a smelly tweed fedora and a poisonous-colored sport coat in the pockets of which were wrapped hard candies you had to work to pick the lint off of. He spoke in plain rhyme—*What's the story, morning glory? Where's the shoe, cockledoo?*—and if it didn't rhyme, he didn't say it. When he died (of family neglect, my mother said) his small green stucco house was immediately sold to the Murphys. This distressed my mother, yet she did the neighborly thing and, the day they moved in, carried over a lemon cake and chipped-beef casserole. She returned, minutes later, appalled. *Beat-all-Catholics*, she hissed, not sounding like my mother at all. *Living like pigs. Dumber than stumps.* She forbade me to play with any of the five children, which thrust an unearned sense of superiority upon me, yet also forged curiosity. What was their offense? What was wrong with Catholics? In our house no one said grace or gave thanks. My father dropped me off at a nearby Episcopal church on Sundays at nine and picked me up one hour later, no questions asked. Hard work, cleanliness, thrift—these formed our creed. No one raised the sorts of schmoozy, profligate questions that led to a need for theology in the first place. In fact, as the Ping-Pong ball zinged over the fence, I remembered it was Sunday, and the nearest we came to practicing religion in our house was the pork roast and apple pie we ate every Sunday night, a dinner to which Donna Rae, being untrustworthy, would never be invited. "There's a way in through the alley," I said.

We prodded around in weeds and nettles and trash, hunted among dozens of volunteer maple saplings that had formed a dense miniature forest, and ended up, without our Ping-Pong ball, beside the mint-green stucco house. The Murphys' dented brown sedan was gone from the driveway, leaving behind a long oily splotch. It was unusually silent, so I figured the Murphys were at noon Mass. We crept to a window and peered in, and what we saw drove us to the next window and the next.

The wild disorder I saw in the hallway, in the kitchen, was repeated in every room—a squalor like I had never seen, a mess that enthralled me. Donna Rae saw Mrs. Murphy first. She was sitting up in bed, her hands steepled on her mountainous belly. I thought she looked sad and martyred. She was also doing nothing, a concept foreign at my house.

"Ish. She looks like a pillbug." I followed Donna Rae who had boldly unlatched the chain-link front gate and was now *glissading* sideways down the street, her arms raised in a *port de bras*, explaining what Mr. Murphy had done to Mrs. Murphy to make her have to sit without moving until the baby was born. "Six fucks, six kids."

"What?"

"It's called fucking, and it's a bad word. Don't say it. Swear."

I swore, and later, as Donna Rae leapt, faunlike, inside her white grove of candles, I lay face-up on the bed, hostage to a vaguely thrilling scenario of Mr. Murphy whating Mrs. Murphy, and, beside them, the five littled whated-into-existence Murphys strung like natural rosary beads, backs turned, sucking on pruny, bitter thumbs.

I agreed to meet Donna Rae outside the Burlingame public library at noon. Having withstood the librarian's flinty glance of disapproval, I now sat on a stone bench, feeling the moral weight of seven Holocaust books on my lap. Books were paths that led away from and back to myself; they were self-selective, uncannily autobiographical. The previous summer I had read everything on ghosts, poltergeists, possessions and hauntings; the summer before had been horses, *Misty of Chincoteague*, etcetera. Now it was the Holocaust, and I had just been made to feel ashamed of my curiosity.

We had disagreed over what Miss Gita's house would look like, and when Donna Rae finally showed up and we walked the block and a half to the address inked on her wrist, my prediction turned out to be the more accurate. Miss Gita lived inside a square, pencil-yellow house with blank, white metal awnings. Neat but ugly. Clean but ominous. Nothing grew. There were even two plots of dark green gravel instead of grass.

I pointed to the sharklike gray fins of an old Cadillac sticking out from behind the house.

"Go knock." I was crabby because my arms were tired, because it was the hottest part of the day, because the house was so hideous.

Donna Rae made it up three of four cement steps before she turned and flitted back to the sidewalk.

"What?"

"I think when you visit, you're supposed to bring a little gift." Little gift? That sounded like somebody's mother talking, but I couldn't say that. After all.

Donna Rae, spurred by disappointment, hurtled through a round of *pas de chat*, *pas de boureé* and a vertiginous series of pirouettes. I worried that either her long-flying hair or her leotard might catch fire. I also told her my mother had refused to let me walk down to Broadway until she realized the dog was out of food; so if I stopped at Fred Borcher's, I could go. George was a dark red bratwurst, a "dashhound," a dachshund, a Rhineland wiener dog. He was twelve, like me, though in dog years that translated into the news that he should be dead. Pink epilepsy pills spiked his specialty food, and his water intake had to be rationed because of incontinence. My mother spoiled George, talking to him in a pippy baby-voice he loved. My fun came from plugging him under a sisal wastebasket in our backyard and watching it twirl frenziedly around the lawn and carom into the trunks of trees.

For what must have been the fortieth time, I studied the photograph of June Earps. With her pixie haircut and round, sad eyes, she made me think of a depressed elf.

"How come there's no picture of your brother?"

I was convinced Donna Rae did not possess the same flesh and bones I did. Dropping into a deep, willowy back-bend, she turned slightly, staring dramatically through glossy streams of hair. Though I loved watching her, I resented being her constant audience.

"People said, except for our age, we could have been twins. We looked exactly alike. Did you bring your money?"

I nodded, having in fact filched five of the newer and less valuable coins from my silver dollar collection, a theft I would record on my secret list and later erase.

Broadway, Burlingame was one long, supple road of neighborly commerce. It began with a sign at the intersection of El Camino Real and Broadway—a wide, licorice-black arch bridging the street, the letters BROADWAY whitely marching across. It ended five or so blocks later at the train station where commuters made the forty-five minute trip north to San Francisco.

My mother had gone to Our Lady of Angels High School with Lou Giotti, now in his corner grocery; with Fred Borcher, now in his butcher shop; with Mr. and Mrs. Swenson, now wearing their red-and-white striped jackets to match their ice cream parlor. There was also a dry cleaner's and a shoe store, where I could stick my bare feet on the metal plate of an X-ray machine, look through the rubber eyepiece and see my green, twiglike, vaporous bones. There was Sprouse Reitz, where I was apprehended by the manager, Herman Lynch, when I tried eating an Abba-Zaba behind the mossy, bubbling acquarium and the pyramind of slug bait. There was a clothing store where, without asking, I could make a beeline straight past boys' underwear, raise the lid of the white freezer and dig out a Neapolitan ice cream cup with a flat wooden spoon taped across it. Near the railroad station was a small, popular restaurant, Vic and Roger's, where we went almost every Friday night so my dad could order what he proclaimed were the best deep-fried prawns in California.

"As usual we're the only non-Catholics in the place," my mother would dryly comment from behind her seafood menu. One time we saw Miss Gita there with a man. Our waiter, when my mother asked, said he thought the man was her brother. "Poor soul." My mother trawled a fried shrimp through red cocktail sauce. "Don't you wonder how he got that way?"

"Fire," my father spoke through a mouthful, "or birth defect." He wiped his mouth with one of Vic and Roger's beige monogrammed napkins. "Could be both. Jaz, quit staring." For some inexplicable reason, my father had recently taken to calling me Jaz.

The only shop I hadn't been in (my mother always breezed disdainfully by) was a gift shop two doors down from Fred Borcher's, run, my mother said, by a Chinese couple who no doubt lived there, like those kind of people do. The shop didn't have a name, so I couldn't be sure it wasn't their living room window I was slowing down to stare into, a window displaying a dusty hodgepodge of European figurines—shepherdesses and lamplighters, embroidered red Chinese slippers, black lacquered chopsticks, imported Irish tea towels and a row of white ceramic Buddhas, like pale, unmollified frogs. A scrim of amber-colored gel paper gave the display a dull, hot empty-aquarium look. Flies, upturned and skeletal, dotted the window's edge. I stood counting them while Donna Rae, hands cupped to her eyes, surveyed the display case.

"No one goes in there," I offered lamely, but she was already pushing open the door. The shop's velvety dark interior smelled sweet with what Donna Rae later told me was Oriental incense. Now she was whispering that her mother always loved doing business with the Chinese in Livermore. As my eyes grew accustomed to the darkness, I saw a lady standing behind a long glass counter, her mouth smudged with the same fuschia color as the rows of curlers in her hair.

Donna Rae spoke slowly, artificially. "We should like to see an item in your display case."

Not smiling, the woman stepped out from behind the counter and with a strange stick, like a pool cue with a metal hook, fished up, by its red cording, the clear plastic box Donna Rae had pointed to. She wore blue terry-cloth slippers, making me think my mother was right. These people lived here, and we were standing, two strangers, in their living room.

Donna Rae took the box, showing me what looked like a bunch of red-foil wrapped bouillon cubes.

"Chocolate-covered bees," she stage-whispered.

"Bees?" I leaned in to read the gold label.

"From Switzerland," the Chinese woman added.

"How much?" Donna Rae asked, sounding more herself.

"Seven dollars."

"Sorry, we have five."

The woman shook her head. Then, because he coughed, I noticed a man in the doorway leading into a back part of the store. They lived there, all right. For some reason, I remembered the joke Tiger Lindemann and Devlin Kuby had taken turns telling me, about a Chinaman, a barrel, and two straws.

"Look." Donna Rae ran one finger across the top of the box, lifting it to show the dust. The man's voice boomed cheerfully. "Five is OK."

Donna Rae turned to me, her hand out.

The silver dollars sagged, a weight of resistance, in my shorts pocket. "Where's yours?"

"I haven't got it yet. Come on, Nors. I'll pay you back."

So there I was setting my large and valuable coins on the glass countertop, everybody but me cheerful, smiling, pleased about the whole thing.

I started walking home, crossing to the opposite side of the street (that's how mad I was) before I remembered: dog food. Not looking at her, I recrossed and headed back to Fred Borcher's, took a number and waited, as always, by the organ meats, staring at the stainless-steel troughs of kidneys, brains, hearts, livers, the sallow waves of tripe. I had never eaten any of these things and wondered if I could. Fred, a tall man whose face reminded me of a tiny wooden mallet, winked as he handed over the dog food rolled in white butcher paper.

I got all the way to Balboa and Cortez before I saw Donna Rae. She was sitting beneath a maple tree, her perfect white legs stuck out, the gift box on her lap.

"Want to try one?" Her boldness as much as anything stopped me. She was undeterred by consequence, maybe even dishonest; still, I reminded myself, these were a far cry from courage.

"We can't. They're a gift."

"See these layers? We'll just take two off the bottom."

She sat unpeeling the red foil, then we set squares of Swiss chocolate into our opened mouths. Chinese bees, bees' knees. I waited to feel a leg, fuzz, the eyes, a head, something. There was only the slightest, bland crunch.

I thawed out a clump of George's dog food on my windowsill, wrote on my list that I had swallowed most of it, and by midnight was vomiting so violently my mother was convinced I had the summer flu she'd heard about. She refused to let me out of bed, much less out of the house to go to Miss Gita's. By noon she'd relented enough to let me sunbathe in the driveway. I was on my back, a pair of green plastic goggles over my eyes, my nose zinced, wearing one of her old suits, a purple one-piece, the built-in bust sticking up in the space between my chest and my collarbone, when I felt something longish and warm-blooded, like George, brush against my thigh. Propping up on my elbows, I blinked off the goggles, then screamed. Charging like a four-legged bullet for the utility room my dad had just built onto our old garage, the rat vanished. Within minutes, my dad was stalking the rat with a snow shovel while my mother, two steps behind, threatened to alert the county health department to the filthy Murphy premises, where no doubt they would find a ship's nest of rats. I picked up my beach towel and went inside to eat potato chips and wish I had stayed calm and courageous. Then the doorbell rang, and there was Donna Rae, in a frilly pink party dress, holding a large, adult-looking book on the Royal Ballet.

We sat in the wide stripe of shade on my front steps. I twiddled with the purple straps of my sagging suit and explained about getting sick and not being allowed to meet her. I told her about the rat. Donna Rae didn't seem interested, so I said, "It's a miracle I wasn't bitten. I could have gotten rabies and died."

"Miss Gita liked the bees."

"She ate them?"

"She's saving them for a special occasion." One step below me, Donna Rae glanced up with an expression I later identified as guilt.

"I'm going back for lunch tomorrow."

Here I spoke from a stupid assumption. "I don't have to wear a dress, do I?"

"Nors. I'm trying to tell you. I'm the only one invited."

"The only one? You didn't say the bees were from both of us? You didn't say that I bought them?"

Donna Rae had a finger deep in her mouth, prodding a loose tooth.

"You didn't even mention me, did you?" I saw myself in Miss Gita's Academy, pudgy, ugly, dodging behind Donna Rae. I stared at the book on the step, at the ballerina on its cover, brilliantly plumaged to look like a bluebird. She wore a hat like a bathing cap, made of blue sequins, with three white feathers sticking up. Dumb.

"If you want, you could come over now and we can . . ."

"No, thank you. I can't." *I have to stalk a rat.* After I locked the front door, I thought I heard the light, half-ringing thwang of a snow shovel. Then my mother was bullying pots and pans around the kitchen, her territory contaminated, and George, in there with her, had worked himself into a series of gruff, self-congratulatory barks.

Sunday had come and nearly gone. The church recessional "Onward, Christian Soldiers" had boomed like a kettledrum through my blood all day. In the afternoon, I'd helped my mother iron handkerchiefs, and polish the silver tea service that had been my great-aunt Mabel's and would one day be mine. I had eaten Sunday's pork roast and scrubbed the pan afterward, thinking it was a strange upbringing where you were expected to behave at prescribed times like a high-class person, then clean up after that person with your secondary servant self. Much later, I came to see this as the signature dynamic of the middle class, perpetually equipped for poverty, in sly practice for wealth.

Now it was dark and I was in the yard, stretched out on the striped, mildewy cushions of our old lawn-swing, an unopened package of Oreos on my lap. I was examining, with my flashlight, photographs of the Holocaust. How to react to this? For a while, I looked just at the faces, sometimes looking for Anne. But they were all Anne, and, of course, none of them was. How to react? I knew I wanted to be heroic. And underneath that, I wanted to be admired for my heroism, to be assured that beauty like Donna Rae's, even grace, weren't as noble or necessary as courage. I was in a state of great confusion. I believe I wept. The pictures shocked me, but there was also some other, personal hurt at work—mixed swells of emotion that had to do with feeling invisible, uncounted, in my own life.

My mother came out of the house and stood on the patio. I trained my flashlight on her.

"Eleanor Ann." Her arms were crossed across her chest. "Your friend is here to see you—at an inappropriate time, I might add." My flashlight picked out Donna Rae's white hair. She looked as if she was hiding behind my mother. I flipped the orb of light back down to my book and heard my mother go inside.

"Nors?" The swing rocked as she sat down on the far end. I drew my feet up and hoped an earwig would bite her.

"Will you forgive me?"

"Why?"

"Because I believe you're smarter than me and you'll know what to do."

I closed the book and poked the light around to find her. Her face was puffy from crying. She wore an ugly shirt with big orange fish on it. She almost looked ordinary; and more important, she realized I was smarter than her.

"It's OK." The words were out before I knew if I meant them or was just curious. "What is it?"

First I heard about Miss Gita's hair, how, out of its bun, it fell straight to the floor and was a marbled white-and-gray river. Then she talked about Miss Gita's brother offering to drive her home, offering to buy her an ice cream (which she'd refused), offering to show her something and then taking that thing out of his pants while telling her what he wanted her to do—a thing she could never repeat to someone as innocent and pure as I was—until she unlatched the car door, jumped out and hid in a hedge of lilac bushes. For the longest time, she said, he just sat there, playing the car radio. Finally he had driven off.

"Tell your father."

"My father? He'll never believe me."

"Why not?"

"I can't."

"You have to, Donna Rae."

"What if Miss Gita finds out?"

Exactly. A small, smug-but-obdurate voice spoke up in me. I

became aware, for the first time, of saying the right thing for less than the right reason.

"Look. If Miss Gita finds out, I doubt if it will kill her, but you can probably keep this from happening to anyone else."

"Weird stuff always happens to me." I heard her soft voice in the summer darkness and—later, upon reflection—wondered if she hadn't sounded just the slightest bit pleased.

Over the next two days, my mother, in one of her moods, put me to work in the front flower bed, tugging weeds, my hands stuck and sweating inside a pair of yellow rubber gloves. When Kristine Leipzig and Sandra Dougherty floated up the hilly bump of our lawn and stared down at me, a purposeful stare, as if they'd thought of a lot to say but had just lost their nerve, I kept churning up pieces of what I would later be informed had been a rare Japanese iris root. Finally Sandra spoke. I had missed three meetings of the Katy Keene Fan Club. They hadn't done much, Kristine added, besides collect twenty-five cents from our one other member, Mitch Nasslund, a too-clutchy, bimbly kid with chronic toe-fungus who sought out the comparative refuge of girls. "Next meeting's Friday," Sandra informed me. I'd about decided the Katy Keene Fan Club was the most pointless thing I'd ever belonged to. I didn't even know who Katy Keene was. Nobody did, except Sandra, who once waved a couple of comic books about her in our faces. Bored by how I kept chipping away at the same iris root, by how little I had to say, Sandra and Kristine wafted down the lawn to the pavement and left me alone.

After lunch, I was helping my mother reorganize her upstairs linen closet—unfolding and refolding sheets, stacking them by color—when, without having rehearsed it, I asked if I could quit ballet. She snapped together the corners of one of our just-for-company bedsheets and held them between her teeth. "Eleanor Ann. Pick up your end. As for ballet, you have three more lessons paid for, and if your father and I succeed in teaching you anything, it's that money means commitment."

At that moment, George, who had been grinding away on his veal knuckle, sent up a nasal howl, *ahwoo-woo*ing out of his silvered snout. My mother, carrying a folded stack of fingertip towels, followed him. Looking out of the bathroom window, she said, "Hell's bells. An ambulance at the Murphys. That family is tragedy in a nutshell."

Two hours later I accompanied her, my hands in oven mitts, trying not to drop her salmon casserole, potato chips crushed like giant's dandruff all over the top. The oldest Murphy girl, who told us her name was Bridget, opened the door, still in her Catholic summer-school uniform. She said her mother had lost the baby and been taken—Mr. Murphy with her—to the hospital. Then Bridget took the Pyrex casserole dish, said thank you. Before she shut the door on us, I heard kids shouting, somebody practicing the piano, news blaring on the TV.

After our dinner, my mother relayed me back with a green Jell-O ring clogged with bits of canned fruit cocktail. I heard her tell my father she felt guilty for having reported the Murphys to the county health department the day before. Maybe because it was just me, Bridget invited me in, though she simply took the Jell-O and disappeared into the kitchen, where I could hear her talking on the phone. I sat by myself on a plastic-covered brown couch, sweat gathering under my knees, until a little boy, whose hair stood in strange orange peaks, like whipped squash, pulled me through the shambles of a kitchen, where I saw my mother's casserole on the counter, untouched. In a dim corner of the screened back porch, the boy knelt beside a cardboard box, stuffed his fingers, all five of them, into his mouth and started stroking the pale yellow down on the duckling nearest us. There were two. The other was tucked into a corner—asleep, I thought. Suddenly, an older girl, about eight, clattered onto the porch in a pair of red high heels, nipped the sleeping duckling by its neck and swung it out of the box. "Duckyduckyducky," she sang. The boy popped his fingers out of his mouth and started screaming. I noticed spots of blood in the box, that the duck's open eyes had a dull, blue film, and one side of its head was mostly a bloodied lump.

"Kathleen Elizabeth Murphy, I know what you're doing." Bridget's voice roared out from the house. "Put that poor tormented creature back this minute or I'll see you don't live till your ninth birthday."

The girl swung the duck by its neck once more before dropping it into the box and clomping back inside. In a fog of nausea and cowardice, I managed to say I had to go straight home. I ran through the backyard, unhooked the gate into the alley, and disgusted with myself, escaped into the relative peace of my own yard.

The following afternoon, Wednesday, I accidentally ripped a hole in the knee of my ballet tights and tried sealing it with my mother's red nail polish. I was late getting to our corner, and when I didn't see her, figured Donna Rae had gone ahead. I arrived at Miss Gita's, panting hard, the thick red blob tugging at the hairs on my knee. A woman named Betty Trower was teaching the class; Miss Gita, she said, was unwell. Noting Donna Rae's absence, I skidded up to my place at the *barre* as Hayley Schmadabeck turned and glared at me. Betty Trower was wearing a purple leotard, and all her hair seemed to be jammed up inside a fat, purple turban. She complimented us. She praised us as if she were blind. She even refrained from ridiculing me, as Miss Gita surely would have, as I wobbled like a damaged top, trying to pirouette across the room. On my turn back, as I strained to exceed myself, my left arch gave way, and I hit the floor like a rock. As Miss Trower knelt and fussed extravagantly over my foot—in the process admitting she was really a jazz and tap teacher—I was inspired to say that whenever this happened, Miss Gita usually let me leave class early and walk home by myself.

⚜

Coming up the weed-choked walkway, I saw him sitting in the over-stuffed blue chair with the torn, ruffled hem. Sprawled, half-concealed behind a lattice losing its battle with an orange trumpet vine, Ray Earps had a can of beer propped on one knee and a cigarette, unlit, dangling from his lips. His head was tilted back, his eyes were shut. The porch was so small I stood right beside him, an anxious girl in a faded leotard and linty, red-splotted tights.

"Mr. Earps?"

He opened one eye.

"Is Donna Rae here?"

Now both eyes were open.

I raised my little plastic suitcase. "She missed class."

He picked the cigarette from his mouth, cleared his throat, set down his beer can, leaned and spat into the bushes.

"You're who now?"

"Her friend, Eleanor Stoddard."

"Well, Eleanor Stoddard, my daughter is no longer here." He looked at my face. "No longer at this residence."

Ray Earps stood up. He had no shirt on. His skin was tanned to bronze, and he looked nothing, in his half-nakedness, like my father.

"I put her on the Greyhound to Livermore yesterday morning, back to her mother." He looked sharply at me. "She didn't tell you? She said she did." His sigh was pained, yet unsurprised. "Hell, I'm sorry. Donna Rae's pretty ticked off at the truth. Meaning she rarely bothers to tell it. Let me get you a soda."

I followed Ray Earps, followed his broad, sweating back into the darkened house. I didn't really need a soda so much as I needed to see she was really gone. The news that June Earps was alive hadn't quite reached me yet. Halfway to the kitchen he turned, saw me looking down the hall.

"You leave something? Go ahead, go on in there."

The room was empty, but it had always been mostly empty; it just felt different. The kitchen chair was gone, the candles—so were all the ballet words I'd helped thumbtack to the walls, except for one still stuck to the back of the closet door, *relevé* (re-le-VAY). I was passing my hand back and forth under the pillow to see if June Earp's picture was still there when I heard footsteps and sat down.

Ray Earps sat beside me and handed me a can of grape soda. "That stuff's too sweet, I don't know how you kids stand it. Now here's the deal. Donna Rae'd come to live with me for the summer; then on Sunday I believe it was, she woke me up with another of her cockamamie stories—this one about her ballet teacher's brother . . . you know anything about that, she tell you about that, Eleanor?"

"No, sir," I lied so fast it startled me. "No sir." I dug in deep. "She never did." My gaze traveled up to the red truck.

"Is that your son's?"

"My son? No, that old fire truck belonged to my younger brother, who died when he was four. For some reason, Donna Rae's always been partial to keeping it in her room."

"Could she touch it?"

"Sure she could. I just told her the special nature of it and to be careful when she did."

"She told me it was her brother's and she wasn't supposed to ever touch it and that he had died. She told me your wife was dead, too." By now I was doing two things, picking the scab of polish off my knee and starting to cry. "She told me they'd died in a car wreck."

"She told you that?" He rested his hand on the part of my back that was bare. Neither of us said anything for a while.

"Donna Rae's mother and I got our divorce a year ago. She is remarried and lives there in Livermore. As for a brother, Donna Rae doesn't have any brothers or sisters. She got herself into some trouble, telling lies about her stepfather, so I told June she was welcome to stay here with me, though I made it clear my place wasn't anything like hers, no Doughboy pool, no red T-bird convertible, nothing like that. But like I said before, Donna Rae, especially since her mom and I split up, runs farther and farther from the truth. It's like she makes things up to be the way she wants. Maybe it comes from her having a drama teacher as a mother. An actress. I told her—one day, it's going to catch up to you, you're going to find yourself, or get somebody else, in deep trouble. Now this business about a man in a car. She's cried wolf on me one too many times, that's the last thing I said to her, her currency's about used up in that department. So I figured the best thing was to put her on a bus back to Livermore. Get her out of Dodge. Then again, maybe it wasn't the right thing. Maybe the guy really did do what she said. I find it hard to believe. I find Donna Rae hard to believe. Hell, you tell me."

He walked across the floor and stood staring out the window. I had stopped crying and was frankly studying the way his blond hair tailed down the nape of his neck, the muscled, triangular slope of his back. This was male beauty I was looking at, sexual attraction, though I had no words or any real feeling for it then.

"It's nearly dark. You live close or do you need a ride?"

"I live close."

"Thing is . . . " Here he turned and looked right at me. "June, my wife—my ex-wife—is the most beautiful woman in the world to me. The only woman. And you know what's funny? One day, some joker, some other clown who I should already start feeling sorry for but I won't, is going to feel that same way about Donna Rae. About my own daughter. What I'm talking about here is time."

I nodded as if I understood. Then he was lifting the can of soda from my hands, his face so close, the smell of his beer so strong, I flinched.

"I would lay down my life for that woman. I've already tried. And to do that for someone who doesn't give a rat's ass about you—it hurts. It plain hurts. I won't get over this, Eleanor Stoddard."

Only then, as he started to cry, did it occur to me how drunk he maybe was.

I followed him back outside. The house had been so dark and sad, even the porch at dusk seemed bright. Before he could land back in his chair, I put my hand out like I had seen my father do.

"Thank you very much, Mr. Earps."

He took my hand, startled. Whatever else I'd thought to say scattered as I looked into his eyes. Ray Earps was courtly and wounded, poor and self-pitying, sensitive and far too handsome, the kind of man I would zero in on for years. But I didn't know that then. I only knew how my heart felt, losing its race, how ridiculous I looked in my leotard, how his hand felt with mine, how we were bound by one, sweet, irresistible pain.

I started for home, half-expecting to see my mother out driving around, looking for me. So when the car slowed behind me on the quiet street and I didn't hear her voice, I turned to see instead Miss Gita's shark-finned, old Cadillac, and hunched over the wheel, staring straight at me, her brother.

I don't remember. I must have had some instinct to run or to scream. Instead, and to this day I don't know why, I did the strangest thing, deliberately, as if obeying the shape of dreams. Backing away until I stood on someone's green lawn, not taking my eyes off the accused, I raised both arms—fingertips touching, *port de bras*; pointing my left foot, *tendu*; striking it twice against the grass, *frappé*; and began to turn. My figure whirled, turning, darkness both supporting and concealing it, until the Cadillac was a blur, until it was gone, until with a sharp, exhilarating cramp in my ribs I ran for home. My mother, who had been taking a nap, had not even missed me.

⚜

On Friday I showed up in Sandra Dougherty's backyard, quieter than usual, drank lemonade out of a Dixie cup, handed over twenty-five cents for the fan club. I took my turn touching Kristine Leipzig's newest patch of psoriasis on her elbow; I laughed at Mitch Nasslund's stupid Chinaman jokes, the two he knew. I tried to forget what I had been thinking about for days—that something lay dormant inside each of us, that only the right constellation of weaknesses could bring whatever it was into the light. And that keeping those weaknesses separated from one another was probably all anyone ever meant by being good.

I returned the Holocaust books, but not before tearing up my childish list and stuffing the bits inside one of them. I began walking past Ray Earp's house every single evening. I had fantasies of being his perfect daughter, or wife, depending. Miss Gita had recovered from the summer flu, and I refused to go to my last two classes. I was punished but did not care. I sat in my room and thought about the ballet suitcase I had left at Ray Earp's house that day, how the time would come for me to go over there and get it back and that I would know when that time came. I stopped reading and did not read again until seventh grade, and then only what I was assigned. My father complained I watched too much TV, though my mother was pleased I was losing weight, walking for exercise, paying more attention to what she called my femininity. The truth is, things had happened, and it helped to blame other people.

I was no longer comfortable with the way Fred Borcher looked at my mother or the way she laughed at his jokes. One day, when I asked, she explained she had been a Catholic until she eloped with my father, after which she was excommunicated. According to her former priest, I, as the fruit of their marriage, was banned for eternity from paradise. I noticed how often my father worked late and, even when he was home, seemed away. I continued to have fantasies about Ray Earps, wrote love poems and letters and stuffed them into a suitcase under my bed. Before long I would be reading again, books I was embarrassed to check out or to bring home. So I stayed at the library, what I chose to read concealed inside more acceptable books. I was catching up to Donna Rae; I would surpass her, for beauty was not to be my protector, nor did I aspire, as I once had through false tests, to courage.

The more I would learn to shape myself into the kind of woman I imagined Ray Earps might grieve over and want to die for (though I was never to see him again—he would take his own life the following Christmas), the more he would become the shadow behind all the boys and men I would open my arms to, *port de bras*, on my back where I thought I belonged and wanted to be, for all those years, passionate and grasping and full of delusion, to come.

Robin Lippincott

The 'I' Rejected

was what she wrote toward the end, what she wrote she wanted to achieve in what would, though she did not know it then, be her last book; and in her life, too, I think. And she did, both in the novel and in her death by drowning, did achieve it, so floats amongst us now a "we," as she stood beside me that spring afternoon and knelt by the pond (two years before her death), knelt that day in 1939, folded that long, elegant body of hers to examine an "emerald" frog on a lily pad, and saw her reflection as a breeze rippled the water's surface; saw herself as she now appears amongst us. "There she is," she said to me, pointing at her own reflection and referring to herself in the third person, "the phantom"; and then she laughed that big, whooping laugh of hers, laughed and said soberly, "I am dispersed," and smiled at me wistfully. And it was after that, that she muttered to herself, turning away, not meaning, I'm sure, for me to hear, muttered: "The only way." That was the last time I saw her.

Who am I? The I of me—my name? I shall remain nameless. Call me anonymous. I, too, am a phantom, a ghostly apparition, an old man almost transparent now in my twilit days; one so terribly lonely.

Then, in 1939, when I was twenty-four, an only child whose parents had recently died, then I was one of several, a "we" of several young men from Oxford, etc., one of a few who, in various and roundabout ways, through Spender and Isherwood and perhaps less so Auden, one of a few drawn into her circle. I saw her perhaps only ten times over the years, but knew her well enough to know, for example, that she liked her coffee black and strong; liked good food with plenty of salt; liked good talk, and liked, of course, her special cigarettes, which she and her husband would roll of an evening. I knew her well enough, too, not to delude myself, and to admit that the way to know her best, to be closest to her, no surprise, was through her work. And so I read and reread, and have recently reread again, everything that she published.

My name is not to be found in any of the published diaries or letters, or in any of the many published accounts of that group, that time, that place. Because I, after all, am a homosexual, and we have often remained anonymous throughout history; a gay man, as they say today, a usage I strongly dislike, and at which she, I'm sure, would have been horrified. "The bastardization of the English language!" I can just hear her saying it in that teasing, sonorous voice she had. Of course there were homosexuals in her own group of friends, "buggers" they were called; her circle was known for them. But they were all distinguished: Strachey, before my time; Keynes; Morgan Forster and so on, through Isherwood, whom I knew, of course, etc. The individual could distinguish himself from the pack, but I did not. Not then. I was just another "bugger."

She was a very personal person, you see, an individualist (quite the opposite of her husband), and had sought, for most of her life, to distinguish herself in a *very* distinguished family and group of friends, which of course she did. *Enormously*. Perhaps *most* successfully. At a price.

It happens to all of us upon occasion, I suspect, riding on the tube one sees a face on the body opposite one thinks is his own. His hand reflexes up to his face—a stroke, a brush—to feel if he is still there; and then one almost reaches out to the face across, so intense and symbiotic is the feeling. He begins to wonder if he is himself after all. And if not, who?

Riding the tube is my daily constitutional, only yesterday there was no one sitting opposite me, and the face I saw reflected in the glass, on my body, was hers. I am now, in old age, rather pink and pinched, as she was late in her life—that which can still be beautiful on a woman but not on a man; but this was *her* face, *her* features, and not my own. It gave me such a fright!

I arrived home that afternoon—I have lived in this same flat in Leicester Square for over twenty years, arrived home feeling all helter-skelter. So I made a pot of tea and sat in the dying light of the day, still feeling shaken; feeling as though I'd lost all sense of myself. Too much time alone, no doubt, I thought. So I rang up Maggie, whom I've known as many years as I taught at the university, some thirty-odd, and dear, inelegant Maggie, a colleague's secretary all those years, an old maid,

Maggie, who doesn't really know me at all, nor I her, said, "Do let's meet for supper then." And so we did, and had a good hoot, and afterwards I felt restored, myself again, and came home, put on my smoking jacket, poured myself a brandy, and a nip in old Tom's bowl, then sat before the fire warming and looking at my hands in the light, and thinking.

I did not mean to suggest earlier, in mentioning that spring afternoon in 1939 as the two of us knelt by the pond, did not by any means intend to imply that the event and what she said that day was at all premonitory or ominous, or that I somehow knew. Not at all. In fact, there is such a volume of water in her work, and in her life; it was commonplace. But I must admit that I was not surprised when I heard *how* she did it, or that she had done it at all, really. (I remember a biographer pointing out that one of her earliest memories was of her mother, and of the water outside her window. The biographer wrote, ending the book, I believe, and I paraphrase: in her beginning was her end. Smashing, to achieve such symmetry!)

Look, for example, at the work: her first novel is set at sea; the third begins on a beach; the fifth and some think finest, set on an island. There is a fluidity in her best work, a rushing liquescence which, when not present, as in that flat second book, makes the work seem grounded. And in my personal favorite, each chapter begins with a description of the ocean at a later, ever-darkening time of day. And then there is the last, that dark, haunted pool of a book, about which my friend John Lehmann showed me shortly after her death (from a letter she had written him):

> "If I live another 50 years I think I shall put this method to use, but as in 50 years I shall be under the pond, with the goldfish swimming over me . . ."

In that last, unfinished, beautiful book, a work I have always thought of, and taught, as capturing, and perhaps prophesying, the atomization that the Second War brought to the world, and that she herself felt so keenly, living in London and Rodmell in her last years and days. In the last book, this is her reference to that pond:

> "It was in that deep center, in that black heart, that the lady had drowned herself."

If I go to a club, which I do now very rarely, but if I do go to a club, I am ignored, and may as well be nonexistent, invisible. Oh, I get waited on all right. "Scotch on the rocks," I'll say to the inevitably blond boy behind the bar. The drink gets plopped down and splashes onto the counter, I hand him the money, say "Keep the change," he smiles, and that is the extent of any intercourse. Occasionally, I'll see other older men there who look at me as if they despise me, because I remind them of themselves, I think, and because they probably figure that one old man, for the chance fetishist, is enough, has better odds. The music is too loud and the smoke too thick, but what I enjoy, what I go for, besides just looking, is the smell—yes, that sense is still vibrant: sweat and aftershave and cologne (there's a difference), and poppers (poppers were common even back in the Fifties), and urine, and even sex, yes, for there is a back room. But then always when I leave I am haunted by my own self-consciousness as I see myself reflected in the glass door on my way out. I walk home to an almost empty flat, Tom brushes against my pants leg, and I sit down before the fire and review my life, which only lends itself to sleepless nights, regrets, recriminations, and resolutions to end the terrible loneliness.

Roland Barthes died, was killed rather, and rather absurdly I must say, struck down by a van as he was crossing the street, on his way to post a letter, in Paris. I have always thought that she would have appreciated his work. And the two of them do rather look alike. Perhaps what set this whole remembering engine running, besides the dark pressing of my last days, was my reading, several weeks back, that Barthes—toward the end of his life (which he did not know, of course, to be the end)—had come to the end of something in his work, and that he, too, had felt the "I" had to be "dismantled." Barthes is, in fact, quoted as having said, or written, that "True knowledge depends upon the unmasking of the 'I'." At which point she, the author of the piece on Barthes, a noted American intellectual, wrote: " . . . the great project of depersonalization which is the aesthete's highest gesture of good taste."

I, myself, sit in my flat. Retired now. A Chair at the University, an office where I can go if I choose, which I don't: I am tired. I sit in my flat by the fire and stare at my hands against the light; I am so terribly lonely. I never did find another, a man with whom to share my life. Oh, there were trysts here and there that became more desperate, more depraved, as I grew older, but never did I find a mate: the great sadness of my life.

Yes, I am tired. Tired of academic life. Tired of books and theories and arguments and abstractions, tired, yes, let it be said, of myself. Odd: one might think I would associate her with all that, but I do not. Instead, I remember her laugh and her conversational flights: she was a fun person to be with, and took one places, if one happened to be sitting next to her at the time, included one in those fanciful flights of the mind.

Birds singing; green leaves, green grass, and a border of brush, darker green, lush, around the pond; sky and pond surface blue, periwinkle blue, and the light, soft; a slight breeze, a shimmering of leaves, and of the water's surface, yes—spring!; the rubbing together, almost whistle, of her brown jersey and long jacket, as we walk along, the group of others fading in the distance behind us; the juices of the grass staining her suede shoes as she steps, sending a sweet, pungent scent up, up, up; but then suddenly, as we near the pond, before she kneels and spots the frog, (yes, between this and the moment she knelt, there had to be a long interlude in which I "explained" myself), she says, "I get no sense of you at all. Do tell me about yourself."

And so whether it was then, in the spring of 1939, when she knelt down beside me at the edge of the pond; or a few days ago (fifty years from then), when she visited me on the tube; or years from now, when I am dead, in a new century, when she lights on the streets of London as a simple shop girl; she is now and forever a "we," a "we" of me, of you, of us all.

And so now "I" will leave my flat one day soon and walk out into the busy streets of London, walk out into the rush of traffic; of the Queen, perhaps, passing by, caught, temporarily, in a traffic jam; of angry, nihilistic, spike-haired youngsters; of the bobby mounted on a horse, oblivious to all, including his horse's droppings, as he talks to a crony on the street corner; will walk out and fling myself ("the only way") against all humanity, the parade, and thus become less myself, more a part of the whole, and finally not alone, yes!

Louella Bryant

Uncharted Territory

Lois presses her right foot against the floor of the passenger side as the car passes the snow plow, lights flashing red and blue.

"It's all right," Rob says. "They're salting the roads."

"There's a traveler's advisory," she says.

"You can't crawl into a hole every time the weather turns bad," he says.

She watches him driving with the fingertips of his left hand curved over the bottom of the steering wheel, drumming his knee with the fingers of his right. It's an oldies station, a Grateful Dead tune. He's wearing a gray shirt and fleece vest that match the ghostly scene outside the window. Thickets of shadowy trees lurk on the sides of the road.

Under the circumstances, she ought to have said no when he suggested dinner out. She thinks Rob is deceived by spring snow, thinks he focuses on the earth coming back to life rather than the layer of ice that still clings to it. He is not rattled by the storm or even by the fact that their son has been gone exactly one year, and it's his imperturbability that maddens her most. He was calm even when the principal called to say Drew had walked out in the middle of his eleventh-grade English test on the Transcendentalists. He'd gotten into the car—her car that he drove to school so he could stay late for track practice—pulled out of the student parking lot and driven off. By inventory of what remained in his room, they know he took his guitar and amplifier, a duffel bag of clothes, the four hundred dollars in his savings account, eighty dollars in cash from Rob's sock drawer, and her credit card.

"Hungry?" Rob asks, turning on the blinker, pulling into a parking space.

"A little." She's lying. She had a bagel on the way to the dry cleaners that morning, nothing since. But she's not hungry, really. Just empty. Hollow. She can almost hear an echo, like footsteps across a wood floor.

By this time the snow has changed to sleet. They have forgotten the umbrella.

"Wait here," Rob says.

She knows waiting. For the school bus, young Drew in hand, double-checking for his bookbag, his lunchbox. In the bleachers at Little League games while he sat the bench, the back-up pitcher. Watching the clock the night of a school dance, listening for a car motor, a door slam. Waiting is what she does best.

Rob pulls a coat from the back seat, covers his head and runs around the car. He opens the door for her and uses the coat to shield them from the freezing rain. His arm around her back, he guides her toward the restaurant. She remembers a warm night before Drew was born, when the stars were out and his touch struck nerves, how they wove down the street like clumsy children, just for the delight of making each other laugh. Laughter came easily then, even in love-making, both of them hoping that in the next weeks the test would come out positive and they'd begin redefining themselves as parents, generators of a good thing they'd made together.

They shuffle up the walk, passing a bar where young people cluster under an awning and music surges onto the street. Bass and drum, saxophone and guitar thrown together in confusion. She scans their faces. Three girls, a thick-necked boy, all smoking and laughing as if it's not cold and wet. The boy wears a green baseball cap with a yellow "V," plump face glowing orange in the light coming from the bar, not like Drew, who is thin and almost awkward, as if his bones grew too fast for his skin. Drew might have changed enough in twelve months that she'd have trouble recognizing him. Taller, longer hair, a growth of fuzz on the chin, a new look to the eyes. This boy digs his hands into jacket pockets and talks around the cigarette between his lips. He leans against the brick wall, against a poster with a picture of three boys—the band. One short, hair parted in the middle, sunglasses. One hefty. One tall, scowling, brown hair cow-licked about his head. A lanky arm reaching toward her. "Tonight. Nine o'clock. Uncharted Territory," the poster says.

She lets Rob tug her along, even though she'd like to stand in front of the poster. At the corner they stop at a restaurant with bright light pouring through the glass front. She steps back. She wants to stay in the darkness, to be cold and wet and miserable. Two women come out, long coats flapping, bringing with them smells of garlic and sage. They grip each other and duck toward the curb, through the light dripping from the streetlamp.

Rob hurries her through the door and shakes water from the coat. Then he hangs it on a hook, unzips the vest and leaves it on. They follow the hostess to a booth against the wall. Rob sits across from her, a red tablecloth between them covered edge to edge with a plate of thick glass. They've never eaten at this restaurant before, although they've passed it several times. The window by their booth looks out onto the intersection where the traffic signal turns red, winks yellow, turns green, reflecting in the wet street.

"What'll it be?" Rob says. His reading glasses hang around his neck on a thin length of reefing line. She once admired his practicality, his lack of pretense. It hadn't occurred to her then, as it does now, that if one wraps reefing line around his neck, he must have a sail to be reefed, a boat to sail. But they have no boat, so he must have made a special trip to the marina store for reefing line. It was odd how he was becoming more of a mystery to her the longer they lived together.

"I'd like a drink," she says.

"I thought you gave it up."

"I have a drink every night. You haven't been paying attention." She tries for a light tone, but her voice ices up.

"Don't get huffy," he says. "What difference does it make whether you drink or not?"

"The difference is you didn't notice." She's looking at the menu, but she's listening for his response. She wants to hear something warm, cheerful.

"I'm trying, Lois," is all he says.

The waiter puts a basket of rolls on the table between them, and she orders a vodka martini. Usually she has her vodka with juice or tonic, but she likes to order martinis when she's out. She hasn't the shaker or the wide-rimmed glasses or the ambition to make them at home. Rob orders a bottle of Merlot.

Reading glasses perched on the end of his nose, he scans the menu, looking more like a philosophy professor reading a student's paper than a middle-aged software salesman deciding what he'll have for dinner. He frowns at the dim lamp on the wall and turns his back to it to throw more light on the menu.

"Emu Marsala with wild rice pilaf," he says. "What's emu?"

"It's like an ostrich," she says. "Where have you been that you haven't heard about emus? The meat of the future. Lean, economical, nutritious."

"I'm not eating anything that walks on two legs."

"Chickens walk on two legs."

"Anything that walks on two legs and is taller than I am." He probably expects her to laugh, which she might have a few years back, even at as faltering a joke as this one.

"You won't know the difference once it's on your plate," she says. "Once it's dead, it's dead." The word "dead" falls onto the table between them.

She thinks of the nights she lay on Drew's bed, looking at the posters on the wall. Jerry Garcia, Jimi Hendrix, Stevie Ray Vaughan, guitars posed like machine guns, firing rounds of silent chords into the dark room. He'd talked of California, but she couldn't picture him there, playing guitar the way he'd played it sitting on his bed, long into the night. What she pictured was her son lying in a casket surrounded by white puffs of satin, hair tucked behind his ears, long fingers entwined over his chest. She tried to push away the pleasure of imagining him close, even in death, of touching his still body, of looking her fill at his thin face, the dark lashes, the narrow mouth, the relief of not having to wonder whether he was safe.

The waiter brings her martini and the wine, and while he opens the bottle, Rob banters with him over corkscrews—the air pump versus the old-fashioned screw-in variety. She needs his good humor and hates him for it at the same time.

After the waiter pours wine for Rob to taste and serves them both a glass, Rob orders prime rib and a green salad. She still hasn't decided, and the waiter shifts from one foot to the other.

"Shall I order for you?" Rob asks.

She doesn't want him to pick out her dinner. He would order something pink and bleeding. She rejects, too, the turkey and the chicken—the pale skin, the featherless little bodies.

"I'll have ziti with marinara sauce. That's all."

"How exciting," Rob says.

"I'm not in an exciting mood," she says.

After the waiter leaves, Rob says, "Here's to you," and taps his glass against hers. He's taken off his glasses, and they hang awkwardly on his chest.

The rim of the martini glass is so thin she could take a bite out of it. The martini is dry enough to be unpleasant and tastes like liquid drunkenness. Both sensations please her. Rob's wine is deep red, the color of maple leaves splattered on autumn frost. He holds his glass under his nose and swirls the wine around.

"Savoring the bouquet?" she asks, her voice cutting the silence, surprising her. She slides the napkin off the table and smoothes it onto her lap. Where the napkin has been, a wing from a small insect—a moth maybe—is pressed under the glass table top. It is the color of sand, and segmented with dark lines. A single wing, smaller than a dime, and solitary.

"What's that?" Rob asks. The traffic signal is green, tingeing his cheek and making him look as if he's under water. She's heard that the surface tension of water is so hard that divers bandage their fingers to keep from injuring them when they break into the pool. It's like breaking through glass.

"Something under the glass," she says. "A wing."

"Lovely. Put your plate over it."

"Do you have something against winged creatures?" she says.

"I'm bothered by insects while I'm dining, yes."

Why is it that winged creatures make her think of that night on Jamaica's eastern coast? They were staying in the Glass House, called that because of the windows looking toward the sea. The surf bubbled luminescence on the shore, and warm rain splashed against the windows. Both of them stoned on rum and ganja, Rob read out loud to her from Siddhartha, a story about a boy, a young man, on a soul-searching journey. She felt she had found her soul-mate in Rob. And when they made love, she settled into the pleasure of his skin against hers, into the rhythms of rain and waves. In the morning, she lolled in bed and Rob brought her scrambled eggs and coffee. When the sun steamed through the glass, she finally rose and drifted across the hot sand for a swim, washing away salty sweat with salty ocean water. Months later, she felt the first flutters in her stomach.

Rob begins polishing his fork with the napkin, rubbing the water spots from the tines, turning it while he pinches a corner of the napkin around the handle. His lips fall open. She has begun to realize that the polishing is a gathering of steam for some thought about to emerge and wonders what will erupt this time.

He puts down the fork and breaks open a roll. "You ought to take in a boarder," he says.

"What do you mean?"

He unwraps the gold foil from a pat of butter and wipes the butter on the bread directly from the paper, without using a knife.

"It wouldn't be any trouble," he says at last. "What would it take—a morning muffin, a cup of coffee?"

She envisions herself as a bent old woman, bifocals slipping down her nose, loose housedress and low-heeled shoes. No—orthopedic lace-ups. The aroma of oatmeal hovering about her. An elderly man in a worn cardigan with leather buttons—the boarder—smelling like an old leather suitcase.

"We don't need the money," she says. She emphasizes "we," bringing him back into it.

"It's not about money," he says.

"That's ridiculous," she says. "We have no space for a boarder. The spare room has the computer and filing cabinet, and where would your mother stay when she comes to visit?" She laughs softly and tries to pretend he's joking, although his sense of humor is slipping. He's usually more acerbic, more witty.

"I don't mean the spare room," he says.

There is the unfinished attic, the damp cellar, the crawl space over the garage, which aren't suitable for anyone, especially for an arthritic old man to spend his declining years. She thinks of any place except Drew's room, the rust-colored carpet, walls the color of an overcast sky, and the single window that looks onto the street.

She looks around the restaurant to avoid looking at Rob. On the bar a figurine of a naked cherub with chubby arms holds up a ball, a serene smile on his face. His skin is pale gray and blue-veined. The bartender mixes a drink. He's older than Drew by at least five years. Decent looking, maybe a college graduate. Like Drew could turn out. She'd like to go to the ladies' room, lock herself in a stall or crawl out the window. She wants to hide from what her husband is telling her. He has given up.

"There's a housing crunch at the university," he says. "And we have a place set up for a student."

"No," she says. "We don't have an empty place."

"He's not coming back," he says.

She rotates her wine glass by the stem. "It's his home," she says. Her voice trembles, and she takes a sip of wine.

"Wherever he is, he's doing what we taught him to do," he says. "He's being independent and learning to take care of himself."

"He's seventeen. He just turned seventeen." She doesn't want her voice to sound as if she's pleading.

"I know when his birthday is," he says.

Of course he knows. He was there when her water broke in the morning and she left a stream between the bed and the bathroom. He was there during the long hours of early labor, reading her quips from *The New York Times* about Spain legalizing divorce, the world population reaching four and a half billion. And when she was in hard labor, what the nurse called "transition," he held the pan for her to retch in, squeezed her hand, helped her focus on the breathing.

"What are you thinking?" he says.

"You wanted a girl."

"It didn't matter."

"When he was born," she says, "you bowed your head. I thought you were disappointed." When he'd raised his head, she'd seen tears drip from his nose. And then he held his son, no bigger than a football in his arms, stared at a little hand curled around his finger, kissed the bald head.

"I wasn't disappointed," he says.

The waiter sets a mound of thick red substance in front of her that undulates faintly as the plate meets the table. Rob's plate holds a lump of meat floating in a lake of dark blood. He saws off a hunk, sticks it between his lips and grinds it slowly.

"Aren't you going to eat?" he says between bites.

The smell of basil and oregano rises from her plate. Outside, a couple cross the street arm in arm and talk with heads tilted toward each other. In the window she sees her own reflection, beads of rain streaking down the glass.

She pokes her fork into the pasta and takes a bite. It is surprisingly sweet and she eats slowly, willfully, and remembers how the neighbors brought in food when news got around that Drew had gone. Lasagnas and pot pies, cakes and platters of cookies. "Keep up your strength," they said, as if he'd died. Later, sausage and mushroom pizza—Drew's favorite—kept her alive, delivered to the door each night by a boy his age. If she ate what he was eating, some assimilation might occur, some psychic link might bring them together and he'd know the pain he was causing. He'd call. The phone did ring, but it was friends, the police, the detective.

The waiter clears the table and brings coffee. Rob circles his hands around the cup.

"Let's review what we know—" he says. He taps his index finger on the edge of the saucer. She feels a stab in her stomach. "—what the police and detectives have uncovered."

The word "uncovered" sounds as if Drew is lying on a street somewhere, someone's coat thrown over his face so no one can see the ghastly look of death. They've been over Drew's drug use, the falling grades, his determination to play in a band. He turned away from his friends and started hanging out with college students who played gigs at downtown bars. When they told him no more going to bars, he went out after they were asleep, and she heard the back door shudder when he came in at one or two in the morning. On weekends he rarely was home at all, and when he was, the guitar squealed and rasped frantic riffs behind his closed bedroom door. They've been over it all, yet she wants to hear it again. She wants to hear it from Rob.

"The last time he used your credit card was in Chicago," he says. "It looks like he headed west, hitting big cities where he could find some work and make a few quick bucks. And he'd be tougher to spot. He could be in Seattle by now, or anywhere on the West Coast."

"If he were a criminal," she says, "they might try harder to find him."

"He's not a criminal," he says. "He's our son." His voice is tender. She thinks about him standing in the doorway while she lay in Drew's room. In the darkness she sensed rather than saw him there, but he never came in. She would like to have spent the night like that, sharing expectation with her husband, as if they were both waiting for their son to pull up the driveway in her car. But she would hear his soft step down the hall, the water running in the bathroom, the click of the lamp switch as he turned out the light.

"Look," he says. He lays his palms flat on the table. "You need some breathing room."

She holds onto the edge of the table, her fingers slipping on the glass. Her left index finger is pressed against the moth wing, as if it is holding her in place.

"Here's the way it is," he says. "I'm going to move out for a while."

"What?" she says.

He presses a knuckle to his upper lip and lays his hand back on the table, like a card player waiting for a hit. "Just until you get yourself together. Until you figure things out."

"You're moving out?" She imagines him being sucked out the front door, clothes and papers swirling out behind him.

"I can't watch you do this to yourself," he says.

"I'm not doing anything," she says, making an attempt to pull him back.

"I know. That's the point."

She wipes her hands on the napkin across her lap and reaches for her purse, pushes things around inside it. Wallet. Lipstick. Glasses case. Comb. Matchbook. She has no idea what she's looking for.

Outside the rain has fizzled to a fine mist. When they get to the bar, the bear-necked boy stands on the sidewalk alone.

"I'm going in," she says, pointing to the poster of the three boys.

"Uncharted Territory?" Rob looks at her as if she is a foreign object, some abstract sculpture in an art gallery.

She goes through the scarred door and up the narrow staircase to the landing where a boy with a crew cut and a silver bar pierced through one eyebrow holds out his hand for money. Rob's hand comes from behind her and passes him a ten-dollar bill, and she is startled, as if she expected him, after two decades of marriage, to abandon her at a college bar.

Thick smells of beer, coffee, and cigarettes heave with the taut, pressing music, and the floor vibrates with a driving bass. The drum thumps inside her, hammering through her chest. Dancers crowd the stage, and lights flicker bright blue, yellow, red. She can't see the faces of the musicians through the smoke. She hears the guitar, though, feels the pressure of fingertips against frets, can almost clutch the familiarity.

"A drink?" Rob asks. He takes off his coat and vest and folds them over his arm.

She shakes her head, slips off her jacket and piles it on an empty bar stool. Then she elbows her way onto the dance floor, through shoulders, backsides and breasts. She lets her arms fall to her sides and sways her hips slowly. Bodies churn around her, and she melts into them, gives in to the rhythm, lets it take her.

When she catches a glimpse of Rob by the door, his coat is still in his arms. He is looking toward the stage, and she sees how he has given Drew the angular body, the straight nose, the full lips. She loves him in that moment more than in all the moments of the last twenty years and at the same time knows she has never known him at all.

The music blows its shrill wind through her, aerating her. Cymbals crash like broken glass and the guitar shrieks. She closes her eyes and spirals into the colors behind her lids, into the pounding noise, twisting until her chest opens and a shadow flutters out.

Roy Hoffman

from *Chicken Dreaming Corn*

THE LAND OF COTTON

Mobile, Alabama, 1916

Down the stairs from the bedrooms to the floor of his store, past the blouses and pants under dust covers waiting for day to begin, Morris Kleinman made his way to the front door thanking God, blessed be His name, for a regular night's sleep, his devoted Miriam, four healthy children, and strength enough, after a nagging cold, to be the first one up on Upper Dauphin Street wielding his broom against the walk in preparation for the Confederate Veteran's parade.

Above him the swallows looped their crazy script against the chalky Mobile sky. They circled above the Lebanese clothing store and

Syrian pressing shop, turned and soared above the Greek bakery where Matranga was baking his New York twist bread that would sell, in today's busy crowd, for a nickel a loaf. As the Holy Cathedral bell gonged six times Father O'Connor scraped his way on one good leg toward the church steps, calling out to Morris, "May peace be with you," to which Morris called back, thinking of the silent, glaring Orthodox priest of his Romanian village, "Good morning, Monsignor, and *shalom* to you."

Horse hair, wood shavings, tobacco, goat droppings, melon rind, ashes, a lone shoelace—his broom whisked away last night's debris onto the wood-brick street. He reached down into the gutter and retrieved the shoelace, slipping it into his pocket for Miriam's scrap box; yesterday she'd kissed him when he salvaged an ivory button.

As he wheeled out the clothes racks he looked down the street, past the red-brick and stained-glass Cathedral, past the tattered Star Theater marquee and the humble mercantile storefronts of Habeeb and Zoghby and Kalifeh, toward Lower Dauphin where the likes of prosperous Greenbaum and Leinkauf were nowhere yet to be seen. *Oh*, he shook his head, the German Jewish merchants still blithely asleep in their canopied beds.

The ritual morning prayers humming at his lips, he turned to go back in, eyeing a crate to be opened. Facing east, *tallit* over his shoulders, he laced the prayer straps through his fingers and intoned the Hebrew, rocking gently, trying not to think about the work pants he'd ordered from Schwartz in Memphis or the dresses from Besser in New Orleans, *landsmen* with their own ties to the Carpathian vistas of Romania. The sun fanned out like palmetto leaves across the storefronts where cedar bread boxes awaited Smith's Bakery deliveries and, in the doorway of the Norwegian Seamen's Hall, men curled hoping for day jobs cleaning stables or lugging bananas from the docks. As Father O'Connor said his first "amen" in the incensed recesses of Holy

Cathedral, Morris said his last "*o main*" standing behind the cash register of his store. He added a prayer for safekeeping of Papa, dwelling still with sister Golda, so far away. "You will join us here in Alabama," he vowed. "Soon."

He folded away his prayer shawl, picked up a crowbar and faced the shoulder-high crate: *Besser Fashions. New Orleans*. Thinking of his sons curled in a lazy cocoon, he went back upstairs.

In the front room, his own, Miriam lay curled in their bed before the French doors half-opened to the balcony. The collar of her embroidered gown came high on the neck, her dark hair coiled in a bun. Without turning she raised her hand to signal she was awake: the eyes and ears of the house even as she dozed in reverie, he knew, of the village lanes and kitchen tables of her Romanian home.

He passed his daughter's room. Lillian had kicked off the covers, her twelve-year-old legs sprawled to the far corners of the mattress, her gown twisted up to beyond her knees. The color was robust in her face, blessed be His Name, but after her rheumatic fever—three years ago, this day of the Confederates—who could ever be sure? He stole in and draped the sheet back over her.

He turned into the front room where baby Hannah snored in her bed. Just the other side of a muslin curtain dividing the room, ten-year-old Abraham and eight-year-old Herman lay elbow to shoulder, mouths open like fish. He leaned over and stroked the back of his hand over Abe's cheek; his son groaned. He wiggled his fingertip on the peach fuzz over the boy's upper lip; Abe brushed away the finger.

"*Gutte morgen, mein boychik*," Morris whispered.

"Mornin'," Abe moaned back.

"*Langer loksh*," he exhorted, using the nickname, "long legs," for his lanky son.

"No school today, Daddy."

"Up!"

"Sun's not even up."

"This son is the first who will make good at Barton?"

"Hm, mm."

"Who will make a good marriage to a nice *shayna madele*?"

He nodded in the pillow.

"Who will help his Papa in the store?"

He was answered with a rising snore.

Morris laid his hand on the boy's shoulder and belted, "*Avraham*!"

The boy bolted upright, but Herman was already on his feet, slipping on his pants, dancing from side to side and bunching his fists like a boxer.

Miriam called out, "You will wake Hannah!"

"Abe will hush her," Morris answered.

"Oh, Daddy!" Abe protested, climbing out now, but Morris instructed, "Stay, you, with the baby."

Abe flopped back down and hugged on his pillow.

On the first landing, with Herman padding behind, Morris fingered up a cigar butt he'd stuck into an ash tray and chomped down on it.

"Daddy, are we Rebels?" Herman asked as they came to the crate.

"Today? Yes, we are Rebels."

Morris jockeyed the box out of the corner and wedged the crowbar into a crevice. Herman reached up and grabbed hold of the bar and lifted his feet off the ground. The boards groaned apart.

Morris lifted out the skirts one by one: pretty pale blues and checkered reds. "Besser," he addressed the spirit of his supplier in New Orleans, "now, you are making good business."

From in the back he pulled a skirt soiled on the side. Holding it close, he eyed the brown stain. "Besser," he fumed, "you try to sell to me this *drek*?"

"Daddy!"

From deep inside the crate came scratching and scuffling. Feathers flashed brightly, then exploded into wings.

"Gall durn bird!" Herman cried. "Shoo." A starling wove toward the eaves.

Morris found the bag of old shoes and brought one out, hurling it upwards. The starling dove away, arcing across overalls.

"Small blessings," Morris muttered as bird droppings missed the table and splashed against the floor. The starling turned back over his head and flew up the steps. Herman raced behind.

Into Lillian's room, back through Abe's and Herman's, the bird coursed. Herman grabbed up a broomstick and jumped onto the bed, dancing around Abe's pillow.

Abe sat up blearily. "What are you doing?"

"Is this fun!"

"Not fair."

"You're the one didn't get up." Herman poked wildly at the air.

"Daddy wouldn't let me!"

"In bed like a bum!" Morris yelled at him.

The bird swooped back into the dining room, veering by Morris's head, who cursed Besser like he was in the next room.

"Y'all leave Abe alone," Lillian said, coming from her room, jaw dropping at the spectacle of Daddy waving his arms in the air and turning in circles.

Morris ran toward the front of the apartment, throwing open the French doors. The starling looped back, veered toward Herman who shouted, "*Go on, git!*" before it banked and hurtled into the calm, bluing Alabama sky.

⚜

After drinking his black coffee and eating a bowl of *mamaligi* that Miriam had fixed—he still preferred to pasty Southern grits this hearty Romanian dish of cornmeal boiled down to yellow porridge—Morris hurried back down to the walk.

Waiting for the parade to assemble, two boys leaned against a hitching post in front of the Lyric Theater, practicing their drums. Their rolls and rimshots climbed the walls of the popular vaudeville venue, by the marquee reading *Al Jolson May 5* and *Alabama Minstrels Tonight*, moving like a prowler up the French grille balconies.

Most, this early, just wanted to converse about that bloody conflict he'd heard called "the Civil War" up North but here was "the War Between the States," or "the Cause." When this subject came up, anywhere in America, he kept his mouth shut. Fifty years had passed since the Yankees had come steaming into Mobile Bay and Admiral Farragut had cried, "Damn the torpedoes, full speed ahead," but it was as if the Jackal had appeared yesterday. Morris had learned, soon after stepping off the train here in 1907, that mention of "Grant" or "Sherman" started a fight. Even in school in Romania, he had heard of the great president named Lincoln, but to repeat his name here, except among the Negroes, was to risk a bloody nose.

Besides, with every holiday there were sales to be made. Fourth of July—bathing attire. Christmas—children's dresses. Last month had been the celebration called Mardi Gras. He had no evening dress to sell—not like Hammel's, run by German Jews, where blue-blooded city dwellers, whatever their origins, spent a pretty penny to outfit themselves elegantly for the occasion.

He watched Donnie McCall saunter in now, panama hat pushed back, red-faced and jowly. Beneath McCall's eyes were always deep circles, like his own Papa's. McCall, an Irishman he called himself, like Papa also had black-black eyes. A better customer there never was.

McCall nodded to his scuffed-up shoes. "Need a new pair, Mr. Morris. Something respectable for today's doings, not too fancy. The colored look up to a man with smart shoes."

Morris fetched two-tone lace-ups while McCall settled into a chair. Kneeling at his feet, Morris asked about the funeral insurance business as he shoehorned on the first pair.

"One thing folks got to do is die. And when they do, God rest their souls"—McCall stood, peering down—"they want to make sure their funeral's a send-off the likes of which"—he wriggled his toes—"has never been witnessed before. Too small." He sat.

"These better will fit."

McCall stood again, rocked back and forth. "Got my name on 'em, don't you think?"

"Right here." Morris patted the tips. "I can interest you in a new panama hat?"

"Could be tomorrow."

"I will put in the back one with your name just in case."

McCall paid for the shoes and said good-day. A tall man shambled in and plopped down in a chair.

"Got these suckers from you a while ago," the man said, tugging off his muddy boots. "Name's Jackson."

"A good price I remember, Mr. Jackson."

The clammy odor of Jackson's feet rose up. "Don't want 'em."

"Is not possible."

"You make it possible."

"How can I take back old shoes?"

"I paid $2.95 for these durn boots! They hurt my feet!"

Morris broke into a sweat. "Come, the wife she does not like when I do this, but"—he coaxed the man to the display case—"if she does not see." He handed him a bottle of 25¢ ointment.

The man turned it back and forth. "What's it say?"

"Dr. Zigorsky's Foot Elixir. A medicine, but for you a blessing. Worth many dollars."

"Cost me nothin'?"

Morris shook his head. "Hurry, before the wife, she sees."

"Got you a deal," said the man, who dragged his boots back on and hobbled out the store.

By eight o'clock the walks of Dauphin Street began to fill with people and Morris positioned Herman on a stool near the door to keep an eye out for passersby with sticky fingers. Some paused before the outdoor racks of M. Kleinman & Sons looking over the newest hats and boulevard ties.

A willowy, red-haired young woman turned into the store with easy gait, heading to the fancy ladies' section in the rear. Lillian came from the back office to greet her.

As they went down the rows, the woman selected a blue cotton dress and Lillian directed her to the dressing curtain which she drew around her. A moment later she rolled open the curtain and walked to the floor-length mirror.

"What do you think?" she asked Lillian.

"You look," Lillian surmised, "like a nice spring day."

"What an enterprising girl!" The young woman turned to Morris. "Now for a gentleman's opinion?"

He saw again the rich hair and pale eyes of the Romanian girl, Theodora Eminescu, turning to him in the window long ago. Her shoulders rose from her gown, the lantern glow bathing her skin.

"We call this, a *shayna klayde*. A pretty dress."

"But how do I look in it?"

"In this *shayna klayde* you are"—he hesitated, not wanting to sound fresh—"a *shayna madele*." He felt himself blush.

"By the look on your face, it must be good. Reckon I'll take it."

Morris quickly turned his attention to the register.

Before long the sidewalk was lined with Mobilians craning their necks for sight of the marchers, the Kleinman children among them. There were squeals and shouts as, far off, the full complement of drums sounded, buzzing along M. Kleinman & Sons' street-front panes. The tattoo of cornets charged the air. The first marchers arrived.

No matter their look—one man was rigid, another bent—or their size—one was tall like a youth, another once tall but shrunk in old age—the men carried themselves with the same tired, but defiant bearing. At ages sixty-five and seventy, seventy-five and eighty, they puffed their chests out against their gray jackets, feeble but cocksure.

"The *alter kockers*," Sam Lutchnik, a Polish Jew down the street, had said of the marchers, "the old men, still fighting their war."

It was a war that lived still from regiment to regiment, in the trudging boots, the gray coats buttoned tight around the sloping bellies of men who years before, lean and quick, thundered across the fields of Shiloh and Manassas, that town, Morris had heard, named for a Jew.

Two men passed, aided by young cadets—the first was missing his left leg, his stump wagging as he hopped on crutches, the second on crutches with no right foot. Behind them walked a veteran with a cane, tap-tapping on the street. With his free hand he waved at the crowd, his ruined eyes cocked toward the sky.

Some veteran groups had banners: the Raphael Semmes Division, honoring one man, Morris had been told, who stood at the helm of a big warship called Alabama and was buried at the old Catholic cemetery a few miles away, and the George E. Dixon Division, memorializing a poor boy from Mobile who had gone under the water in Charleston Harbor in a hand-cranked submarine called the Hunley to blast a hole in a Union ship, and was entombed in those waters.

The music rose, a tune called "Bonnie Blue Flag." It changed to a melody Morris knew well.

It was not a song that belonged to him like the Yiddish melodies he loved to hum from deep in his boyhood, or the religious songs like the soaring "Aveinu Malkeinu" of Rosh Hashanah, or the stirring "Kol Nidre" chanted at Yom Kippur. But these piccolos playing out the spirited melody gave him goosebumps. "Dixie," it was called. The song piped its sad merriment through the streets, where the onlookers clapped and stomped.

Behind the last division of men followed a crowd of marching ladies: A-frame dresses sweeping the street, silver hair up in buns or down in thin gray tresses reminiscent of the days they had waited for their young Johnny Rebs to return from the battlefields. Many had waited, and waited, their faces caught still in that moment fifty years ago when an emissary stepped onto the porch and announced, with deep consolation, that Jack Mayfield or Curtis Kellogg or Ira Glasser would never be returning, sweet Jesus be with you in this time of great need.

Among these women Morris saw Ira's widow, Dolores, who'd later married Joseph Levy, a German Jew who himself had died the year before. Today, though, Joseph was forgotten; Dolores walked mourning her bright, Confederate youth.

Young women now passed who smiled and waved in the modern way. These were the Daughters of the Confederacy: Spring Hill Chapter, Oakleigh Chapter, Saraland Chapter, Bay Minette Chapter. Girls no older than Ira must have been when the word came back that the young man's life had bled out of him at Chickamauga.

Behind a drum and fife corps filed the cadets of Mobile Military Academy, grave-faced adolescents restless for President Wilson to make a declaration of War, allowing them to jump into trenches alongside the Frenchmen and Brits, having at the dirty Huns. Some had already found action with General Pershing on the Mexican border, chasing the wily Pancho Villa back to his desert lair; the heroic tales they brought back had ignited their friends. The way they stamped their feet reminded Morris of Cossacks, rifles locked on their shoulders. Abe put two fingers to his lips and shrieked a whistle.

A towering lout bumped into Morris and veered into the store.

"I can help you, sir?" Morris asked, following behind.

The man wove toward the rack of hats, reached for a Stetson and knocked several hats to the floor. He stepped back, tottering.

The smell of corn whiskey soured the air.

Miriam looked in from the street. "*Shikker*," Morris said to her.

"What did you say about me?" The man wove toward the counter, steadying himself on the cash register.

"I said you are drunk."

"Don't talk *Yid* talk."

"Out of the store, mister."

"I can do what I Goddamn please!"

"Do not curse the Lord God in here."

"*You're* telling *me* about . . . ?" The man gazed up blearily at the ceiling, then back down to Morris. "What business you people got hoopin' and hollerin' today?"

"Leave this store."

"This ain't your war."

Miriam had disappeared from the door; a band played a weary dirge.

"Passed by a woman here," said Morris, "Dolores Glasser, who lost a husband in this War. How old was he? Only a boy, fighting in Chickamauga, I have seen the place, such a sadness. Passed Molly Friedman, her brother today walks with two crutches and no legs, boom. Fighting for a Jew named Proskauer, I have seen his picture. A proud man from Mobile, too, with a fancy beard. He was not like you, not a horse's behind, not a *putz* making trouble in an honest man's store."

The man fell back from the cash register and glared at Morris. "You're a scrappy cuss, ain't you?" He took a step closer.

Morris picked up the crowbar.

Miriam came hurrying in with Officer Flynn, who gripped the troublemaker's collar and shook him. "You giving Mr. Morris trouble? I got a hole at the jail for a stinkin' mongrel to sleep in."

The man looked helplessly at Morris. Abe and Herman had appeared.

Morris shook his head. "No, he will not bother us again."

The man nodded dumbly as they went outside. When Flynn had gone his way, the man said, "You ain't such a bad Joe," and brought out a flask of whiskey.

Morris grasped it, took a swig, and, as the man stumbled away, spat it out behind him on the walk.

"*Ach*, my shoulder." Morris spoke to himself, sitting in the rocking chair near the door as a lull came in the procession. The sky had clouded over and rain threatened the day. Wearily he rubbed at his shoulder. Since the November night he'd first slept on those feed sacks in the Eminescu barn, he'd felt the Romanian cold haunting his body, like a sliver of ice deep in his wing. He ceased rubbing, wishing he had swallowed that hooligan's whiskey now, a nice elixir to ease his shoulder's ache.

Sheeted men with hoods over their faces trod silently by, on the shoulders of one a large, rugged cross. The Klan members were met with polite, steady, applause. Morris had learned it was prudent, when Klansmen passed, to look straight ahead, nodding, while revealing no emotion at all. What bone to pick anyway, could they have with him? Wilder enthusiasm greeted the wagonloads of farmers who waved Confederate battle flags and hollered and whistled back at the crowd.

At the same time as the children went cavorting down the street going *bang bang* at enemy soldiers there was the crack of real rifles from the direction of Magnolia Cemetery. The sharp report came again in salute to the Confederate dead, scattering swallows from the telegraph wires down Dauphin, igniting a spark in the feet of the children.

Morris rocked back, looking up at the pressed-tin ceiling of his store, seeing the brocade of ice on the window of his room as a boy with his brothers and sister close by, hearing the blast of rifles again in the frozen night. Under the blanket next to him stirred Chaim, who burrowed down deeper against the shattering noise. There was another volley of shots and, from the adjacent bed, Ben leapt up and came to join him at the window. Frantically they rubbed their palms across the thick, muted glass, trying to see. Golda began to cry in the next room.

Everywhere snow swirled through darkness, hiding the rattle of steel and the pounding of hooves, hiding the screams until it drew back like a veil revealing a man sunk down into the drifts and another alongside, tugging him up, and a horse, like a black ghost flying. Voices, shouts, villagers emerging from doorways running toward the figures in the snow. Another horse crowded the darkness, then another came thundering, and the door of Morris's own house opened as Papa, nightshirt flying, headed toward the courtyard, and Mama was at the door of their room holding Golda, putting her finger to her lips, exhorting, "*Sha shtil, kinder*, be quiet, children, do as Papa has asked and pray to the Almighty."

The night stilled a moment, then held sobbing, and angry, rising voices. Morris and his brothers rubbed busily at the window, wiping away their own curtains of breath, watching the men disperse, hearing the sobbing fall away and the voices receding into houses across the *shtetl* square.

Papa's face was long and dark when he came back in, and the next day when he went off to work at his distillery, and when he returned; and the next day and next, when sitting by the fire, prayer book open on his lap, he gazed off at the dancing flames. He said nothing until that night he came home, eyes sunk into deep moons, and told them the soldiers had visited him with swords and guns, with padlocks and chains, pronouncing his distillery closed: it was a law, they said, barring Jews from this business, as others had been barred from being doctors and men of the courts. Who knew, they said, what mischief Jews might perform on grains and yeast and water; on the magic liquor they sold to the good Christians of Piatra Neamt? How much money the Jews had accumulated, they complained, at the expense of the good people of the village! As Papa spoke his face darkened still, as though wanting to let loose tears like those that had come when they marched to the cemetery with his own father and tossed the dirt onto the casket and sat solemnly for days until the black veils were lifted from the chairs.

But he held back the tears, and sat one week, and then another, with prayer book open while gazing only at the fire. He called Morris to him and explained there was little money left for the family, and word had come throughout the region of Moldavia, from Dorohoi to Iasi, that others had businesses that were being closed down. He told Morris that he must leave school and go to work at a farmhouse on the edge of the Romanian plain; that he had contacted a grain farmer he knew through the distillery, Stefan Eminescu, a good Christian man with a son and two daughters, who could use a boy with good hands and a strong back.

Mama's hand rested on Morris's shoulder. "Azril," she said, "don't be so hard on him, tell him more gently," and he nodded and said her name, "Shayna Blema," pretty rose. "Pretty rose," Morris repeated, reaching up to touch her slender, soft hand. She started to walk away, but he held her hand firmly now; "*gai nisht*, Mama," he whispered, don't go, feeling the floor drop away.

"Morris?" Miriam's voice was exhorting him. Her hand jiggled his shoulder. "Chicken dreaming corn?"

He shook his head. "Not so good."

"The parade is over, and more customers will be coming soon." She moved away toward the cash register to go over the morning's receipts.

He stood from the rocking chair, the floor still dropping away, and stepped outdoors to steady himself, breathing in Mobile streets.

Julie Brickman

from *An Empty Quarter*

MESSAGE FROM AYSHA

I was never so excited in my life as the day my father told me he was hiring an American woman *to run his new business. Well, not run, but co-run. And she was to be on equal footing as a director with my brother, Samir! Samir was not happy, in fact he was furious. He flushed to a bruised purple and stayed that way throughout the evening.*

My nervous system electrified like a hot wire fence, sending little zinging feelings crackling through me, until even my liver trembled, my kidney, my heart, though I tried to conceal my elation. I wish they would send me to school in England; I'd come back broadened. I am proud of my father. No one else in this fossilized country would dare do such a thing, except my father. He is so cool, don't you think? The first with new ideas, western technology, change. I wanted to throw my arms around him, but of course I didn't because I am seventeen and my father is a man.

Though I wish, sometimes, he would listen to me.

I've dreamt about you. Emma Solace. What a funny name. I looked it up in my English dictionary. "Solace: To console. To make cheerful. To amuse." I thought, she will make me laugh. My mother claims I shouldn't laugh because something bad will happen, but you, Emma Solace, laugh in your picture, your mouth wide and open like you could swallow the world, your hair the color of moonlight on water, frothy like a whipped-up sea, and completely uncovered. The top button on your blouse undone so anyone can see the milky skin on your chest covered with freckles like specks of gold in the sand.

I sneaked your visa down to the tourist photo shop where I could get a copy of that picture. The very look of it declares independence; what I will *have in my life. Idolatry is a sin, my mother would say, quoting our imam, because it distracts from devotion to God, but what she really fears is diluted respect for the family. Even my father, who is probably the most influential person in this country, not counting the royals, had to get special permission to put a statue in front of his new building, a Bedouin with a camel. So I figured the sin was small enough to be worth the risk. After all, you had the photo taken yourself. It wasn't as if I were stealing a piece of your soul. Not that I'd mind. I think you must have a soul of steel to come to Arabia all by yourself.*

I take out the photo and stare at it every day. I have memorized every line on your face, even the tiny ones that look like sandpiper tracks by the sea. It is a lived-in kind of face, beautiful but homey, as if the person wearing it got weatherbeaten from being so real all the time. I try to learn from those eyes. To look into the secret parts of myself for vision is power and I need all the power I can get. When I gaze into your eyes, aqua like a sundrenched sea and set so far apart they can watch every direction, I feel an acceptance of things I can't say to anyone. I plunge further into myself, deeper into the murk of rage and desire. I hear myself shouting with anguish. No, I won't! I won't follow unjust laws of God or man! I won't obey my parents! I won't be forced to marry! I won't obey God or Mohammed his Prophet and Messenger (Blessed be his name). Emma Solace is from an atheist country; her eyes permit this terrible doubt, forbidden here, punishable under charges of apostasy, yet my father doubts, he doubts and together with curiosity it has enabled him to develop and progress, to become wealthy; he doubts but won't let me. But I will *go to school and develop my mind, I* will *select a career and push it as far as I can. If I can't do what I want in this pathetic country I will emigrate to Where I Can.*

And listen to me, listen. I won't have children. No Children.

I want my eyes to behold a thousand mountains, my ears to hear a thousand tongues, my mind to rove as far as strong minds can launch it, to the stars and to Europe and to the United States of America. I want to see London and San Francisco and Paris and to live in New York. In New York at Columbia University, where my father went, I will learn everything there is to know. I will wear slinky dresses and date men who hand me glasses of wine and tilt through the air between us just to hear what I have to say. My skin will feel the wetness of snow and sheets of rain, my ears will hear the timpani of thunder and the melody of harps and flutes, my lips will be kissed. I will eat pork in restaurants and go out with Jews. I will get a doctorate in the history of infidel ideas and work at the United Nations or at a university.

The eyes in your photograph understand. They say, yes, Aysha bint Khalid bint Maryam al Rashid you can go to Europe and America. You are smarter than Samir or Abbas or your sister Nura, fleet of wit like your father. It hurts to neglect a brilliant mind. It hurts to chain it forever to a common mind or to expose it to no more than gossip and the swish of silk dresses. You can get a doctorate in any subject you choose, those eyes of iron assert. You can marry whomever you want.

My thoughts are so vivid I think they have happened. If I hear an interesting story about a man I instantly dream about how he might brush my hand or my neck and I feel this liquid in my body that makes me want to rock myself. I recite verses of the Qu'ran *to remind myself about what happens to bad women, but I think badness is a barrier to keep men away from women's souls and my thoughts just get stronger. Like last night when my father said to tomato-faced Samir, "The cowboy had another great idea." The Cowboy. That salty admiration in my father's voice. The sizzle of Samir's envy. The choice of a man is the choice of how to live. Emma of the oasis eyes will be able to answer my questions about differences between men. I must know if this liquid feeling is love, if every man can set it off or only the right one. I must know if who I choose will matter or if all men will be uninterested in the depths of my being. I must know if a woman's life is better alone.*

For months I have pondered what to offer so we can become friends (and now at last you are here!). My father must respect you immensely to hire you to manage a branch of his business. He claims you have romantic silly notions about the desert and the Bedu, but a surprising amount of real knowledge too. He says you are a Catholic Christian. I guess that means you believe in some kind of god (but surely not without thought? not absolutely?). Everyone here thinks that the reason there is so much robbing and killing in the big cities of the west is because they believe Man is more important than God.

I wonder how love grows if you don't believe in God.

I wonder if doubt incapacitates love.

God. Love. Ideas. There's so much I need to talk to you about.

My father refused to let me go to the airport when you arrived. I argued with him, but he had decided. "You are not to go. You will go to school. You can meet her later when she's not so exhausted. After she's had a chance to settle." "After you've decided if I should!" I accused. "It's because I'm a girl. You're taking Abbas and Samir." "They are out of school," he said. He was lying. He did not ask Nura and she is out of school. But Nura didn't care if she went to the airport or met Emma Solace the American at all. Nura only cares about music. It's like she's not even in the family.

"I'm going to go live Where I Can Go to the Airport by Myself," I muttered, though not loud enough for him to hear. My mother heard. "He is trying to do what is best for you," she insisted.

If I hear those words one more time, I am going to slap her. Why does she have to perfume everything he says? He's not right all the time. And she has her own ideas. I can see them in her eyes. Once, just once, I want to hear what she thinks, not what he does. You'd think he was Allah and she was his Prophet. I started making as if to prostrate in front of her and she yanked me upright by my shoulder. "Oh Mother," I sniveled, "How could he leave me out?" She put her arms around me like I was a little girl again.

But she didn't take my side.

The minute she left, I whipped back to this e-mail to you. Here's what I can do. I can show you underground happening Arabia, the cafes where girls go, the music and video clubs, the secret gatherings where we discuss reform, everything you will never find in books or on your own. Dearest Emma, I have been writing to you for months. Meet me for coffee at the Sultana Cafe.

If you are hurt because my parents turned around about your staying with us, understand it is because of me. My father wants to make sure you are a fit companion for his precious daughter. Since you're not married, he's afraid that you may have turned into one of those flirty, sexy types or become discontented and bossy. He'll send you right back on the next plane if he doesn't approve of you. I'd absolutely die if that happened.

My mother worries your reputation will suffer if you live alone, but she completely panics—goes nutsie with prayer—over the thought that Samir will fall for you. She thinks he's obsessed with English women since he was at Oxford. As if marrying an upper class blonde with skinny lips would get back at all the men who snubbed him because he was Arab and brown. And you know what? I don't think it was the prejudice that offended him. I think it was the way sin is so cool there.

The day you came, I put on my favorite abaya and went to school. The abaya felt especially heavy and hot, like a gag over my whole body. I kept imagining what you would be wearing when you stepped into view. You would be dressed in pastels, as you were in your picture, strong colors that conjure images of rainbows and sunsets. The kind of colors that sparkle from crystals and sunlit water. The colors of nuance and doubt, of life lived at its most supple.

And I would be covered in black. The color of limousines and stars that disappear, of newsprint on the Khaleej Times *and the ropes around my father's white ghutra. The color of oil and thirst-swollen tongues. Of shadows and midnight and the unknown. Of death and slavery and domination.*

The color of Gulf women.

Luke Wallin

Collecting Butterfish

My wife was away, visiting her family, so I didn't have to explain myself as I rushed around our house turning on lights, sliding into my boots, trying to imagine what I'd need. Within ten minutes of Chap's call I was backing my pickup down the drive, heading out into the cool night. I didn't believe his kidnapping story at all, but I wanted to help, and to see how this night would unfold.

Soon I was flying south on the straight highway through cattle country, breathing rich hayfields and clover, and the roadsides of freshly mown grass. I loved the Mississippi prairie in May, and I'd always loved traveling to Chap Stewart's place, which seemed a trip into the Southern past.

Ten miles from town he'd inherited land so vast he'd never seen it all. Chap was from the kind of family where this can happen—they'd owned the property since 1820, and the black families on his farm—he wouldn't use the word plantation—were descended from his ancestors' slaves.

Butterfish Brown, the legendary bluesman, was chief among these people now. At eighty-two, tall and gaunt and erratic, he'd come home to rule in the little community of Oak Hill. With his bad temper and bad heart, his fat wad of hundreds in one pocket and small pistol in the other, he acted as a kind of godfather to the people, helping those in need, threatening anyone who misbehaved. And he always had young women around, a mystery to me. He still picked well on some days, and he was Chap's special project. Chap drove him up and down the road, bought his groceries, took him to the doctor. And sometimes they played guitars together. I never lost a chance to sit and listen, when Chap invited me.

Chapman Forest Stewart was a heavy-set young man with hurt blue eyes, prominent in his full face. This created a startled and wild look, as if something had just been taken from him. In 1970 he'd entered Tulane University, down in New Orleans, and studied the history of jazz and blues. He'd discovered the incredible legacy of Mississippi blacks to world musical culture, and experienced a kind of spiritual conversion.

"You know what," he said to me on one of our rare visits, "white people in the South will be remembered for one thing only."

"What's that?"

"They created slavery. And slavery created the blues."

He really believed this, and tried to live up to it by moving back home after college and devoting himself to the old bluesmen and women alive in our corner of the state.

I turned off the highway onto a gravel track, and drove east toward the Tuckabaloosa. Chap's farm was the last broad expanse before the land sloped to the woods and swamps of the river's floodplain. It was one o'clock by now, and I hoped Reinhart had just taken Butterfish out driving in his excuse for a car, and that I'd arrive to find them safe and home again. Reinhart was a thin humorless German, a young blues collector with some beautiful recording equipment small enough to lug around and set up on the front porches of shacks and in the living rooms of trailers. He was living hard, eating vienna sausages and sleeping in his car, but building a fine collection of master tapes that would make his reputation back home.

For all Reinhart's earnestness about the blues, Butterfish didn't like him much. The old man seemed jealous of other artists Reinhart had found and recorded, and they argued loudly about royalty arrangements on the tapes Butterfish had made. Butterfish had put down the tracks—but so far hadn't signed any releases. Reinhart couldn't use the material unless they came to terms, and his year in the States was almost over. Chap had used the words 'Reinhart' and 'kidnapping' in his telephone call, but why hadn't he called the police rather than *me*? At his insistence I'd brought an old revolver, but I was determined to keep it unloaded and under my coat.

I pulled into the muddy yard near Butterfish's cockeyed trailer. Beneath a yellow lightbulb, Chap and a young woman I recognized, Luleen Rice, stood slapping mosquitoes and waiting for me.

"No sign of him yet?"

"Surely is not," Luleen said. She was pretty, slightly plump, and she wore a purple tank top and jean cut offs. "Reinhart *took* him," she said. "Took him to the swamp."

"Maybe," Chap said.

"His guitar is gone. What *else* has Reinhart been talkin' about all spring 'cept before he leaves, he's *going* to record Butterfish, singin' with the bullfrogs down in the swamp."

"That's true," Chap added. "And—" he pointed to Reinhart's dusty brown Ford settled a short distance away, "the tape deck is gone."

Luleen's voice cracked as she said, "Reinhart *warned* Butterfish! Said he better *give* him that recordin' in the swamp!"

"He can barely walk a block without heart pain," Chap added furiously.

"But I don't get it," I said, "Butterfish gives all the orders. He's the one with the money and the pistol."

"That's why I'm worried so," Luleen explained. "Butterfish wouldn't anymore go off like this. That German has *pulled* somethin. That's what I *say*, and that's what I *know*."

"You ready?" Chap asked.

"I guess."

Chapman led me across a short pasture and through an old barbed wire fence gap. Here the weeds grew thick and tall along the rutted road. "You know the way now don't you, down to the lake in the woods?" He wanted me to draw on memories from our hunting days, all the way back to high school.

"This old path?"

"That's where the bullfrogs are."

"Yeah," I said slowly. "We used to gig them all night."

He was silent and I remembered how he'd disliked the killing. For a moment we were boys again, with our different ways of loving his farm.

I led the way with my six-volt spotlight, and sure enough there were two sets of deep tracks in the soft grassy earth. We entered the woods, moving downslope, and the smell of strong plants and vegetable mud rose around us. Great Horned Owls hooted in the distance, mellow but sharp, and as we swished through thick reeds we heard creatures slither from our steps. The swamp was scary, and I remembered the cottonmouth moccasins we used to see. Already redbugs and mosquitoes worked my neck.

"*Listen!*" Chap said, pinching my arm.

Faintly, the clear notes of a guitar came sliding over crickets and cicadas.

"*He's doing it!*" Chap whispered. "Butterfish shouldn't *be* down here. I don't think he can get back up this hill."

We kept moving, and Butterfish's rasping wail rose up out of the night like he belonged down there, like he was kin to other screamers in the swamp. Then we reached a spot where the trail divided, and I remembered it well because we used to sneak along there to ambush mallards on the surface in the fall. "This way," I said, leading Chap to the left.

"You sure?"

"Positive." I felt proud the map was still in my bones.

We eased between scratchy, broad-leaved plants and emerged on a bluff above the lake. A half-moon hung over treetops rising from the opposite shore, and its twin lay in a broken ribbon on the water. Lily pads in yellow bloom spread over the surface, and below us, beyond a tangle of muscadine vines, we saw shadowy silhouettes.

Butterfish finished his song, and Reinhart flipped on a small light and fiddled with his tape deck.

"Now!" he announced in a bark. "This is the moment, old man! Count down for *I left Mississippi.*"

Butterfish chuckled. Then he coughed and it sounded bad.

"*Two, Three, Four*" . . . Click!

Butterfish began to play his most famous song, the one he'd recorded three times, his autobiographical song. He opened with a line of descending bass notes, repeated them again and again, and the frogs took notice. First the tiny ones set up an answering pulse, the little high-pitched peepers, and baby bullfrogs down in the moss. They sang in a joyful alternating 2/4 time, not quite matching Butterfish's beat but forming a weirdly responsive background. Then he added falling treble runs, keeping the bass notes going too, and the larger bullfrogs began to stir.

I left Mississippi in the dark of the moon, Butterfish sang so clearly he seemed younger than his frail eighty-two years. He answered himself musically down the neck of his National steel, repeating in guitar language his intonation and lament, and the bullfrogs knew the stakes were raised, and they lifted their volume to match.

I left Mississippi in the dark of the moon
Everybody said it was none too soon
Yeah none too soon
I left Mississippi

he answered himself on the steel again, a joyful three finger picking style suddenly, counterpointing his sad words,

Left Mississippi
Well I left Mississippi Lord, Lord it was none too soon.

He finished the first verse and chorus as the bullfrogs established themselves into matching choirs, one on each side of the lake to Butterfish's left and right, their amazing voices alternating with the pulse of an accordion or a bagpipe, creating a vast authorative bass ground for the treble cheeping of tree frogs and cicadas.

I left Mississippi in the middle of the night
Left Mississippi in the middle of the night
Said I done somethin wrong but it sho felt right
Yeah sho felt right
I left Mississippi, Left Mississippi
Yeah left Mississippi Lord, Lord yeah it sho felt right

Well a rich man raised his gun to me
yeah a rich man raised his gun to me
I hit him side the head Lord set him free
I set him free child
Left Mississippi, Left Mississippi,
Yeah left Mississippi Lord, Lord yeah set him free.

Now he played in earnest, mixing the high clear sliding notes that can break your heart with a raucous chording pattern that cried anger anger anger; as suddenly, he broke into the three finger picking again, that melodious, upbeat sound, and carried his break for a few sweet seconds.

Everybody try to steal the way I play
Yeah everybody try to steal the way I play
Added three mo strings, Make 'em lose they way
Make 'em lose they way
I left Mississippi, Left Mississippi
Yeah left Mississippi Lord, Lord make 'em lose they way.

The bullfrogs sang their hearts out, and the cicadas and crickets solidified into a massive silver sound like castanets in sync, while far across the water Great Horned Owls offered single piercing notes as pure as the steel guitar's shocking high sliders. Then Butterfish arrived at his last verse with a raging power I hadn't heard since his earliest records.

Some say when you travelin' back?
Yeah Mama say when you travelin' back?
Say soon as the blood seep to the bedrock
Seep to the bedrock
Goin' back to Mississippi, Yeah back to Mississippi
Go back to Mississippi
When the blood reach the bottom of the world
Yeah I'll go back to Mississippi
when the blood reach the bottom of the world

and he slowed down like always for the finish

Said I'll go back to Mississippi when the
Blood reach the bottom of the world.

He brought his hand down the neck in a final run and cut off quickly with an E minor chord, a sudden Robert Johnson type of ending to leave you in surprise and full of energy and response.

⚜

Chapman and I held still, held our breaths until we heard that quiet expensive click of the recorder snapping off.

"Wow," I said.

"*That bastard*," Chap replied, already running ahead in the darkness. He tangled in the wild grape vines, came up slapping his arms, and waded down the grassy trail again. I was right behind him, shining my spotlight over his bouncing head.

In a moment we stood at the water's cool edge. Butterfish sat on a mossy log watching Reinhart pack his tape deck into its case.

"Ya'll hear me?" Butterfish asked, smiling. His speaking voice was raspy and chordal, a wheezing smoker's sound. "Hear them frogs? Man that was fine, fine. Wadn't that fine, Chapy?"

"Yeah, it was."

"Course, I ain't told Reiny he can *use* any of this," he laughed briefly and bitterly.

"I'm going back to Germany," Reinhart said in a cold tone. "If you want your legacy to continue, you had better come to an agreement quickly."

"*Don't you tell me!*" Butterfish cried. "You damn baby. *All* you babies. Don't tell me nothin'. I tell *you*, understand? I tell you."

"How'd he get you down here?" Chap asked.

"He brung up them frogs again. I told him how they sing with me when I want 'em to, and them horny owls, too. But he didn't believe me, did you Reiny?"

Reinhart was packed and rigid, ready to depart. "I must get the tape out of this dampness," he said. And with that he walked past us and up into the bushes of the trail.

"*Stop him!*" Chap commanded me. "He's not stealing Butterfish's work and taking it out of the country. *Pull your gun!*"

"Butterfish," I said, "don't you have a gun?"

"*Not with me!*" he fired."*Get yours out!*"

I slowly drew my unloaded Colt. It seemed my duty to point it at Reinhart.

"I have given him back his voice, and his glory," Reinhart said haughtily. "If I produce the record in Europe, I will restore his faded reputation. Will you shoot me for that?"

I felt unbearably foolish during the long moment that followed. Then, slowly, I slipped my revolver back into its holster beneath my coat.

"*Don't let him leave*," Chap said.

Reinhart gave us a final, contemptuous look. "You Americans—you don't even know what you have."

With that he vanished into the darkness, and the magical tape was gone.

We stood in silence, my spotlight shining on Butterfish's shoes for want of a better place, and he said, "Help this old man up the hill."

He rose, steadying against the log. Then he handed me his guitar.

When I took it he held on, and gripped my wrist. He grinned wickedly into my face. "This what you want?"

"I'll be glad to carry it for you."

"Carry it for me, yeah, carry it for me. But this right here, this touchin' me, touchin' my National. And hearin' my song with those frogs—nothin' like it, is there?"

"No," I said, "there isn't."

"You heard those stories about the devil and me? You heard I met him one night and shook his hand?"

"I've heard that."

"Shook his hand and he tuned my guitar, have you heard that too?"

"Yes."

"And after that I had my gift. I could play any song, I could tune any way. And every time I played it was different. Always different. Have you heard that too?"

"I have."

"But he's got my soul. That's what *he* wanted. And now it's 'bout collectin' time, 'bout collectin' time. You heard that part as well?"

"Yes I have."

"That's right, that's right. *And you not sure what to believe about it*, are you?"

"No," I smiled.

"But you *half* hopin' it's true. You hopin' I touched him, and you can come touch *me* some kinda way."

"Something like that, I guess."

"Yeah," he said, thrusting the National firmly into my hands. "*That's what all ya'll want.*"

Then Chapman wrapped a meaty arm around Butterfish's thin body, and the old man laid one arm over Chap's shoulder, and they slowly made their way back up the hill. I came close behind, holding my spot high, shining it over their heads to light their way.

The National was heavy in my hand. It seemed full of its history, the recording sessions in Chicago, and its life as a weapon in the jukes of Mississippi. Swamp smell was strong, blending the tannin of oak leaves in the springs that fed the lake with the rank weeds and mud and blossoming trees. They had to rest a few times, and Butterfish's breathing was a delicate sound, shallow and quick. But we made the trailer and Luleen shoved Chap aside, and helped the old man into his bed.

He lay on the frayed patchwork quilt, with its faded yellow and lavender squares, and looked into the weak bulb overhead. After a moment he sucked air loudly and motioned for his steel guitar. I gave it to him, and when he held it tight it seemed to ease him.

"Chap's a good man," he breathed. "You a good man too."

"Ya'll can *go* now," Luleen announced. She held a mason jar of gleaming ice cubes and whiskey and water. We glanced at Butterfish and he smiled. With his long fingers he shooed us away. His heavy-lidded and intense eyes were only for her.

Butterfish lived another year after that. Reinhart brought out his five-album set in Germany, and rode it to fame. *I Left Mississippi*, with the frog and cicada chorus, was the talk of the blues circuit on two continents. Reinhart sent no letters, and no royalty checks. That seemed mockery of a great man's art, and seemed to confirm what Butterfish had said about our desire to be near him, to take something from him. *That's what all ya'll want*, he'd said to me that night. Chap proposed to sue, since Reinhart must have forged the old man's signature on a contract, but Butterfish closed his eyes and waved his hand, said let it go. Chap served Butterfish until he passed, on another spring night after he'd played for some Oak Hill neighbors in the packed-dirt yard of his trailer. Hundreds of people attended the funeral, and his obituary appeared in *The New York Times*. The writer described him as "an American legend who, like many before, had disappeared from the hearts of his aging audience."

Chap rented out his farm to an agribiz corporation based in Chicago, and they sent down a team of young MBAs to manage the land. The company paid Chap a lot of money for a multi-year lease, and right away they bulldozed the old trailer and cut down the osage trees that had shaded Butterfish from the sun. They eliminated all the tenant families on the place, and farmed it with just two employees. These men rode air-conditioned machinery all day long, up and down the rows, wearing headphones while they worked.

Chap moved to Memphis and bought a recording studio. He hosted a late-night radio program, and taught courses in the blues at Memphis State. The last time I heard anything about him he'd written a review for *Blues Journey* magazine, in which he critized some young musicians for not knowing their own history.

And me, I went back to grad school in American Studies, and wrote a dissertation on the white blues-collecting movement of the 1960s and 70s. I read everything ever written about the collectors and the artists, and interviewed every one I could find. Of course I made my own story the lead chapter of my book. And when it came out it was well reviewed, and got me tenure in a northern university.

As time passes that night in the swamp becomes—for some reason—more important to me. I remember the broken moonlight on the water lillies with their yellow flowers, and Butterfish's smell of tobacco as he gripped my wrist and smiled into my eyes. I dream of the bullfrogs and owls and peepers and even the insects singing with him, and in my dream I can feel the weight of his steel guitar. I wake up sometimes and lie there, and in the stillness I can feel it exactly as it was, when I carried it up that hill in the weedy dark.

Mary Clyde

Krista Had a Treble Clef Rose

Anne and Nicole at Lunch

Perched on bar stools at Johnny Rockets Diner, Anne tugs at the lettuce ruffle of her sandwich; Nicole smears a puddle of ketchup with a French fry.

"We're freaks," Anne announces. She says it mildly. Though she believes it, she's said it before.

"We are." Nicole's slow nod accelerates in agreement.

Poster teenagers, they call themselves, though they're not. Still, they are aware it's only the survivors who get to represent their disease.

A girl in cutoff jeans and combat boots pauses in front of the frantic shapes of a mall theater's movie posters.

"Cute hair," Anne whispers. She straightens the turquoise shopping bag resting by her sandaled feet. Inside is a clam comb of imitation tortoiseshell and wands like chopsticks to twist up her hair.

Nicole says, "The anesthesia made my hair fall out. I've got three hairs left. I'm playing up my eyes." She bats them as proof. Then: "Dr. Stafford is the cutest of the junior doctors. Don't you think? He told me I remind him of his sister-in-law."

"Except when he pulled my wound drain, he didn't warn me."

Nicole sighs. "The Jackson Pratt drain."

They wince and smile, knowing smiles of well-tended teeth.

Nine months ago, they were Garden Grove Honor Cotillion Debutantes. Anne had giggled when she told her mother about her nomination because wasn't she just exactly not the type? But wasn't it a kick to be one?

Anne now says, "My dad wants to buy me clothes. Suddenly he can't buy me enough clothes."

Nicole says, "My mom will say, 'Would you like something to eat, sweetie?' Then doesn't even blink. Brings it like some genie and stands there watching me eat."

"They feel guilty."

"It's no one's fault."

"We're not going to die, not now."

"Saved by stomas."

"Ileostomies," Anne says, a word that suddenly sounds like a flying dinosaur.

ANNE'S BOYFRIEND

Anne's boyfriend Jeff left for college while she was still in the hospital. Before he left he visited her often and brought roses in a vase. Like a wedding anniversary or an apology for forgetting one. Florist flowers, but all different colors, which showed he had no taste. Part of why she liked him, was that he didn't pretend he did.

When an alarm sounded, he ran to get the nurse. "It's just a pump," Anne called, but he was already in the hall. He played ice hockey; he was fast even without his skates.

They went for walks in the halls. Jeff pushed the IV pole and kept a wary eye on the pumps. He was prone to giving himself titles: Amazing Microwave Chef, Consumer Math Repeat Kid. "Supreme IV Pole Navigator," he now said. His smile looked like his old smile, goofy and a little shy. It made her miss him and understand how that part of him was already gone.

Once they rode the elevator to the cafeteria. The cashier spotted some label on Anne's equipment and radioed for help. It came in the fast-moving form of an efficient Asian nurse.

"Must not leave floor," she scolded, wrestling the IV pole from the startled Jeff. "Never, never. You N.P.O."

Nothing by mouth. It sounded contagious, deadly.

Anne said, “You think I’d eat something?”

“Been done,” the nurse said, commandeering the IV pole.

Jeff looked as if he might cry.

What to Wear in the Hospital

As her condition worsened, Anne abandoned her appearance. She quit plucking her eyebrows, didn’t bother with her contact lenses, sent home her makeup and earrings and her nightshirts with a prostrate Snoopy and Jesus Christ as a superstar.

It took concentration to stay alive. She wore hospital gowns because of their utility and as an admission of how sick she was and because she now belonged. Soldiers wear fatigues. She rolled up her sleeves, lost the knack of good looks, forgot the need.

When she came home from the hospital, just shaving her legs exhausted her.

Anne’s Father and Mother

Afterward, she heard her father whisper in the hall, “Do you think she understands?”

Her mother said, “Do you?” It sounded fierce.

The Psychiatrist Visits

The psychiatrist told her about his brother who had been hospitalized with the same thing when he was a young boy. “They took him off food, too.” The psychiatrist untangled her IV tubes, expertly. He said he didn’t want to see the photographs of her ulcerated colon, but the way he said it was kind and made Anne hope the pictures weren’t as important as the doctors made them out to be. “My brother watched TV all day. It was when McDonald’s was just introducing Chicken

McNuggets. All he talked about was how when he got out, he'd get some. It helped him get through it, gave him something to look forward to."

("Talk to him," her mother had pleaded before he came in. "Annie, just try. He can help you.")

Tubes brought things into Anne's body, other tubes took things out. It seemed like math, a hospital story problem. "If a teenager is not responding to medication and has two tubes for feeding and one tube for blood, and if the tube in her nose . . ."

"Anne," the psychiatrist said, "visualize a healthy colon."

ANNE AND NICOLE GO SHOPPING AT J. CREW

Anne buys a high-waisted dress of fluttery fabric with the colors and spots of overripe bananas.

"Is it too short?" she says.

Nicole shakes her head. "You've got nice legs."

"Look how my calves go in. Right there. Look how deformed."

Nicole holds out her freckled arms. "You think that's bad? Look at my fat arms." Anne has seen Nicole's mother; she has seen these arms before. "And my knees are kind of baggy." Nicole pinches her knees where Anne now notices they sag, something like a zoo elephant's.

WHAT TO EXPECT BEFORE SURGERY

The enterostomal therapy nurse will visit your hospital room to mark the ileostomy site. The placement is based on several factors: skin creases, scars, navel, waistline, hip bone, how you sit and where you wear the waist of your clothes. Proper location makes ileostomy care easier after the surgery.

Food Dreams

Frequently: mashed potatoes—the gastro-intestinal patient's last food friend.

Occasionally: Chocolate Cornflake Crunchies. Anne's mother hadn't made them since kindergarten. Anne thought she'd forgotten them, didn't remember even liking them; now she had Chocolate Cornflake Crunchy fantasties. A steep yearning, sweet as homesickness.

Recurring nightmare: Popcorn—salted, buttered, white-cheddar-cheesed, carameled, balled, pink-candied. She'd been told she could never eat popcorn again, which scared her and proved her vulnerability as nothing else quite had. Because who could be undone by popcorn?

Friends

Krista had a treble clef rose, a tattoo three inches long on her thigh, because she was going to major in music.

Jen had blown out her knee cheerleading, but she refused to have it operated on until after basketball season. As a concession to her parents she wore a brace for tumbling.

Richard said he'd been born with an extra finger. Its ghost helped him catch. It gave him ESP.

Anne's Father at the Hospital

Sometimes her father seemed as difficult as the illness. He washed her undriven car and replaced the burnt-out taillight. He bought her a Rolling Stones CD. Mick Jagger looked desperate.

He brought Misty, their golden retriever, who stood beneath Anne's hospital window, dismayed by the circumstances. She sniffed the air. When a doctor knelt to pet her, she gratefully wagged her tail.

When Anne's pain was intense, she thought no one else could have ever experienced anything like it. She learned what morphine demanded in exchange for its not-quite-heroic rescue. She worried about becoming addicted.

Her father's experience with pain medication included the nitrous oxide from the dentist and Tylenol with codeine from the time he broke his leg skiing. "I heard it snap," he said, still in fond disbelief.

"Annie, what can I do for you?" he said.

Out of kindness, she or her mother came up with errands: lotion from home? a blanket from the warmer? He forgot them. Instead, he wired her hospital room for stereo sound from the VCR and replumbed the bathroom shower.

"This way," he yelled over the clank of his tools. "when you're ready for a shower, you can direct the spray."

Hospital Routine

The hospital gave medication, recorded vital signs, changed linens, and offered sponge baths on a rigid schedule.

Unscheduled but with frequency, Anne bled, cursed, wept, vomited, and prayed. Whatever she did the staff called her brave, and she understood how saying it helped them.

The Boyfriend Leaves for College

Anne wore white surgical support stockings and two hospital gowns. Jeff wore a baseball cap. The logo was No Fear. They walked by the surgery waiting room, where the occupants regarded their progress with ill-concealed anxiety or encouragement.

Back in Anne's room, Jeff sat in the chair one of her parents slept in at night. He stroked the IV pole and told Anne about work at the furniture rental store. How his dad kept asking what kind of people have to rent furniture. Anne realized a boyfriend was an exhausting luxury like reading or crossword puzzles.

Jeff didn't talk about how he was going away to school, which proved to her how badly he wanted to talk about it, how eager he was to go. He didn't talk about Anne either, but she knew he watched her carefully to see what she expected or wanted from him and if she were in any way still the same.

She thought, *We are in love* and also, *This relationship is probably doomed.*

Anne and Nicole Shop at the Sports Watch Counter

Nicole says her goal is to kiss a guy of every race. Every religion, too. "But with a system," she says, "like starting with boys from extreme far-right religions and going to extreme left. Or from short guys to tall ones. Something to make it challenging."

The watch Anne is looking at doesn't have numbers, but has weird geometric shapes instead.

"Or older men to younger," Nicole says, taking the watch from Anne. "That way I'd be shocking when I was young fooling around with old men and again when I was old, kissing young guys."

Anne says, "Do all religions allow kissing?"

"Who could be against kissing?"

"I don't know. Amish? Do they?" Anne says.

"Yuck, who'd want to kiss some Amish guy?"

Anne takes the watch back. "Do you think after I got used to this watch I'd be able to tell time on it?

"I mean he'd never forget me, an Amish boy. He'd be so grateful."

Mother of pearl makes one watch face appear chaste. Another is no bigger than an aspirin.

Anne says, "I'd like something plain, but gorgeous."

NICOLE'S MOTHER

Nicole's mother banned popcorn from the house, as if it were responsible. When the popcorn ads were flashed before movies, Nicole said her mother clucked her tongue and said, "Honestly!" the same as she did for cigarette or beer ads. Popcorn became a vice.

Nicole's parents were divorced. Her father moved to New Mexico and kept urging her to join him, telling her how the fresh mountain air and exercise could help her. Once her mother yanked the phone out of Nicole's hand. "Rodney," she screamed, "she doesn't have tuberculosis!"

ANNE'S MOTHER

Anne found even if she didn't respond to her mother, her mother continued to talk to her. She jabbered cheerfully. Anne hadn't thought her mother was a jabberer. Sometimes she didn't bother to listen while her mother changed her hospital gowns or shampooed her hair. She looked away when her mother bathed her, her earlier modesty forgotten. Once, she thought, this must have been how she spoke to me when I was a baby before I learned to talk.

Then one day Anne heard her: "Anne," she said. "where are you when you don't answer us? Where is it you go?"

Anne looked at her mother then, saw how bruised her eyes looked; how she'd lost weight. She is suffering, Anne thought, and it frightened her.

"Sometimes I just don't feel like talking," Anne said, but she thought, I'm holding my breath, balancing on life's thin edge.

FRIENDS

Coach hung Richard's jersey from where the rafters would be if the high school gymnasium had them. He said the team would finish the season playing in his memory. In all his years of coaching he'd never seen anything like what Richard could do to an opposition's defensive line. Coach hugged his clipboard to his chest and swore it: Richard could just plain read their freaking minds.

Nicole

Nicole threatened her brother when he wouldn't give her the TV remote control. She said he'd show him her bag. "You use what you've got," she explained sensibly to Anne. "It's what America is all about."

Nicole said she's never flying on an airplane, because what if the bag exploded? Nicole said stoma means mouth. Nicole's scar was purple. It puckered thick as masking tape.

A Letter from Anne's Boyfriend

Dear Anne,

I tested out of freshman English. Awesome! I've got a great roommate. He's from around here and knows about everything.

He signed it love, not love you. Anne guessed that it mattered, wondered what she could do.

Nicole's Mother and Aunt

Nicole's mother and her aunt stayed with her in the hospital. Nicole's aunt called Nicole's mother sis or sister. "Sister, you need some coffee." "Sis, it's high time we got the doctor in here." Anne asked Nicole if her aunt sometimes got grossed out. "No," Nicole said, "she's a Republican."

The Jackson Pratt Drain

Anne read about it. "Drains remove fluid from the surgical sites. Once the drainage decreases, they will be removed." It sounded simple enough, hardly brutal.

But cute Dr. Stafford knew better. She wondered what he should have said when he pulled the drain shaped like a lawn-mower starter from the surgically punctured hole in her side—a lawn-mower starter with a long, long deeply embedded cord.

But she couldn't find a warning that would not have alarmed her, a caution with the right amount of sympathy, words that would have bolstered her courage and respected the suffering that had come before and was about to be inflicted.

But: "This will sting a little"? No, not that.

FINDING THE PERFECT GOWN

Your cotillion dress must be pure white. Because of its variability in color, silk is not allowed. It must be sleeved. A cap sleeve is flattering and feminine. It must not have detracting decoration, such as feathers, sequins, beads, or pearls. A pearl necklace, however, is acceptable.

Anne's dress was drop-waisted cotton brocade. Nicole's had a sweetheart neckline. It was taffeta. She said she thought the rustle of it sounded sexy and cheap, undermining the whole virgin-maiden thing. They wore slips, layers and layers of white netting.

Anne said, "If my period starts, I'll kill myself."

Nicole said, "If your period starts, you'll never find it."

POSSIBLE RECURRENCE

This fear hangs heavy as a stage curtain: like a cursed mythological figure, Anne may be forced to repeat this misery. But what will the surgeons cut out then? She must not think about it. She cannot stop thinking about it.

Hospital Visitors

Batman, with a plastic pectoral chest and a cape that swished like Nicole's cotillion dress. He gave Anne a picture of himself signed "With Bat wishes."

The team mascot for a minor league ball team, a shaggy bull who kept banging his horns on the door frame. He gave her a blue and white pom-pom and a red baseball bat. He was led around by a uniformed batboy.

Raggedy Anne from the Ice Capades, whose real red hair stuck out from under her red yarn hair. "Lose this place, babe," she said in a husky whisper.

Anne's grandmother. She left a plate of peanut butter cookies, Anne's favorite, long after everyone else seemed to have forgotten Anne had ever eaten. Confused by Anne's mother's explanation of her condition, she sighed. "I don't understand what you're saying to me."

Leaving the Hospital

Going home from the hospital you get ostomy bags, one- or two-piece-like swimming suits. You get ostomy wafers, a spray-on skin barrier, an ointment to heal the skin the skin barrier misses, adhesive for the ostomy wafers, solvent for the adhesive. You get instruction from the enterostomal therapy nurse, long-suffering as a piano teacher. You get a subscription to *Ostomates*.

Nicole wore clear bags. Anne wore flesh-colored bags. She said she thought they were more feminine.

"What?" Nicole said. "You think they're more what?"

Friends

Johanna had ridden her bike late at night along the canal. Her killer folded her clothes neatly beside her. Johanna had signed Anne's yearbook, "See ya this summer!"

The Psychiatrist Visits

The psychiatrist tugged on his soaring-and-diving-seagulls tie and told Anne about a young woman in his parish who had the surgery, how glad she was to be well. "Anne, visualize your return to health. Visualize no more pain or bleeding."

The psychiatrist actually had the disease. It wasn't just his brother. He told Anne's mother in the hall, who told Anne after he'd left.

"Why didn't he just tell me himself?" Anne said.

"Maybe he thinks it would undermine his authority," her mother said.

"Because I'd know he got sick?" Anne was being what her mother called petulant. But she knew she'd slipped, like Alice, into a world with nonsensical rules.

"How sick?" she said. "Can he eat popcorn? Does he wear a bag?"

"Can't you call it an appliance?" Her mother turned toward the window.

Personal Ads in *Ostomates*

Female, 32. Diagnosed with colitis at 18. Colon cancer discovered two years ago. Had ileostomy and pull-through. Having rough time right now. Enjoy poetry, movies, my cat, Spike. Will answer all letters.

I am a girl, 15. Just diagnosed and had surgery. I had never heard of it before. I like music and love to dance; take gymnastics. I don't care about your age or anything. Am scared.

Single male, 32, from Seattle area. Would like to hear from any female interested in friendship and support. I'm a great listener.

Anne's Colon

After the surgery the surgeon asked Anne's parents if they would like to see Anne's colon. Anne's mother, who had never yet looked away, said, "I couldn't." But her father looked, so he could say what he now says: that Anne is better off without it. He also calls it names, says, "More holes than Swiss cheese," "craters deeper than the moon," "pock-marked," "pitted," "ravaged," "U-G-L-Y."

The surgeon's hands were red and cool. He stood next to a bobbing balloon bouquet and talked to Anne about colons. He said they are inelegant. Big, dumb organs whose agility is limited to spasms of contraction and whose perception of pain is dim and inaccurate.

But Anne thinks of them—of hers—as shy. A mole, maybe. Loathsome, but gentle. A homely animal taken out and shot. And her stomach, her heart, her soul—whatever they've left inside—hurts with the cruelty of it.

Anne and Nicole Shop at the Cosmetic Counter

They are walking past the wooden gleam of a bookstore and a pyramid of soap, multicolored and clear like Jell-O, in the window of a bath shop.

"I almost fell on the cotillion runway," Nicole says, referring to a time Anne thinks seems as long ago as counting sheep with Bert and Ernie or begging to wear a bra. "Eric gave me his right arm instead of his left, and it threw me off. I kind of wobbled."

"I didn't see a thing," Anne says. She is lying—recalling the gracelessness of it—because what are friends for?

The mannequins have erect nipples but no facial features. A glass elevator rises as if with grace. They walk by Surf, Sea, and Swim where empty bathing suits float disembodied in the blue-tinted display. (Visualize, Anne thinks, a red bikini, sun glistening off the baby oil of an unseamed abdomen.) Escalator teeth endlessly recycle. They hear the patter of the computerized water fountain, brown-bottomed with penny litter. At a table in front of Coffee Breaks, a woman says to a young girl, "But everyone uses a napkin."

"How's Jeff?" Nicole says.

"Fine." Anne makes a face to say, "Like it matters." It's a save-face face, in case she needs it when he comes home.

Nicole says, "I've been feeling ugly as a dog dish. Let's get new makeup."

"I saw this eye shadow that goes on white and changes color in the sun."

"Have you seen that lipstick? Black Ice? It's dark but light at the same time."

They rearrange their bags and retrace their steps, heading for Dillard's cosmetic counter. Anne tries to remember the name of the eye shadow. Glimmer Glow? They pass the movie theater. Nicole points to a coming-soon poster, says while she's kissing she wouldn't mind kissing Johnny Depp. Does Anne happen to have any idea what religion he is?

From the snack bar comes an explosive burst of popcorn, as well as its urgent smell.

"Christian Scientist?" Anne says. "And I think he might also be part Indian."

Nicole grins, as if it's all but done.

In the Music Box Company, someone is trying one out. Anne and Nicole hear the mechanical plunking of "Camptown Races," a tune they do not know.

Connie May Fowler

from *The Problem with Murmur Lee*

Charleston Rowena Mudd

In Boston they know me as Charlotte, for in that Northern city, positioned as it is in the bread basket of higher learning, I became a geographical liar. My goal? To hide my true origins. And not simply because people outside of dear old Dixie have unfairly pegged us all as shiftless, ignorant, backward, inbred—should I go on?—but because I, Charleston Rowena Mudd, am a Self-Loathing Southerner.

As such, I have developed various airs and voices appropriate to whatever name I'm using in whatever region I find myself in. For instance, in Boston I truncate my vowels. "My name is Charlotte." Quick as a darting bird: five syllables compressed into one quick wobble.

But after two or three bourbons, I sometimes slip up. "My name is Chaaaarlut, rhymes with haaaaarlot."

Very few of my friends back at Harvard Divinity find my seldom revealed but ribald Southern humor charming. Only Happy Jim, a fallen Franciscan Brother with the smile of an angel. An easy audience, for sure.

And now I have returned to my old haunts—the sandy coquina-laced beaches that build and recede at the whimsy of the tides, the lesser known shores of Anastasia Island, Crescent Beach, Iris Haven, Marineland for Christ's sake—where I am known simply as Charlie. Charlie Mudd.

And I must admit, the name fits.

I never imagined I would return to this place. I left in order to become an educated woman, to escape redneck culture, to become worldly and intellectual and Yankee-fied. And I pretty much succeeded.

True, I didn't manage to totally stamp out my good manners and, as I said, the old drawl lifted its ugly magnolia scented head occasionally. And even after coming to terms with the awful realization that rednecks are universal as is racism, sexism, and plagiarism, I still managed to live my life using my brains versus my body. Which, come to think of it, was actually my main goal when I set out from the South. You see, at the time of my exodus at the age of twenty-five, I was convinced that female brain-driven success was a peculiarly Northern tradition. I never stopped to consider that those Cotillion Queens whom I loathed both out of envy and disgust might have had more going on upstairs than I was willing to give them credit for.

So, yes, I could pass as Northern on most days. I learned to make a phone call and get to the point immediately, rather than engage in the ritualized politeness which is the glue that binds all cultures of the South into one huge dysfunctional gossip tree. You know, How's your daddy, your great grand daddy, your camellias, and your mama doing? when the point of the call was to ask, Can you please turn down your stereo just a tad, the baby is trying to sleep?

I could meet someone for the very first time and discuss world issues without knowing who their people were. I could bully my way up to the front of a line without ever once saying, "Excuse me." I quit addressing people as sir or ma'am even if they were over seventy. This, alone, would have killed my mother had she been alive. I ate grits only in private. A store in St. Augustine shipped them to me. I hid them in a tin canister I kept tucked out of sight on the top shelf of my kitchen cabinet. The raised black letters on the canister identified the contents as flour. If a friend happened to spy the leftovers in my fridge I would lie, saying that it was couscous. I once spent a weekend alone in New York City. I rode the subway. Hailed a cab. Wandered Central Park without police protection. I've been known to dine out by myself. I learned to stop asking for sweet tea—I grew tired of the dismissive waiters saying, "The sugar is on the table" and me trying to explain it's simply not the same. I paid scant attention to football, claiming not to know that the Florida State Seminoles were anything other than an amalgam of lost tribes chased into the Everglades by the U.S. Army and disease. I owned an ice scraper. I pretended to like, even understand, Phillip Glass. I never ate supper anymore. Dinner. Let's go have dinner. I joined the ACLU.

But there is one fact above all others that illustrates how far I had traveled from Iris Haven and my Deep South roots. My fiancé, the man who dumped me two weeks before we were to say our vows in a Unitarian chapel close to campus, hailed from Nigeria. Ahmed. Ahmed Al-Kuwaee.

His was a lilting, London influenced, perfect-grammar accent. A Muslim by birth, training, and choice, he considered my Catholic upbringing exotic, naive. He was, as my Southern cronies would say, black as the ace of spades.

We were a perfect match, a complement of old world and new, cream and coffee, intellect and passion, seaweed and salt.

But he had a secret. One that he revealed, if you will indulge me, in the most startling fashion. It was a Saturday night and Cambridge was hot, humid, and smelled faintly of rotting garbage. Ahmed was to be at my apartment at 7:30 for dinner. He had his own key, which he used. I was in my tiny kitchen that was, if the truth be known, an afterthought carved out of a closet, chopping cilantro—a must-have ingredient in the spicy Thai lemon and shrimp soup I was serving. Ahmed loved my cooking. And I admit, I'm not half bad in the kitchen. But I digress. There I was, standing at my kitchen counter, concentrating so singularly on the task at hand that I didn't realize Ahmed had let himself in until he cleared his throat.

I spun around, thrilled—I was wild for him—the knife still in-hand, and then froze. Ahmed was pale. I swear. His ebony skin resembled chalk. Beside him stood a petite young thing with downcast eyes. A child, really. Shy, maybe gentle, definitely out of her element. I could read nothing else about her.

He spoke softly, a slight embarrassed smile revealing a thin flash of white. He explained it succinctly, with all the emotion one uses when reciting a textbook passage. Theirs was an arranged union, an agreement entered into before he or she had any inkling of puberty. They were married the day prior to him leaving for America and Harvard. His conscience wouldn't allow him to go forward with a Christian marriage. He asked that I forgive him.

Despite my Northern, sophisticated, and tough as nails in an urban way attitude, I didn't take the news well. He had barely finished his plea for forgiveness when I heard myself screech, my drawl in full bloom—anger, hurt, and disbelief fueling the elongation of my vowels, "Why you no good lily-livered shit ass!"

He could have run me over with a Jeep and I would not have felt as injured. I feared my eyes were darting about in my head as I tried to recover some semblance of control. My best friend from home, Murmur, scattered like light through my foundering brain. She never let anyone get the best of her—she never showed it, anyway. She could have a cobra sitting on her head and remain steady. I had to slip into another dimension. If only for a moment. In my mind's eye Murmur gathered. She was smirking, not a drop of fear betrayed, not even in her squinty blue eyes. It did the trick. Briefly, a calm pushed at the thunder clouds roiling through my veins. And I did it. I got righteous.

My voice deepened. I slowed way down. I enjoyed the heft of the knife which I gripped ever so sweetly.

"How dare you. You have taken advantage of my honor. My good nature." I pushed an errant strand of hair off my forehead with the point of the knife. "Even my honest heart." I pursed my lips as I conjured my next face-saving line, all the while struggling not to collapse at his feet and beg and howl in true Belle fashion for him not to abandon me.

"You are dead to me. Do you understand? And if you don't walk out that door this very second, you will also be dead to your sweet little bride." I tossed the knife—one revolution—and caught it by the handle. For the first time in my life I was grateful that in high school I had been a baton twirler.

Over the top? Certainly. Effective? Oh, yes.

Ahmed backed out of my cellblock-c-sized apartment, shielding his poor shocked bride with his own body, stunned I believe not only by the spin of my knife but, most importantly, by my sudden Southernness.

Yes, it's true. I had deceived him, too. Told him I was from Chicago. My friends at Harvard warned me that I would rot in hell for telling such a lie and that surely he would find me out. But I felt the need to hide my origins because he truly hated Southerners, too. We had so much in common. He had seen George Wallace footage and believed everyone in the South was just a bunch of little Georges blocking school entrances throughout the region, yelling racist epithets into bull horns, and swiping sweat out of their pale, beady eyes. Their intention? To prevent Ahmed from stepping foot into any of their hallowed halls of second-rate education.

Playing devil's advocate, I once asked him, "What about Jimmy Carter?"

"What about him?" He stared back at me, unblinking, unwilling to admit I had scored a point.

"He's from the South. He's not prejudiced. He's a good man."

"He's not truly a Southerner," Ahmed said thoughtfully, stroking his new growth goatee, seemingly at peace with his flawed logic.

Of course, my deception was minor, indeed barely counts, when compared to not disclosing you already have a wife. My God, he had turned me into an adulteress—and nearly a polygamist—without my informed consent.

So upon learning that my fiancé was already married, the guilt I had borne these last seventeen months transformed itself into seething satisfaction even as my heart was shattering like a K-mart wine glass dropped onto a Terrazzo floor. In the face of my solemn death threat, Ahmed had exited my apartment with a soft shush of the door, but I flung it open and before he and she had made it down the hall to the elevator I screamed triumphantly, pointing that trusty blade at what I presumed to be the upper chamber of his heart, "Yes, you fucking asshole, you have been sleeping with a Cracker!"

Then I slammed the door so hard that my outsider art wall calendar fell off its hook. I started bawling and headed for the kitchen where I poured myself a water glass full of bourbon and ate cold leftover cheese grits right out of the plastic container. I planned all manner of revenge. I could have gay smut magazines delivered to his mail box in the divinity department. I could call Immigration from a pay phone and say I believed he was in the country on an expired visa. I could tell the FBI that he often had clandestine midnight meetings with men of Middle Eastern origin and he once admitted he'd like to bomb the State Department. Lies. Lies. Lies. I could, I could, I could . . . But I did not.

Instead, I dropped out of school. One class to go—three credit hours: Christianity and Ecology. Course description: "A rigorous exploration of sound Christian environmental thought." As opposed to? And then there is the matter of my dissertation which, if ever done, will explore the thorny subject of the Historical Jesus. My committee head, Dr. Wise, was hoping for something a bit more traditional. Not my style, I told him breezily.

The truth is, despite a life-long pre-occupation with religion—and yes, I'll say it—the Holy Roman Catholic Church in all its many genuflections—I have lost my faith. I'm not sure when it left. Or was I the one who walked away? Beats me. All I know is that in my current state of lapsed faith I cannot possibly write about a Christian Jesus. A political strategist? A social maverick? A revolutionary par none? Yes. God? No. Not right now.

I am newly home—three days—haven't yet unpacked. The coastal plain of Iris Haven feels as familiar to me as skin. But I am not the same person who left here five years ago. If we are, indeed, defined by the friends and lovers who fill the lonely hollows of our hearts, displacing for a moment our sadness and alienation (those twin sisters of original sin), then I am ash. Not bone.

Ahmed wasn't solely one more attempt on my part to wrestle free from the South's wide guilt. I loved him. When he held me, I felt free. Surrounded. The pain of past traumas receded. The fear of failure faded.

Two days after he jilted me, Murmur died. Alone. In the Iris Haven River. How does a woman who spent her entire life fishing and surfing and snorkeling these waters die by drowning? And what condition was her faith in as she took her final breath? Did anyone care? Did the Christian God—so important to her in girlhood—whisper into her fading ear, "My child, you are a woman of many sins: adultery, drink, promiscuity. But you indulged honestly, with a fair heart, meaning no harm. So welcome home"?

I always knew that I could gallivant anywhere. Recreate myself a thousand times over. Charleston. Charlotte. Cher. Hell, you name it. I could pass as a Yankee. I could fall in love with a fine-boned man from Nigeria whose dreams were of places, colors, smells, textures more foreign to me than the surface of Mars. I could fall off the edge of the earth and never be honest about the consequences because I had Murmur. Murmur was back home, keeping the world straight, sending me letters about new dune lines and turtle runs and the metaline sound of dragonflies on the wing at dusk. So no matter what new plot I was hatching for myself, at the close of the day, by the time I got to that last flourish at the end of the page—Love you lots, Murmur—I knew once again who I was. Charlie Mudd. A simple white girl from North Florida who loved grits and sea oats and, sans racism, most all things Southern.

Brad Watson

BILL

Wilhelmina, eighty-seven, lived alone in the same town as her two children, but she rarely saw them. Her main companion was a trembling poodle she's had for about fifteen years, named Bill. You never hear of dogs named Bill. Her husband in his decline had bought him, named him after a boy he'd known in the Great War, and then wouldn't have anything to do with him. He'd always been Wilhelmina's dog. She could talk to Bill in a way that she couldn't talk to anyone else, not even her own children.

Not even her husband, now nearly a vegetable out at King's Daughter's Rest Home on the old highway.

She rose in the blue candlelight morning to go see him about the dog, who was doing poorly. She was afraid of being completely alone.

There were her children and their children, and even some great-grandchildren, but that was neither here nor there for Wilhelmina. They were all in different worlds.

She drove her immaculate ocean-blue Delta 88 out to the home and turned up the long, barren drive. The tall naked trunks of a few old pines lined the way, their sparse tops distant as clouds. Wilhelmina pulled into the parking lot and took two spaces so she'd have plenty of room to back out when she left. She paused for a moment to check herself in the rearview mirror, and adjusted the broad-brimmed hat she wore to hide the thinning spot on top of her head.

Her husband, Howard, lay propped up and twisted in her old velour robe, his mouth open, watching TV. His thick white hair stood in a matted knot on his head like a child's.

"What?" he said when she walked in. "What did you say?"

"I said, 'Hello!'" Wilhelmina replied, though she'd said nothing.

She sat down.

"I came to tell you about Bill, Howard. He's almost completely blind now and he can't go to the bathroom properly. The veterinarian says he's in pain and he's not going to get better and I should put him to sleep."

Her husband had tears in his eyes.

"Poor old Bill," he said.

"I know," Wilhelmina said, welling up herself now. "I'll miss him so."

"I loved him at Belleau Wood! He was all bloody and walking around," Howard said. "They shot off his nose in the Meuse-Argonne." He picked up the remote box and held the button down, the channels thumping past like the muted thud of an ancient machine gun.

Wilhelmina dried her tears with a Kleenex from her handbag and looked up at him.

"Oh, fiddle," she said.

"Breakfast time," said an attendant, a slim copper-colored man whose blue smock was tailored at the waist and flared over his hips like a suit jacket. He set down the tray and held his long delicate hands before him as if for inspection.

He turned to Wilhelmina.

"Would you like to feed your husband, ma'am?"

"Heavens, no," Wilhelmina said. She shrank back as if he intended to touch her with those hands.

When the attendant held a spoonful of oatmeal up to her husband's mouth he lunged for it, his old gray tongue out, and slurped it down.

"Oh, he's ravenous today," said the attendant. Wilhelmina, horrified, felt for a moment as if she were losing her mind and had wandered into this stranger's room by mistake. She clutched her purse and slipped out into the hall.

"I'm going," she called faintly, and hurried out to her car, which sat on the cracked surface of the parking lot like an old beached yacht. The engine groaned, turned over, and she steered down the long drive and onto the highway without even a glance at the traffic. A car passed her on the right, up in the grass, horn blaring, and an enormous dump truck cleaved the air to her left like a thunderclap. She would pay them no mind.

When she got home, the red light on her answering machine, a gift from her son, was blinking. It was him on the tape.

"I got your message about Bill, Mama. I'll take him to the vet in the morning, if you want. Just give me a call. Bye-bye, now."

"No, I can't think about it," Wilhelmina said.

Bill was on his cedar-filled pillow in the den. He looked around for her, his nose up in the air.

"Over here, Bill," Wilhelmina said loudly for the dog's deaf ears. She carried him a Milk-Bone biscuit, for his teeth were surprisingly good. He sniffed the biscuit, then took it carefully between his teeth, bit off a piece, and chewed.

"Good boy, good Bill."

Bill didn't finish the biscuit. He laid his head down on the cedar pillow and breathed heavily. In a minute he got up and made his halting, wobbling way toward his water bowl in the kitchen, but hit his head on the doorjamb and fell over.

"Oh, Bill, I can't stand it," Wilhelmina said, rushing to him. She stroked his head until he calmed down, and then she dragged him gently to his bowl, where he lapped and lapped until she had to refill it, he drank so much. He kept drinking.

"Kidneys," Wilhelmina said, picking up the bowl. "That's enough, boy."

Bill nosed around for the water bowl, confused. He tried to squat, legs trembling, and began to whine. Wilhelmina carried him out to the backyard, set him down, and massaged his kidneys the way the vet had shown her, and finally a little trickle ran down Bill's left hind leg. He tried to lift it.

"Good old Bill," she said. "You try, don't you?"

She carried him back in and dried his leg with some paper towels.

"I guess I'd do anything for you, Bill," she said. But she had made up her mind. She picked up the phone and called her son. It rang four times and then his wife's voice answered.

"You've reached two-eight-one," she began.

"I know that," Wilhelmina muttered.

". . . We can't come to the phone right now . . ."

Wilhelmina thought that sort of message was rude. If they were there, they could come to the phone.

". . . leave your message after the beep."

"I guess you better come and get Bill in the morning," Wilhelmina said, and hung up.

Wilhelmina's husband had been a butcher, and Katrina, the young widow who'd succeeded him at the market, still brought meat by the house every Saturday afternoon—steaks, roasts, young chickens, stew beef, soup bones, whole hams, bacon, pork chops, ground chuck. Once she even brought a leg of lamb. Wilhelmina couldn't possibly eat it all, so she stored most of it in her deep freeze.

She went out to the porch and gathered as much from the deep freeze as she could carry, dumped it into the kitchen sink like a load of kindling, then pulled her cookbooks from the cupboard and sat down at the kitchen table. She began looking up recipes that had always seemed too complex for her, dishes that sounded vaguely exotic, chose six of the most interesting she could find, and copied them onto a legal pad. Then she made a quick trip to the grocery store to find the items she didn't have on hand, buying odd spices like saffron and coriander, and not just produce but shallots and bright red bell peppers, and a bulb of garlic cloves as big as her fist. Bill always liked garlic.

Back home, she spread all the meat out on the counter, the chops and steaks and ham, the roast and the bacon, some Italian sausage she'd found, some boudin that had been there for ages, and even a big piece of fish fillet. She chopped the sweet peppers, the shallots, ground the spices. The more she worked, the less she thought of the recipes, until she'd become a marvel of culinary innovativeness, combining oils and spices and herbs and meats into the most savory dishes you could imagine: Master William's Sirloin Surprise, Ham au Bill, Bill's Leg of Lamb with Bacon Chestnuts, Bill's Broiled Red Snapper with Butter and Crab, Bloody Boudin à la Bill, and one she decided to call simply Sausage Chops. She fired up her oven, lit every eye on her stove, and cooked it all just as if she were serving the king of France instead of her old French poodle. Then she arranged the dishes on her best china, cut the meat into bite-sized pieces, and served them to her closest friend, her dog.

She began serving early in the evening, letting Bill eat just as much or as little as he wanted from each dish. "This ought to wake up your sense, Bill." Indeed, Bill's interest was piqued. He ate, rested, ate a little more, of this dish and that. He went back to the leg of lamb, nibbling the bacon chestnuts off its sides. Wilhelmina kept gently urging him to eat. And as the evening wore on, Bill's old cataracted eyes gradually seemed to reflect something, it seemed, like quiet suffering—not his usual burden, but the luxurious suffering of the glutton. He had found a strength beyond himself, and so he kept bravely on, forcing himself to eat, until he could not swallow another bite and lay carefully beside the remains of his feast, and slept.

Wilhelmina sat quietly in a kitchen chair and watched from her window as the sun edged up behind the trees, red and molten like the swollen, dying star of an ancient world. She was so tired that her body felt weightless, as if she'd already left it hollow of her spirit. It seemed that she had lived such a long time. Howard had courted her in a horse-drawn wagon. An entire world of souls had disappeared in their time, and other nameless souls had filled their spaces. Some one of them had taken Howard's soul.

Bill had rolled onto his side in sleep, his tongue slack on the floor, his poor stomach as round and taut as a honeydew melon. After such a gorging, there normally would be hell to pay. But Wilhelmina would not allow that to happen.

"I'll take you to the doctor myself, old Bill," she said.

As if in response, a faint and easy dream-howl escaped Bill's throat, someone calling another in the big woods, across empty fields and deep silent stands of trees. Ooooooo, it went, high and soft. Ooooooo.

Wilhelmina's heart thickened with emotion. Her voice was deep and rich with it.

Hoooooo, she called softly to Bill's sleeping ears.

Ooooooo, Bill called again, a little stronger, and she responded, Hoooooo, their pure wordless language like echoes in the morning air.

Neela Vaswani

THE PELVIS SERIES

I.

Eve's father swung her onto his shoulders and gave her a ride to the indoor forest. She pinched his ears. She was farseeing: a giraffe.

"Duck," her father said as they passed through a door hanging with vines.

A white, plastic sky arched above. She heard a trickle of water, distant screeches of birds. She grabbed a hunk of her father's hair and gently kicked him; he lowered her to the ground.

At a fork in the path, they peered through the simulated fog seeping rhythmically from vents. Set back against the plastic horizon, between the trees, a small door framed a patch of real sky. Moisture dripped from the ceiling.

Her father raised a hand, cupped his ear. She heard crickets chirping; she nodded. To the left, watching them through a glass wall, was a chimpanzee.

Eve and her father walked down the Ape Path. The chimp kept pace, his brackish eyes inscrutable, his thick lashes feminine and curious. Eve watched the chimp, close enough to touch, to understand. She squeaked her fingers along the glass. In the dense foggy air, she knew the chimp by his steps, his eyes; she knew her father by his neck, the wedge of his back. Her tongue was flat in her mouth: blank, unnecessary.

When the path veered away from the glass enclosure, the chimp disappeared from her view. She yanked on her father's hand, and he lifted her to his shoulders.

II.

On a dig in South Africa (fieldwork for her linguistics doctorate), Eve unearthed a chimpanzee. It was 3.5 million years dead. She gazed into the empty eye sockets and beige muzzle of the intact skull. An hour later, she found shards of spine.

She worked on the computer, reconstructing the placement of the chimpanzee's larynx. The partially reassembled skeleton lay on a table covered with black velvet, a cushion and contrasting background for the bones. With the help of the resident biologist—a timorous man with clumps of red back hair welling above his collar—Eve deduced the larynx to be high in the throat, restricting the range of sound.

She massaged her own larynx, low, like all *Homo sapiens*. She hummed a high note and made a cage of her fingers around the vibration.

That night, Eve got drunk. Three beers for each member of the American team and four each for the Africans because they haggled better, with charm. The hairy biologist produced a bottle of tequila and the Africans clapped and shouted for Eve as she tossed back five shots in five minutes. "You look like Ghana woman," one man said, and touched her helixed hair. "Where are your people from?"

"Could be Ghana. Could be anywhere," she said.

A game of charades was organized by the paleontologists who insisted on dividing: one team named Leakey, one, Johanssen. Eve sat next to the biologist and his tequila. When the Leakey group said that sound in charades was as legitimate as Piltdown Man, the game turned into a fight.

Eve leaned into the biologist: "So, Red, do you feed that animal on your back, or what? We all want to know."

He laughed and pulled a comb from his pocket. "Want to give it a whirl?" he asked, and rapped the comb sharply against her forehead.

"Not here," she said and staggered from the lab.

In the dark, on a mound of mistakenly excavated twentieth-century rabbit, lion, and hyena bones, Eve sat with her legs sprawled in front of her. The titanic sky rolled down to the earth in every direction, so that Eve stared straight ahead and still looked into the black star-crowded night, a piece of velvet studded with white bones. The biologist tapped her shoulder, and she leaned her head back.

"Gimme that comb," she said, "and take off that dirty shirt." A primitive fear, of decay, of the unknown, taunted her from the tar-pit sky. She knew it was eternal and complete. She was fragile, an inevitable fossil. The biologist removed his shirt.

Eve looked at him, at his red-fringed pelt and triangular head. Against the night, his silhouette rose pointed and stout, blotting stars. She felt safe; his shape, like a tent, spoke of community. Reaching up, she pulled him onto the pile of bones. "They're sharp," he complained, and shrank from the triumph in her voice when she said, "I don't feel anything," and closed her eyes against the sky and the words and the unknown.

The biologist sat meekly, allowing her to tug at his red back hair, wincing when she untangled a snarl. "It's nice," she whispered to him, her legs clamped around his pale fleecy waist, her fingers wielding the comb like a crude weapon.

III.

For her dissertation research, Eve took a job in Texas working with language-impaired children. One of her cases could not speak; eight-year-old Jamie vocalized and gestured, but was usually unable to make herself understood. During her frequent tantrums, she wrapped her hands with her blonde, waist-length hair and punched her mother mechanically.

No matter how her mother tied Jamie's hair, the child shook it loose. When she began yanking it out in fits of frustration, her mother cut it into a bob that curved around Jamie's face in shaggy points. With her short hair, Jamie was unwilling to punch, so she created a new expression of anger. By pointing at the fridge she demanded a juice box and then emptied it in one crushing squeeze, one livid slurp. She tossed the flattened juice box to the floor, then pounced on it and tore it to shreds with her hands and teeth, saving the mutilated plastic straws as trophies. If seriously confounded, she pulled out her own eyebrows and eyelashes and would not allow her mother to attach fake ones. Both speech therapy and sign language failed to help Jamie.

Eve investigated alternate methods. She read about a pygmy chimpanzee, or bonobo, named Kanzi, who learned to communicate through a system of lexigrams, a language called Yerkish.

The system pleased Eve: a computerized board covered with arbitrary symbols, each symbol representing a word: noun, adjective, or verb in the shape of a spiral, square, semicircle, rod. She saw possibilities: *I want pasta, I miss you, I'm tired.* A total of seven hundred potential words lined the lexigram board. The center performing the chimpanzee research also sponsored a program for speech-impaired children.

Eve wrote letters, e-mailed, telephoned the center, bombarding anyone who would listen with her credentials and interests. She said she would move to Georgia and agreed to learn the lexigram process first with chimpanzees, then humans, as the center requested.

She was granted a three-year internship (with no pay). She promised Jamie and her mother that she would send for them as soon as she began work with children.

IV.

When they met, Lola grabbed Eve's hand and brought her to the TV. They spent the afternoon watching a *Discovery* program on the migration patterns of monarch butterflies. Lola was a bonobo, with immense gaps between her teeth and hands textured like olive meat. She was fond of placing towels on her head; when she pulled the ends around her face, she looked uncommonly like Mother Theresa, benevolent and wise. In sunlight, red highlights streaked her long, black fur. Her ears wiggled when it thundered. She laughed easily, explosive, sounding like seagulls cavorting around a dumpster. Because of a mild case of arthritis, she was not very dexterous, even clumsy when climbing. The red of her lips bled almost up to her nostrils, and a deep cove of wrinkled forehead interrupted her soft hair. If embarrassed, she covered her face with her hands.

"Lola, Lo-lo-lo-lo, Lola," Eve sang to her.

What amazed Eve most was the level of comprehension she read in Lola's eyes. She showed her pictures of Jamie, her own parents, her cat. She learned that Lola was pregnant and that her mother had died when she was eight. When Eve was twenty-four, her parents died in an airplane crash. As soon as she told Lola, she found herself clasped in a vigorous embrace.

The pregnancy was Lola's third; all her babies had been stillborn. Lola told Eve this using the lexigrams to say, "My babies quiet." She also told Eve she liked bananas and oranges and disliked the woman with white hair who mopped the floors ("Dirty White Head"), and she hid Eve's car keys at the end of each day—always in a different spot. Arriving home, Eve worked on her dissertation and wrote letters to Jamie and her mother. She sent them pictures of Lola playing dress-up and drinking vodka and cranberry juice with the American Sign Language chimps: Fouts, Jane, and Darwin. From the ASL chimps Lola learned the hand-signs for "Gimme," "More," and "Hurry," which she eventually combined into a sentence, "Hurry, Gimme More." In turn, she taught her friends the lexigrams for "Lola Pretty" and "Please Hug."

Hats and scarves and accessories of any kind thrilled Lola. She loved to try on clothes and look in the mirror; sometimes her hands flew to her face in embarrassment, sometimes her smile stretched happy and gapped. She had a collection of postcards, reproduced prints by Frida Kahlo (her favorite: *Diego on My Mind*) and Georgia O'Keeffe (she ignored the flower paintings but was fascinated by the bone and sky pieces). She adored UPS deliverers; ripping open packages was one of her assigned chores. She danced to polka music, L. L. Cool J. She played darts—the bullseye a photograph of Noam Chomsky. But only one activity, car rides, evoked cheers of delight. When Eve told her they were going for a drive, Lola wrapped an orange silk scarf around her head, Grace Kelly style. She took her backpack and stuffed it full of bananas, audio tapes, magazines (she demanded *Playgirl* whenever she was in estrus or if she had just encountered her favorite man, a grad student with green eyes who was studying bisexuality and face-to-face copulation in bonobos). Beethoven remained her favorite composer, from childhood through adulthood, particularly the Seventh Symphony conducted by Herbert von Karajan. Once she and Eve turned onto the open road, Lola put Beethoven in the deck, rolled down her window, and stuck out her hand, tapping against the side of the car and causing many near accidents. She had a hatred for policemen on motorcycles, especially if they wore sunglasses, and Eve always had to speed in case Lola tried to unseat a cop with her long arms.

In winter, Lola pouted. Forced to stay indoors, she used the lexigram board to sign "Bad oranges" and "Dirty Eve take Good Lola outside." The year Eve came to the language center, the winter was unusually long. Mid-April, the first warm day, Lola followed Eve around, sensing a treat. "Yes, Lola," Eve told her. "We're going for a car ride."

Lola donned her maternity tank top, her gravid stomach bulging, her baby due in two months. She waddled around, fanning herself with the portable lexigram sheet as Eve packed a picnic basket with grapes, cheese sandwiches, a jar of pickles, and napkins. She stowed the basket in the trunk of the car.

With all the windows rolled down, orange scarf wrapped around her head, and wind rippling her sleek, conditioned fur, Lola waved at houses and children looking out the back of a school bus. She whipped her face into a frenzy of terrifying expressions, the children laughing encouragement and forcing their arms joyfully out the side-windows to give her the finger. She gave it back. The wind inflated the orange scarf and she broke the sideview mirror trying to look inside her mouth.

When they stopped at a gas station, the attendant ran from Lola, who got out of the car and stood on one leg, stretching the other above her head. He locked himself in the booth and stared at Lola's pendulous breasts, full stomach, and red engorged sex. Since Lola was always allowed to pay for gas, Eve handed her a ten dollar bill and told her to slide it gently under the slot. The attendant whimpered and cried as Lola gave him the money, grunting her friendly grunt.

As they neared the park, Lola became pensive and quiet. Usually when Eve asked her what she was thinking about, Lola ignored her. Eve reached out and touched Lola's head. She asked her, "What are you thinking about?" Lola poked at the lexigram "Mommy."

"Are you thinking of your Mommy?" asked Eve. "Wuhh, wuh, wuh," Lola replied in her guttural voice and twisted her toes. Eve patted Lola's stomach, sagging under the bottom of the tank top. Tilting the lexigram board, she tapped "Mommy," then patted Lola's stomach again and wondered if she herself would ever be a mother. At thirty-eight, three years younger than Lola, she did not feel ready for children.

"Tell me, Lola, what's in your stomach?" Eve asked, and Lola pointed triumphantly to the symbol, "Baby." They turned into the park.

Black fur gleaming red, Lola led the way to a path they had used once in the fall, peeled off her tank top and unwound the orange scarf from her head. She hardly walked bipedally now, preferring the protective four-hand stance, her back shielding the life inside her. The woods smelled faintly of scallions. Lola gathered sorrel for Eve and daffodils for herself, some of which she ate. Nostrils flared, she loped ahead, scouting. When the sun drifted behind clouds, the air turned cool. Eve mimicked thrush and sparrow calls, trying to engage the birds in conversation. Lola swatted at mosquitoes and ate the ones she caught. "Good protein," Eve told her.

On the bank of a small creek, they spread out a blanket and unpacked the picnic basket. A crow circled above them and called out, the sound echoing. The crow chased its own voice, spinning in wide, flirtatious circles. "Too bad humans understand echoes," Eve said to Lola. "We could have been spared some loneliness." She folded the paper napkins into triangles.

Once Lola gave birth, the center would concentrate on teaching her baby and monitoring how much he learned from his mother (they already knew it was a boy, but did not tell Lola). When the baby turned three, Lola would stop working altogether—money at the center had to be reserved for learning chimps and post-retirement upkeep was expensive. The center tried to accrue money to study old age in chimpanzees, but no donors were interested, and Lola would be sent to a conservancy with other retired chimps and bonobos, a better fate than the last set of aged ASL chimps who had been shipped to a research institute and injected with hepatitis.

Eve wondered if she would be friends with Lola's son as she watched her trying to open the jar of pickles, grunting in frustration. Holding the jar out to Eve, Lola mimed a twisting motion with her right hand and furrowed her brow pleadingly.

They ate the entire jar of pickles, Lola teaching Eve how to eat with her toes. When they finished eating, they lay on their sides and flipped through magazines. It began to rain. Plashes of water fell onto the magazines, sticking the pages together. Out of the blanket, they made a roof and huddled together.

V.

Lola retired at forty-five, Jamie's second year in the children's program, and the year Eve finished her dissertation and was hired as a permanent member of the center. It was Eve who arranged for Lola's send-off picnic at her favorite park. Numerous guest speakers signed up for the event: a specialist on hominid teeth Eve knew from her days on the dig, an ethologist, a cultural anthropolgist. Eve had ordered round tables, white tablecloths, and peach napkins folded into swans (in honor of chimpanzee Washoe and her creation of WATER BIRD) for the wealthy sponsors' table and Lola's center table where Pan—Lola's three-year-old son—Eve, Fouts, Jane, and Darwin also sat. Green and white balloons tossed above the back of each chair. Eve was wearing a new spring dress, white and sheer, flecked with little pink roses. She had twisted her hair and forced earrings through her long-closed piercings.

Lola jabbered to Pan and fed him carrots. She tried to rub up against a handsome paleontologist from Kenya. A few children chased stray programs skipping across the lawn. Eve's group of speech-impaired children sat at the next table, Jamie happily among them. The child's hair was long again, almost to her waist. She sat on her mother's lap and used a lexigram board to demand more coleslaw. After only three months in the program, Jamie had begun to communicate. Lately, she combined sign language with lexigrams. Sometimes she said "Mommy" or "Eve" in a whisper. She and Lola wore the same pink party hat.

The paleontologist from Kenya gave Lola a plastic model of a human pelvis. She sniffed it lovingly and toyed with herself. One speaker remained: Eve. After her introduction, she walked up to the podium and stood under an oversized green umbrella stamped with white chimpanzees. She tapped the microphone, unexpectedly nervous. She saw Lola lying on her back with Pan balanced on her hands and feet, playing airplane. Pan giggled, sounding like a small seagull. His fur glowed with a red hue.

Eve talked about Lola and her accomplishments as a student and mother, her generosity, her love of paintings, dogs, Mississippi John Hurt, her long sentences. She told the story of Roger Fouts and Washoe, the ASL chimp, and the day a deaf girl came to the house to visit. Sitting in the kitchen, the child saw Washoe through the window, and at the same time that she signed "MONKEY" to Washoe, Washoe signed "BABY" to the child. Human-raised and cross-fostered, Washoe thought of herself as a *Homo sapiens*. The first time she met other chimpanzees she disdainfully referred to them as "Black Bugs," but after a few days she called them "Man" or "Woman," deciding they were all one people, all primates.

VI.

The picnic was over. Stars crammed the sky; the moon was a tilted crescent. Lola had consumed three pounds of grapes and seven chili dogs. Pan was frisky from too much iced tea. Eve supervised the removal of the tables and chairs, and made sure the microphone was returned to the soundman. She took out her earrings and put them in her backpack. She was tired.

At ten, the lights in the park went out. Eve, Lola, and Pan ambled to the van together. The crickets buzzed like power tools: screwguns, circ saws, drills. Lola carried the plastic pelvis and led the way through the woods. She knew where the van was parked. Eve always forgot.

When they came out of the trees and onto the blacktop, they stopped and looked at the sky. The stars pulsed and blazed; the Milky Way cloudy, like the wax on a plum.

"Orion," Eve said to the chimps. "And look! There are the Pleiades."

Lola waved the pelvis. She stood bipedally, and so did Pan. Silently, they gazed up. The crickets buzzed and clicked. A thin cloud sidled in front of the moon. Eve stared at the stars, searching for a pattern.

She asked Lola for the pelvis. She looked at the sky through the hip sockets so the stars were framed in white circles of bone. On the back of Lola's "Pelvis With Moon" postcard she had read that Georgia O'Keeffe held flowers and bones against the sky to see the objects clearly, to get a sense of foreground and distance.

She pulled her eye farther away from the hip socket: the curve of white bone; the black sky pitted with light.

"Pelvis With Stars," she said to Lola, and gave the bone back to her. "Like your painting. You know the one?"

Lola held the bone up to her own eyes and hooted. She signed "SKY" to Pan, who copied the gesture, sweeping the air with his hand. He begged for the pelvis in high, pleading grunts.

"Good. Yes. Sky," Eve said to Pan, making the motion herself.

Lola watched Pan's hand, then grabbed his thumb and moved it away from his fingers.

"It was a bit slurred," Eve agreed.

Pan tried again, his hand in front of his face, the arc smooth, expansive. He kept his eyes on his mother: "SKY."

Lola chuffed and gave him the pelvis.

"That's right," Eve said, looking up. "Sky."

Kirby Gann

Disasters of the Catastrophic Kind

Horse wasnt his real name. We all called him that because his real name—Horace—was odd and old-fashioned and people here in Kinard prefer salutary names of a single syllable. He never took issue with anyone over it, though even after a year he went around introducing himself still as Horace Cash from Montreux, Kentucky. A problem is a problem whether you got the name right or not, and Horse was a town-wide mistake and a problem for me especially as for what he did to Norba, sweet and usually-strong woman that she is. Him with all his savior-ideas to rescue her motel, the Beachside.

Not to say it was entirely his fault. It aint like he believed that to save the world you got to start in the swamps. We all share a blame.

He pulled up slipping steam under the car hood, pulled into my garage flying curses and slamming the wheel with his bony arms. Its a Shell station what you cant identify as such coming in as tube lights are all thats left of my typhooned sign, and me not being an official franchise you cant get a replacement no more than you can get true call label whisky at Poppydocks Saloon down the road. My rule of thumb at the time (and now) was that any job I did took an entire day. I tell roadsters passing through to take dinner at Junes Cafeteria and to stay the night at the Beachside Motel—not the most obvious name of choice, that, as the nearest beach to Kinard is Port St. Joe, two hours south.

Thats why the original owners designed a beach of their own. Its still there in the parking lot, bigger than it used to be but cracked through with weeds struggling in from the swamplands. They dumped a ton of white gypsum sand around a saltwater pool, Cyclone fenced it in, and hung a sign marked No Gators Allowed, gators being curious of the pool because it is home to one Common Bottlenose Dolphin. It was that dolphin what convinced Horse he couldnt leave once his car was fixed; in his opinion, this was a situation in need of fixing, too. And there he was, just the enterprising young man begging to be of use.

Now. I am not young but I am no less enterprising, and Horse and me started off wrong-footed from the very beginning, his arrival being nothing more than an unwanted break from my plans, his skidding tires breaking the spell of my daydream as my thoughts turned on my hearts desire—that desire being how to figure an approach to Norba Calhoun, to move ourselves up to the next level, as they say. For a long time now I been ready for my companion, somebody to listen to the hiss and snaps from all these surrounding swamps with, someone to sip the lemonade beside, and in all that time Norb'n'me had worked hard, real hard, to build ourselves something founded on mutual affection (whether she knew it or not). Then came Horse, and then came problems.

So here is me taking sun at my station, tipped back calm in my white wicker chair, and here is Horse raising the hood himself with the rose petal-tipped fingers of another class, leaning his frail womans body over a mess of Italian machinery. Told me later he saw the car in a movie and asked Dad if he could get one and his Dad being the doting kind, he found a Alfa Romeo ten years old and gave the gift of constant headache; say what you will about Italian cars but lets not start on reliability. Horse goes past me to the soda machine without so much as one hailing word, swigs half the can before he slumps against the wall; says, Hey. I been on the interstates nearly fourteen hours, Horse said. He says, Can you believe that? I kept telling myself, just drive and you will rest soon enough, and now I am wired to run the rest of the way to the coast myself.

I didnt congratulate him, if that was what he was waiting for. Horse always did seem like he was waiting for congratulations.

Last three hours engine temps been on the rise but what do I know about cars? How to check the oil and when to refill the gas tank is all, he said. His eyes were tiny behind thick, foggy glasses

But it looks like the fan wont turn on, he said. Then he laughed and added, Damn. Guess I am at your mercy now.

I told him everybody is, stopping here, but dont you worry friend, we will give her a fair look, and already I am thinking this will be a two-day job at least. He says his Pop told him any time a businessman calls you friend to get the hell out, so I ask whats he want to do? and he looks at the other station across Route 73 and shakes his head. They dont work on cars over there anyway, its just gas'n'snacks. He looks at the Beachside and tells me he aint have much money. Its a cheap bed, I said, and off he went, and thats where this whole story starts, with me thinking I done Norba a big favor sending him over when in reality I had just introduced bad luck to our small Florida community. For that I blame myself; I saw right off it was a circuit job that could have had him on the road in an hour. But money is money and often this can affect your judgment.

Off he goes into the Beachside front office to find the wallpaper mural of an orange Florida sunset stretched above a chiminy-red gulf, and Norba—Norb—Calhoun, whose hair kind of matches the mural. She colors her hair herself and never has got it right, yet she still looks good, which is an uncommon mark of true beauty. She has a stack of *True Detective* magazines and a box of creme-filled pastries always on the desktop, and a portable TV playing the day long. Norb told him to pick a key and that the poolgate locked at dark, so if he wanted to check out the dolphin he best do so soon.

Now, as he later related all this to me, he didnt yet know what from what and had ignored the billboard outside where a dolphin reclined, holding a Sloe Gin Fizz in one curved fluke. So he goes, You keep a dolphin here?

Yep, said Norba. Isnt that why you come? She being innocent of my doings to help her out.

No, he said, and already he is out to the parking lot to look. Horse had never seen a dolphin outside TV before. First thing you noticed was how the dolphins size smalled the pool. He wasnt so big when they first got him. Horse stood and stared with his hands on his hips. He kicked a beach ball across the water, but the dolphin didnt go for it (having always been pretty moody). He clapped his hands and called, Go fetch! and the dolphin shifted like it wanted to obey, then sank down to pace the bottom. When it came up for air Horse cried Go fetch! again, louder this time, only to be ignored. That dolphin tapped the ball out of the way with its snout, and cruised to the opposite end of the pool.

I was watching from my station. He scooped a wadded Marlboro pack—probably one of mine—off the surface and tucked it into his shirt pocket, pushed his hand back underwater, stirred it about and called out. That eggsmooth dolphin head popped up. Horse dropped to his stomach, bare feet in the hot gypsum and both hands in that green water. He said something like *Come here*, quietly; but just as he did the dolphin went under again, drifting around the bottom edges of the pool. Horse went silent then.

When Norb come out to lock the gate he asked if he could stay on a while, which took a bit of cajoling and him getting suddenly actionable, which had me standing concerned wondering if I was needed to back her up—none of us knowing yet that Horse was just an oddly excitable boy and physically harmless—but she let him stay. In fact he remained there a long time after dark, on his stomach with one hand in the pool, watching that old fish wander in circles, both of them lighted by the neon sign flashing VACANCY.

⚜

I called it a mystery when Horse didnt leave once his father wired him the money to pay for the car; that red convertible grunted off onto 73 and I figured that was that, and me with three-hundred new dollars in my pocket for a circuit job—money me and Norb could might someday enjoy together. But there he was later, crossing the parking lot with arms loaded full of inflatable toys, and Norb out there smiling, the gate held open for him.

Now I did not feel jealousy at this. Though it is true I am protective when it comes to matters of the heart, with Norba I was allowing myself to walk the line; so lets put down here that Horses welcomed return to the Beachside netted my intense curiosity. It was still Norbs business far as I was concerned.

I should have started suspicions when Horse convinced her to let him stay out by the pool late that first night. He was much younger than me after all and had the kind of belly and charm that I can only remember when prodded. She did not usually permit bends to her rules—I have seen solicitors thrown out of her office by the nose, rowdy guests ejected in the middle of the night, non-payers finding their doorlock bolted and their car wheels locked, too (by me). See, Norb'n'me were making our history before Horse arrived. Before Horse it was Zebb you got time to help me rollpaint this room? and Zebb Honey can you hold this door while I set the hinge? and then those two A.M. phone calls, Zebadoh Parker I am sorry to wake you babe but we got a problem and I need them tire locks. Before Horse it was shared cigarettes and hands touching and me bringing over my wicker seat to sit in the evening shade out front her office, listening to the loons in the swamps and spotting the herons. During Horse it was *Zebb honey I aint got time*. And now that we are After Horse I am still waiting to see what happens.

But this is to get ahead of myself.

Horse come back with his inflatables and Norba was too busy that evening for loon-listening. I steered clear and kept watch, allowing my curiosity to run all over me until it turned hurtful. Horse appeared everywhere over the next few days; I couldnt speak to a customer without seeing him out on that manmade beach. Several nights later at Junes Norb gave me the rundown:

Tell me where I got the good fortune of finding such an able assistant—and at no cost to me!

Boy knows about dolphins, does he? I asked.

No, not much; at least, not *yet*. But since I showed him how to keep the pool clean and the thing fed he almost dont let me out there anymore! She and June laughed. He is so badly sunburned he takes my umbrella with him everywhere now, poor thing.

Which answered one of my questions. That umbrella. Norb was eating her danishes. Her face pinched as she swallowed and she cleared her throat in a girlish way that made me think of sweetness.

But I got concerns, she whispered. Horse thinks something might be wrong with it.

He should know, being from Kentucky, is what I said, and you would have thought I had told her Florida motels were outlawed, the way she reacted: Zebb Parker, dont you try to tell me—look here, I need the help; that dolphin is a twenty-four hour job all himself. To hear Horse talk youd think he had studied dolphins all his life. He got himself a book in Blountstown.

A book!

He means well, sweet Norba said. He did go to college, you know. And I say he is a sight better to look at than any of you old bloodhounds around here (which I thought showed more malice than was called for, but Norb is pretty sharp).

Like I said, already I had my suspicions. Here was a boy with education enough, all right, accepted; and he had money but apparently nothing much to do except play with what he did not understand, whether he meant well or not (is what I said). Lord knows nothing good ever came from a man his age—what could he be? twenty-three, tops?—who didnt have enough to keep preoccupied. Me, at his age, all we had were our fights and beer. Not to say this wasnt a good enough way to grow up; nossir! My point being that the boys I fought then knew well that none of us was going anywhere and we had our entire lives to straighten each other out. Thing with Horse, he had nothing to keep him here, no roots.

He has that dolphin, June said, but June has never known nothing from nothing.

All I am saying is you best insure he makes no move without you clearing it first. That Alfa Romeo works just fine now, you understand? He puts the key in and he is gone.

My only point. Norba told me to just hush.

By the far side of two weeks Horse had it arranged to stay at the Beachside rent-free in exchange for light maintenance duties and dolphin care. Quickly he became one of the accepted sights about Kinard—new blood, as it were—in his sandals and baggy shorts, dim eyes peering through those thick glasses, his girlish body aglow from the sun warming the nylon blue of Norbs umbrella, a beat-up shield he now carried everywhere.

And me? I was yesterdays news, buying smokes for myself only, listening to loon calls at night in my chair by the humming soda machine, alone.

His first big step was to get into the water—the book said dolphins were social creatures, and this one looked lonely. Horse couldnt swim so well but still he had the courage to jump in and splash around, hollering loud enough that we all in the highway pulloff could hear, him later explaining this was to encourage the animal to react in more typical dolphin fashion: that is, playfully. Courage too that he could openly admit how the dolphin avoided him when possible, and tended to stay at the opposite end, where it was too deep for him to go safely.

He tried to overcome this by the lure of food. They made a game out of it—least Horse did, grabbing the dorsal fin as the dolphin lunged for the fish so that it had to carry him in order to eat. Horse called this progress. He didnt seem embarrassed when he tried to show us what he had accomplished, only to end up being thrown from the dolphin each time he tried a ride. And each time the animal managed to snatch the snack.

At the very least, my swimming skills are improving, he said.

I dont think the dolphin likes you much, I said.

Its hard to tell when the dolphin is happy, Horse answered, because it smiles in all cases.

They sing when happy. When he first got here there were nights we couldnt shut the fucker up. What you feeding him, anyway?

Same stuff Norba has always fed him. Fish . . . He motioned to the steel pail where a small pile stenched under the sun. Why? You think we need to change his diet?

How would I know? What kind of fish you feeding him?

Horse shrugged in the water, his shoulders peeled and boiled. He said: Fish fish.

I glared at Norb with finest certainty, content to have made my point. This boy was bad news in the brew for her.

You hush, she said.

So pass three months like that. Horse was a decent kid and I was mature enough to accept evenings without my belle, though this was not my first choice. You cannot net a fish that knows you lay in wait. I even allowed Horse to come fish with me because if nothing else the boy was earnest, coming by my garage saying he had to learn all there was to know about fish if he was going to do this right. Although in the same breath he admitted he never had been able to stand fish of any kind.

One morning we meet out where Cypress Creek opens into the lake, and I notice him moving real stiff. He limps, and keeps setting down his gear and umbrella so to put his palms to the small of his back, or else clutch one shoulder and stretch. He was so sore he had a hard time pitching his lure.

A fight, he said.

This was hard to believe. First, Horse was obviously no fighting man—not unless he had a death wish. Second, the only place to drink within miles was Poppydocks Saloon and Grill in Kinard, town proper, and I pass nearly all night there myself. I would have known of any fight. But Horse said it wasnt with anyone in town. The dolphin, he said.

You got your ass kicked by a fish, I said.

Its a mammal, dammit, said Horse.

Asskicked by a mammal then.

During one of their "games" things got out of hand and he must have fiercely pissed off the fish cause it started to butt him hard about.

Next thing I know half the beach is soaked from the pool and I cant breathe. Had to scramble just to get the hell out.

This didnt sit well with me, even if I never did care much for that dolphin. That dont mean I want to see the beast harassed. So I said to him, I says, Listen, Horse, heres my bitch: Why work so hard to help a creature that obviously dont want it? Has it ever occurred to you to let the sleeping dog lie?

To which Horse responded with only a stare at his bobbing lure. He tugged on the line, said, Ah, he likes me, Mr. Parker . . . I get on with animals. He took off his glasses and rubbed those saucer-eyes with the pad of his thumb. And something I read back at college, he said, something that always stayed with me, goes: Where man is not, nature is barren.

Just bad luck in the brew. And my doll right in the middle standing arms wide open.

I have my own ideas, said Horse. We fished with no more words from morning to noon with only one catch between the two of us, a freshwater bass the dolphin didnt hardly take to.

By February I had become suitor to a ghost; seemed I only caught Norb out the corner of my eye, through window shades, or on the arm of that boy. He was feeling even more grand than usual as he had a plan figured. For whatever reasons, he told me first. We were playing our weekly bottlecap poker game at Poppydocks, and I was a bit high on the fact that I had nearly all American caps—worth more than imports in my book, and we played by my rules—when slightly-slurring Horse fesses up to his new ideas for settling our "dolphin problem" once and for all, what problem no one knew of until he showed up slipping steam that day. I said exactly: She will never allow it and it is a damn fool thing you are talking.

Oh, Norba. She listens to whatever I say.

Well then I wont allow it. Miss Calhoun listens to me over you if she knows what is right for her.

Which bellowed Horse into one of his excitable fits: What do you even know about it, Zebb? You have never so much as got your feet wet in there!

A fact. But doubling a problem wont fix it, any mechanic knows that.

Norb is a good girl, I said, you should be figuring her out of debt, not further into it.

Just drop it, lets play. Horse answered.

Fair enough. He set his cards down to add another cap to the pile and we put to the game again, adding caps to the pot with each one we drank. But ghostly women and pool-bound dolphins had me in knots. After while I was no longer on top, and my mood can alter in direct relation to the amount of American caps lost and imports gained, and the beer had its effect on me, too. So I was getting a little aggressive. I hate to lose to anybody and wasnt about to lose to Horse. This new idea of his set me off too, set me to muttering is what it did and when I started on about the *goddam dolphin* Horse up and shoots back:

Just drop it, Zebb, you know nothing about this and dont deceive yourself into thinking you do!

I have never been scared off a confrontation in my life and stated as much, along with beerfueled feelings about young boys charging into where I lived all my life and how I couldnt figure Horse for a snake-oil salesman or just some bleeding heart, believing what they taught in his highfalutin college had some relation to life in the real world.

Horse tossed down his cards and slapped the table. His voice had a quiver.

Damn you, Zebb . . . Never before have I encountered a mind so small, Mr. Parker, so narrow—

He spoke loud enough that others nearby could hear him over the jukebox. That is when I reached one of my hands—still strong from teenage-meatpacking days—and whacked that boy across his face, sending bottlecaps skittering off onto the floor along with Horses beer. We held still a moment, waiting as we decided where to let this go, my arm out and Horses glasses hung skewedways on his face, skinny Poppydock himself watching intently from the bar with his hands clutching his peacekeeping Louisville Slugger.

We were on. Horse, skinny and quicker than me, popped up and pushed the table into my belly, and the cards cleared fluttering down to join the bottle caps. He managed a clear punch as I was slow to extricate myself from the mess, but said punch fell just short. Then it was all over. By the time Poppydock arrived swinging wood—a true friend, he walked around the end of the bar rather than springing over as you would expect—Horse had got thrashed pretty good, for which I am sorry now but wasnt then.

He lay sprawled half-in and half-out of the doorway with the saloon doors flapping above him, his mouth bloody and glasses broken, moaning into his hands. He said, *Oh that is just cool, you are a real big man for doing that*. A four of diamonds stanched a bleeding over his left eye.

Let it be a lesson to you, I said. Keep that in mind whenever you decide to talk to Norb Calhoun about those ideas of yours.

I removed Poppys hand from my shoulder and apologized for the drama; I like to think I have left such behavior to my wilder years. And then I went home, in my pride, stepping lightfoot over Horse to do so—still managing a last stomp to the boys scalp on the way out, to which I added a polite *excuse me*, having not meant really to do that. Really.

Again I figure that is that and I was a kind of hero for saving our small community from the likes of honest-but-misguided Horse. Excepting Horse wasnt so easily dissuaded, and once he set his will to his mind then you needed a natural disaster—which I am not—to stop him, or else stonewall until he lost interest—which should have happened sooner but I dont know, nothing else came across his line of vision and Kinard never has been a home to many pretty ladies. Norb is not so pretty but she has a ton of charm. So in this case he did manage to schedule himself a brief moment of glory, and rather than try to cause scandal by stopping him I admit I was curious to see what he was going to bring about. Small-town life being what it is.

It was the first week of April, and whatwith a months full of Spring Break students and everything in the motel working now due to Horse—give him credit—and the winter rains having long ago stopped, Norb was flush for the first time since the same month last year. Evening comes when Horse strides into Junes with my belle on his arm. They attract all kinds of immediate attention, laughing out loud and haw-haw shushing one another and playing kiss-kiss, making toasts with glasses of lemonade since Norb never has been much of a drinker. Soon a small crowd of us gathered about their table.

I have given Horse the okay, announced Norb, though nobody but me knew what that meant. A new dolphin! she said, and crowed hard enough to shake her gently-fleshed arms.

Perhaps I should explain, Horse began. I have been observing our dolphin (our dolphin!) for close on a year now, trying to figure what could be bothering it so. It is obviously disturbed, and lonely, and I thought all it needed was a companion—somebody like me to keep an eye on him, play with him, be his pal, right? But thats no good. You ever been in a place where you didnt know a soul and there was no one to talk to except yourself? Its awful; it is demeaning. What our dolphin (OUR!!) needs is his own people. He has been doing solitary for some five years now. So I see two options: we either let the thing go or he gets a companion.

Two dolphins in that little pool? I asked, in case anybody had missed the point.

No! Horse shouts. My father is sending plans to have it expanded. He knows all the hows and whys.

The boys eyes looked huge without his glasses on, but he couldnt hardly see without them. He ignored me trying to be the elder standing over and behind him, listening with slow shaking head and chewing on my beard—a habit I am trying to lose as it bothers Norba.

Hard to believe, I said to June once they left. Hard to figure that Norba, good old Norb who nobody could ever bullshit—if you will excuse me—just sat there listening to this kid explain what she is gonna do. Two dolphins! What she need two dolphins for? As if dropping two dolphins in your parking lot was a Florida tradition for every motel between here and St Joes.

June, being a careful woman, quietly mentioned that though she didnt understand completely, she thought Horse had made sense in his explaining things—which just set me to chewing that much more furiously on my beard (bad habit be damned). Because piss on hellfire if it didnt make some sense to me too, at least right then it did. But I wasnt about to let baggy June know that.

Day comes with the swamps hissing in the heat beneath our sky hard and blue and never with character. Along the edge of the new pool a thin glaze of muck had already formed, it being impossible to keep off for long due to the humidity, and you got your swamps festering bacteria, you got your low-circulation saltwater providing a nifty nest; you got your furnace heat working to give all lower forms their chance to prosper. The design connected two pools by a short passage, half-hidden beneath a Fiberglas foot bridge. From there Norba was to pull a divider out once the new dolphin had arrived. State wildlife officials were coming to publicly offer the custody papers for her to sign. A real shindig. Our new arrival was a calf bred in captivity by an already-pregnant catch.

And get this: I myself even helped build the road signs for the grand reopening. Thinking dolphins would appear more tasteful without the sunglasses or gin fizzes of the old billboards, I paid a local car-detailer fifty of my own dollars to have them springing out of the 'i' in Beachside. Me and Horse planted the signs miles apart on the freeway and the motel had no vacancy for the first time in I cant remember when—your typical vacationing Joe with wife and kids in the wagon cant pass the chance of seeing two dolphins face-to-face.

Except the Fish & Wildlife men forced all visitors out of the parking lot for fear they might intimidate the calf on arrival. Tourists had to watch from the porch at Junes across 73 while me, Norb, and Horse stayed nearby on pretext of service. Among great festivity the calf was slipped from the truck and into the new pool.

It made a hardy splash, and sank to the bottom without much in the way of moving. Then, just before we thought it dead, the calf upped himself for air and started swimming excitedly among our wild applause, making a racket of clicks and whistles—a real racket—as it inspected the limits of its new home. When it broke through into a gentle leap, the entire crowd was running from Junes deck with cameras flashing. After another hour Horse conferred with the officials and they announced that the new dolphin was acclimated enough for Norba to go on and lift the divider.

She did. Slowly the old dolphin swam into the new pool. It followed the outline without once bothering for air. The calf rushed over but the bull seemed as uninterested in it as in everything else, but like I said that fish always had been moody. When the dolphins bumped heads it pushed away irritably and Horse moved as though to separate them, but there wasnt need and we passed an hour cautiously, the next hour tucking away under lesser concern, and by the end of the afternoon the bull appeared to have grudgingly accepted the calf into his world.

I said, *Maybe they fall in love, Norb, and you can start advertising to come view two fruits of the sea*—the kind of line which used to set her to jiggle-laughing, but she told me to shush (a response I was by now used to). By evening the dolphins were chattering wildly and we were all of us happily entertained.

Horse beamed. At the time I thought well, he was right, you cant win every hand and all that, the disappointment of which had me looking at old June for a possible companion someday. Kinard presents a man slim options. June announced she was starting a cookout, everybody come on over. The crowd lingered the day long between the cafeteria and the motel, and a sweaty man from the Tampa paper eventually showed up to ask questions, with Horses comments turning more and more slick and Norb cheesecake—posing by the pool in her purple bikini top and madras shorts pulled up within an inch of her breasts, to cover her small belly.

Near sundown they shut and locked the gates for the night. The sky reflected oily gold and red on the pools. Norba disappeared along with the tourists and I did not follow her. Horse stayed behind, too, he had to, he couldnt leave and not indulge himself on his handiwork, right? It was his day for sure. I went back to my station and took my wicker seat and thought things over while I watched him. By the time he left, the moon was casting orange over the pool, and he turned once while walking away, seeing the two dolphins breaking the surface in rhythm, like two wheels rolling through the waves.

That upset us most: the picture of our two dolphins frolicking together like they belonged there. Without that picture in mind, what we discovered the next day wouldnt have been such a spectacle, such a mess, and we could have accepted it all much easier.

I awoke in the dark forlorn and beaten. I walked over to the fence in boxers and workboots to regard the reason for my defeat. And what I saw set me to shock: a disastrous smell reeked all over, and the water was bloody burgundy with big clouds of gore lapping its way through the small passageway under the bridge. I run over to Horses room hollering to get up and come see what happened, the water gone black and oh jesus, the dolphins . . . He was up and running barefoot and I was left so far begotten that I hardly noticed sleepy-faced Norba sitting up delirious, not even taking into account that she was bare before me. Not the way I would have chosen my first glimpse of her in all her glory, needless to say. Courtesy turned me quickly and I went out to help Horse, only to receive him raging at me through the fence, shouting What the hell, Zebb? and How could you? I set to ranting too telling him to fuck himself and all else that it had nothing to do with me, did he really think I could do something like that?

The calf was dead; it was as still on the water as one of the inflatables. Horse pulled him out and inspected the wounds—punchmarked holes and smashed-skin bruises the same width of the business end of a baseball bat—and he looked at me and again I was swearing I would never do that and could he suspect me?

Slowly he came around, staring at the bull minding its own business with the black inner tube over his snout. We shared a Eureka moment, then. We both put two-and-two together.

Horse covered the calf with a beach towel. He called to the bull, but it ignored him as always. When he approached, it swam away.

I am not going to hurt you, dammit, come here, he said. But that dolphin wasnt having none of it.

He kicked the water as the animal moved off. Fine! Have it your way! he shouted. And there Horse bellowed again into his excitable self. I could only watch as he slapped his thigh and tore at his shirt and kicked over sandcastles the kids had made the day before. He slammed the gate shut and locked it. He emptied the steel bucket, usually filled with stinking fish but now seeping out a bit of viscera and guts from yesterdays meals. Next he was in the water.

You dont like it here? You want a way out? Heres a way out! he hollered, and Horse, he coughed a gulletful of saltwater. This did not stop him. He moved to where his toes could still touch bottom. From there he plunged the pail deep into the water and emptied it out over the side, smashed the bucket back under and pitched the water out again. The sand got dark and began to seep through the diamondback eyelets of the Cyclone fence. He swung the bucket in another direction and the sand there thickened until a wide stream funneled back into the water.

You think I dont care? he yelled again. Think I dont understand? Bring it on! Take a piece of me!

Horse was roaring now, and I didnt have idea one on how to get him out of there, me standing around booted and boxer-shorted and with people beginning to dip their sleepy heads outside their motel doors.

The dolphin went under, then rose right next to him. Horse snarled and smacked the pail off its body, pushed it away even as the swell it caused thumped him into the poolside. He flung the pail at its head but that quickfish ducked under and swam for the divider, coming up to look at him again, laughing at him with that permanent dolphin-smile. Horse must have sensed this too as now he seemed beyond anger and into wild rage. His voice shot high and shrill. He scrummed to the dolphin and winged his arms out and gathered as much water as he could within his span and pushed his best attempt at a rogue wave at the animal, splashed it uselessly. Then he retrieved the sinking pail and began his task in earnest again, cursing the dolphin all the while, ignoring me.

Neither of us bothered with Norba once she ran outside (well, I bothered enough to note she was properly dressed). And we none of us reacted to the guests who now came mingling dazed and stupored and yawning around the fence. It wasnt until Norb screamed that Horse stopped bailing long enough to glare at her, as though to say *dont you start.*

Horse! she shouted. Horse dont you ignore me you let me in right now! She shook the gate and the whole fence rang. HOORRSSE! Then she noticed me and said *Dammit Zebb let me in*, but I didnt have the keys and couldnt find them and she gave me the finger for that, kicking that gate and running back to the motel to come out next instant with some papers and one extremely large key ring. She tried each key until she got it right, storming onto the foamslick beach and doing her best to hold her balance as she furiously waved the sheaf of papers. Yesterdays mascara had run all over her face and she shouted that there was no insurance, she hadnt filed yet and what now was she gonna do?

I said, Aw baby, and held my arms open to accept and console her but she wanted none of me. She shook those papers at my face now and managed only: *Insurance!* I held her arms just below the elbows and told her to get hold of herself and looked at Horse and at the dolphin in the water and then at the small corpse peeking out of its floral beach-towel shroud. Norba kept screeching. Finally this got to me and I told her SHUT UP, louder and more firmly than I meant to, which made me a feeling like my stomach shrunk inside, but she did calm down. I took her back to the office and settled her with some coffee—extra cream and sugar, the way she likes it.

Back outside, Horse sulked and was out of breath. He made a long slow take-it-all-in gaze over what he had wrought, at the wet beach and cloudy water, at the guests leaning with fingers poked through the fence and faces up close to the chain links. A couple very small kids took turns stamping their feet in the water that now fed into the parking lot.

Now . . . I am not a vindictive man, and I told Horse this. But at the same time it seemed meet and right to point out that he had been wrong in his ideas. I told him that was natural and that it happened to everybody, but could he help me out a bit as I had no idea myself of what to do next?

Horse made a tired wave. He sagged like a dog that hadnt wanted to get wet, said he couldnt think right now. We stayed quiet for a long time while I waited for him to get ready to start thinking again, but it didnt look like anything was going to change. Finally I came out with Well fuckall, Horse, there is bound to be somebody to call but I am damned if I know who, now this is your business and I dont appreciate you leaving me this to care for. Helluva way for any of us to wake up, is what I said, thinking how I should have stomped his head a bit harder at Poppydocks that one night.

Man, I never could stand fish of any kind, Horse said. He closed his hands over his face.

Back in the office to check on Norba I found she had managed to recover somewhat. She was shuffling papers and talking on the phone and she had found her admirably firm tone of voice—you cant give Norb a hard time for long, she will let you know. Here we were in the midst of catastrophic disaster and already that girl is making plans. And you know she looked as beautiful to me then as she ever did?—despite the goings-on between her and Horse and him laying down with her and looking her over with those big blind eyes and using those child hands of his over her gentle flesh and—well, some things are best left unimagined. But like I said she was beautiful enough for me at least and all I wanted was to help fix this catastrophic disaster and have her look at me again in that peculiar light that shines on the one you have the special attachment for, so I hung around the office and refilled her coffee and waited for her to get off the phone and when she did I said, I says to her *Norb, I am sorry*. She looked at me with the hurt and fright in her eyes of a little girl.

This made a fine moment. I reached out to take her hand and bring her to me and when she didnt resist, when she curled herself into my arms and let down that stingy guard of hers and began weeping into my chest like the real woman she truly is, I wanted to pull the shades right then and turn the sign on the door that says come back later and forget all and have the day.

But Horse was Horse and he had to ruin all that. We jumped at the kicking engine of his Alfa Romeo with enough time only to sprint out the clatterdoor and see him roaring off onto 73.

Not that this was enough to stop my girl. She ran off yelling and screaming and shaking her fist at him until you couldnt see her anymore, gone past the swamps next door, then you couldnt hear her as she had run too far.

I still cannot figure that boy for a snakeoil salesman or a bleeding heart whose plans went awry and who didnt have the guts to face that fact.

But Norb came back, as I knew she would. She had to, its her place. She came home hours later down in the mouth and weepy, muttering about issues like Loyalty and Trust. I had taken care of the guests who wanted to check out and thanked them for their sympathies the way she wouldve done. And she did appreciate that. I even got a snort out of her, too, describing this office filled with seriously depressed travelers.

And disasters of the catastrophic kind bring people together. All we needed was time, and this I have always been able to offer Norb Calhoun. We lost that day to cleanup around the pool. We passed the next day drinking and swearing at Poppydocks. I was gone the day after, taking down signs advertising two dolphins as luck being what it is it wouldnt surprise me if some rascal tried to sue Norba for false promotions.

We have all noticed the change in her since. She has lost more weight than is good for her and she keeps more to herself. But she is accepting of me again coming around her office with a flask to share, which we pour into our coffees just like we used to (though Norba is not much of a drinking woman), and talk. We pass evenings listening to the crack and hiss and whooping calls from inside the swamps, and not talking about Horse. And I am taking my time as always I did before, being near when she wants it, staying away when she dont. Patience is on my side, because none of us are going anywhere. June says so, too; she keeps her eye on our sweet Norba and agrees it wont be too long before it is safe for me to make my approach.

Mary Yukari Waters

THE WAY LOVE WORKS

I was thirteen when my mother and I flew back to Japan on what, unbeknownst to us, would be our final visit together. I was eager, after a five-year absence and eleven hours of flying, to see our family. But when we emerged from airport customs into the path of countless searching eyes, it took some moments to spot them. They were standing shoulder to shoulder, pressed up against the rails: Grandma, Aunt Miho, Uncle Koku, my cousins, Grandpa Ichiro with his special-occasion beret. A fraction of a second later, I felt Mother's carry-on bag swipe my arm as she rushed past me toward her mother.

The rest of us watched, keeping such a respectful distance from Mother and Grandma that several travelers used the space as a pathway, momentarily blocking them from our sight. The two women faced each other and gripped hands, their knuckles white. Being Japanese, that was all they did, but with such trembling intensity, like lovers, that I almost shriveled with embarrassment.

Mother and Grandma stayed indoors during the entire month of our visit, chatting away with hardly a break. They paused only out of politeness to others: my aunt Miho, who lived ten blocks away; Grandpa Ichiro, asking vague questions about America (do they eat bread at every meal?); phone calls; visitors. "I'm *bored!*" I said. "Can't I go swimming? Can't I go to Summer Haunted House?"

"Go with your cousins," they suggested. "We'll just stay here." They waved good-bye from the doorway as Aunt Miho, with us four children in tow, headed down the alley to the bus stop under the glaring summer sun. When we reached the corner and looked back for a final wave, the two of them were bending over some potted bonsai trees, already engrossed in conversation. They saw us, quickly straightened, and waved in unison.

I grew familiar with the ebb and flow of their talk. In the mornings—while cooking breakfast, washing up, walking to the open-air market—it was bright and animated, bubbling over with bits of gossip, or additions to previous conversations, which had risen to the surface of their memories during sleep. Afternoons, in the lull between lunch and four o'clock (when the local bathhouse opened), gave rise to more sustained, philosophical topics. Since Grandpa Ichiro took his nap then, it was also a good time for whispered confidences. "Nobody knows this except you," I heard Grandma say many times. They sometimes discussed mysterious financial issues: in the trash can I found scratch paper with hastily scrawled calculations using multiplication and long division.

I hadn't caught such nuances when I was eight; I now watched these comings and goings with avid foreign eyes. But even more fascinating than these allegiances was the change in my mother.

Five years earlier, my mother, my Caucasian father, and I had sold our home in Japan and moved to a small logging town in Northern California, surrounded by miles of walnut and plum orchards. "Did you meet up with your husband when he was in the service?" Americans always asked Mother. She hated that question. "Don't these people think?" she fumed in private. "Do they even realize what they're insinuating?"

"No . . . he was never in the service . . ." she always replied, as if in apology. "I have never had the honor of meeting a service man."

"Oh, honey," the neighbor women told me, "your momma's just precious!"

Back in America, Mother spoke English: heavily accented and sometimes halting, but always grammatically correct. When she felt lighthearted, she broke into Japanese with me. For the most part, however, she was a severe disciplinarian. She never lounged. She never snacked between meals. She scrubbed, gardened, hand-laundered, even in cold weather when the skin on her fingertips split open in raw cracks. She pulled back her hair, which was glossy even though she used nothing on it but Johnson's Baby Shampoo, into a French twist. Only occasionally at bedtime would I see it undone at shoulder length, making her face look unformed and girlish.

But here in Japan, she gossiped, giggled, teased. Once or twice I caught her watching me with that eager, open look of someone in love. While Grandma made the miso soup for breakfast, Mother stood before the cupboard and nibbled on red bean cakes, beckoning for me to join her. I did, warily.

"Koraa!" Grandma scolded, coming in from the kitchen with the tray.

"But, Mama," Mother protested in a loud voice, with a conspiratorial glance at me, "these taste so good . . . Meli-chan and I are so hungry . . . "

I remember thinking that each language carried its own aura, its own mood, and that people fell under its spell.

⚜

"I suppose it's only courteous," Mother said, "to visit Miho's house in return. After all, she's always coming over here."

"Yes, you're absolutely right," Grandma said. "But hurry back."

"How come Grandma likes you best?" I asked my mother as the two of us walked toward Aunt Miho's house.

She laughed it off with her new playful air. "Saa, I happen to have a lot of special qualities," she said. "I'm irreplaceable."

Aunt Miho was young and pretty; I had often fantasized about having her for a big sister. She and Mother were half sisters, due to some family complication I grasped only dimly at the time. Aunt

Miho's father was Grandpa Ichiro. Mother's father—my own true grandfather—was long dead.

"How's your visit so far?" Aunt Miho asked me at the lunch table. "Are you having lots of fun?" Her intonation was gentle and courteous, like that of a JAL stewardess, with each word hanging in perfect balance.

"Yes, Auntie," I said.

"Hajime said he heard lots of laughing the other night," she said, "when he passed by your place on his way home from work." We all looked at Aunt Miho's husband, who glanced up, discomfited, from his plate of skewered miso dumplings.

"Oh—there must have been something funny on TV," Mother said. "The Nishikawa Gang, probably. Do you ever watch it? That is a *hilarious* show."

"Soh, it is!" I assured Aunt Miho. "Grandma was saying she hasn't laughed like this in years!"

"Oh," said Aunt Miho. "How nice."

On the tatami floor, right under the low table where we all sat, I noticed a leather-bound Bible. By overhearing—or eavesdropping—I knew that Aunt Miho had turned Christian during our absence. I lifted the book out into the open; Mother frowned and jerked her head no.

I put the book back.

"You can look at that anytime you like," said Aunt Miho in her serene voice. "It's filled with strange and wonderful stories. About loving without limits. Despite anything others might do."

"Even if they're murderers?" I asked. Mother shot me a cold glance.

Aunt Miho smiled. "There is no power," she said, "greater than forgiveness." Aunt Miho's husband, a quiet man, got up and went to the bathroom.

"A hilarious show . . . ," murmured six-year-old Mikiko. I glanced over at my three small cousins, sitting quietly at the far end of the table.

With what must have been ease of habit, they had filled their glasses with exactly four ice cubes each and lined them up, side by side, on the table. They peered, unblinking, as their mother poured the orange Fanta, the children hunching down at the low table so as to be eye-level with the glasses, thus ensuring that no sibling got a milliliter more than the others.

"Did you see them with those drinking glasses?" Mother said on our way home. "If you had brothers and sisters, that's what you'd be doing. See how lucky you are, being an only child?"

I did. I would undoubtedly lose out in a competition of favorites. With a flush of shame, I remembered my behavior back home: how I constantly contradicted Mother in an exasperated tone, taking advantage of her ineptness in what, for her, was a foreign country.

But my behavior had changed since our arrival; the language also cast its spell over me. I was fluent in Japanese—it was my first language—but since our move to America, my vocabulary had stayed at a fourth-grade level. So in Japan my speech, even my thoughts, reverted from those of a cocky teenager to those of the more innocent, dependent child I had been five years ago. Here I was no longer capable of arguing with the contemptuous finesse I used back home. Here I was at a loss.

"But don't worry, Meli-chan," my mother said. "I could never have feelings for any other child but you." I was still unused to *chan*, that tender diminutive to a little girl's name for which English has no equivalent. Hearing such words, after all those years in America, made my throat grow tight. I could not have talked back, even if I had the words.

Mother took advantage of my weakened state. She slipped her hand into mine, a big girl like me, right in public. During the course of our stay, she would do this several times: tentatively at first, then with increasing confidence as the month wore on. This would not last once we flew home; the mere act of standing on American soil would destroy that precarious balance.

Now Mother strode along, leading the way; among the local Japanese, she seemed much taller than her five feet three inches. Near the steps of Heibuchi Shrine, we ran into Mr. Inoue, her former high school principal. "I hope you take after your mother," he told me. "She was the first girl from the Ueno district to pass Kyoto University entrance exams." I stood with my hand damp and unmoving in my mother's, still bashful from our newfound intimacy. I watched the old man bowing with slow, ceremonious respect. I heard their polite conversation, replete with advanced verb conjugations. My mother's sentences flowed sinuously, with nuances of silver and light, like a strong fish gliding through Kamo River.

The next day, I asked Mother whom she loved best in the world.

"My mother, of course," she replied. We were coming home from the open-air market. She was walking ahead of me; the alley was too narrow for the two of us to walk abreast. Dappled shadows jerked and bobbed on the back of her parasol.

"And my dad?"

"He's number two."

"Who's number three?"

"You! Of course." But I suspected, with a flash of intuition, that I was a very close third, probably even a tie for second. Not that I deserved it. I was an unpleasant teenager, whereas my father was a good, kind man. Nonetheless I belonged to this Japanese world, whose language and blood ties gave my mother such radiant power, in a way my American father never could.

"Who's number four?" I asked, assured of my good status. "Who's number five?" Too late. Mother's thoughts had drifted somewhere else.

"When you come first in someone's heart," she said, "when you feel the magnitude of another person's love for you . . ." Her gait slowed, along with her speech. "You become a different person. I mean, something physically changes inside of you." Her voice choked up behind the parasol and I hoped she was not going to cry. "I want you to know that feeling," she said. "Because it'll sustain you, all your life. Life . . . life can get so hard."

So hard . . . Was she was referring to my behavior back home? Guilty and defensive, I trailed my fingers along a low adobe wall in nonchalant fashion, over its braille of pebbles and straw. A smell of earth, intensified by midsummer heat, wafted toward me.

My relationship with my mother was not a bad one, by normal standards. I understand this now. But back then, the only yardstick either of us had was the bond between Mother and Grandma; it must have been a disappointment to my mother, as it was to me that summer, that we could not replicate it.

"You're Grandma's favorite grandchild," my mother said eventually in a recovered voice.

"Really?" I said, gratified. That question had been next on my agenda.

"Don't flatter yourself," she said, "that it's on your own merits. Not yet. It's because you're my child. You reach her through me. Remember that."

"Okay," I agreed. The *k'sha k'sha* of gravel was loud beneath our sandals. The buzz of late-afternoon traffic floated over from Shimbonmachi Boulevard, several blocks down.

"You and I are lucky," Mother said. "Some people never come first." I thought of Aunt Miho, how she had turned back at the corner to wave.

In silence we entered the shade of a large ginkgo tree, which leaned out over the adobe wall into the alley. Its fan-shaped leaves, dangling from thin stems, fluttered and trembled.

Mother stopped walking and lowered her parasol, turning her head this way and that. The *meeeeee* of cicadas was directly overhead now, sharpened from a mass drone into the loud rings of specific creatures; each with a different pitch, a different location among the branches.

"Take a good look around, Meli-chan," she said, attempting to make a sweeping gesture with an arm weighed down by a plastic bag full of daikon radishes and lotus roots. "This alley hasn't changed a bit since I was a girl. It's still got the *feel* this whole city used to have, once."

I looked. My eyes, still accustomed to California sun, registered this new light of a foreign latitude: a hushed gold approaching amber, angling across the alley in dust-moted shafts as if through old stained glass. An aged world. I pictured Mother playing here decades ago, to the drone of cicadas and the occasional *ting* of a wind chime: countless quiet afternoons, their secrets lost to the next generation.

"Ara maa!" Mother said regretfully. "Somebody's gone and replaced their slatted wooden doors with that all-weather metal kind."

Aunt Miho visited us frequently. Several times, when the grownups were reminiscing about old times and everyone sat basking in familial warmth and intimacy, she took the opportunity to slip in something about Love or the Lord. Our laughter trailed away, and we fell silent as she talked: Mother, nodding with restless eyes (when did Miho start using that *voice*, she said in private), Grandma, her gaze averted with a certain sorrowful submission.

Aunt Miho targeted Grandma and Mother. Grandpa Ichiro was spared; he was losing his hearing, usually off in a world of his own. I too was excused, since my vocabulary was insufficient for grasping the finer points of Christian theory. "Wait, what does that word mean?" I demanded anyway at crucial moments. "Wait, wait! What does it mean?"

In the late afternoons, I overheard Grandma and Mother talking. "Childhood insecurities," Mother whispered.

Grandma sighed. "It's all my fault," she said.

"It is *not* your fault!" Mother said.

It came to a head one week before our departure. My cousin, six-year-old Mikiko, came into the kitchen, where Grandma and Mother and I were sitting. "Mama says you don't want to come with us to Heaven," she accused, clasping her tiny arms around Grandma's knees and gazing up at her with moist, reproachful eyes. "Ne, is that true?"

"Miki-chan, it's very complicated," Grandma said.

"How come you aren't coming to Heaven with us? Don't you want to be with us?"

"Ara maa. . . ," Grandma protested, and stood helplessly stroking Mikiko's head over and over.

Mother's lips took on a compressed look I knew well. I followed as she strode down the hall to the room where Aunt Miho was watching a cooking show on television. Mother slid shut the shoji panel with a *pang* behind her. I listened from the hallway, on the other side of the panel.

"Raise your child any way you want, but don't you dare use her that way against my mother." My mother's voice was barely audible. "Can't you *realize*, how much pain she's had in her life?" she said. "How many times, since we were children, have I *pleaded* with you to protect her in my absence?

"And speaking bluntly," Mother continued, "what you want from our mother is impossible. *My* father's in Buddhist heaven, waiting for her. And when she dies, I'll be at the temple chanting sutras for *her*.

Third-year anniversary, fifth, tenth, fifteenth, thirty-fifth, fiftieth! For the rest of my life. Even if I burn in your Christian Hell for it!"

Her wrath was magnificent and primal. At that moment, it didn't even occur to me to feel sorry for Aunt Miho. I was swept up in an unexpected sense of vindication as well as a powerful loyalty to our trio. Over the following week, I was to sit before the vanity mirror and practice pressing my lips together the way Mother had. I would watch my face, with its pointy Caucasian features, become transformed with authority and passion. It would be many years before I felt the poignancy of Mother's belligerent, childlike loyalty, with which she shielded Grandma from the others.

Mother's voice now softened, for Aunt Miho was crying. "Someday," she said, "you'll understand, Miho. You'll understand, the way love works."

⚜

Even then, I sensed that my grandfather—not Grandpa Ichiro but my true grandfather—was a key catalyst in our family relations. That summer, for the first time, I was shown my grandfather Yasunari's photograph album, concealed in a dresser among layers of folded winter kimonos. "Now remember," Grandma and Mother told me, "this is just among us. The rest of them wouldn't like it if they knew. Grandpa Ichiro either. Especially Grandpa Ichiro!" The album was bound in ugly brownish cloth which, according to Grandma, was once a beautiful indigo; it had matching brown tassels that were still dark blue in their centers. I was discouraged from touching it. Grandma and Mother turned the pages, with hands smelling of lemony dishwashing soap.

Mother never knew her father; she was only five when Yasunari died in the war. Throughout her childhood she, too, had been shown this album, during stolen moments when the others were away. It was hard to believe this young man in the black-and-white photographs, her own true father, was as much a stranger to her as he was to me. Yasunari was handsome, like a movie star, with fine molded features and eyes like elegant brushstrokes.

"We were happy, very happy," Grandma told me. "Yasunari-san loved children. Every minute he had free, he was carrying your mother. Walking around, always holding her in one arm."

"I think I remember being held by him," Mother said.

"When he finally set your mother down, she'd cry. And keep on crying. Your mother, even back then, she could read people. And sure enough, he'd laugh and pick her back up. She even sat on his lap at dinnertime."

I learned the rest of this story when I was nineteen, after Mother's sudden death from mitral valve failure. Holding an adult conversation with my grandmother was an adjustment; I was so used to being the nonessential part of a threesome. But in the wake of Mother's death, we took on new roles: she as surrogate mother, I as surrogate daughter. In this new capacity we spent hours discovering each other, with all the obsessions and raised hopes of a courtship.

Before the war, Grandma told me, Yasunari was a highly paid executive in the import-export business. When he died, he left young Grandma with a sizable inheritance. But her in-laws, determined to keep Yasunari's money in the family, pressured her into marrying his elder brother Ichiro. Family obligation, they argued. A father for the child. Protection from wartime dangers.

Ichiro was a dandy. Despite the grinding poverty of those war years, he insisted on sporting an ascot and not a tie. A social creature, popular with both men and women, he drank with a fast set and then, flushed with sake, shook hands on tenuous business deals. In a short time he had gone through much of his younger brother's inheritance. In contrast to his outward persona, Ichiro was surly at home, irritable and quick to find blame for the smallest things.

Even today, more than a decade after Mother's death, Grandma revisits this as she and I sit alone, looking through Yasunari's album. She speaks in a whisper, the same whisper she once used with Mother in late afternoons, even though Grandpa Ichiro is dead now and we two have the house to ourselves.

Many nights, Grandma tells me, she stood at the kitchen window while everyone slept, gazing at the moon caught among pine branches. Many nights she dreamed the same dream: Yasunari was outside in the night, standing silent in the alley. She could not see him, but she knew, as one does in dreams, that he was wearing a white suit like that of a Cuban musician.

"Take me with you! Please! Don't leave me here!" she screamed after him in the dream, and woke to the sound of her own moaning.

Grandma went on to bear two children by Grandpa Ichiro: my uncle Koku, then my aunt Miho. In old photographs little Koku and Miho are always out in front, their beaming, gap-toothed faces playing up to the camera; although Grandpa is out of the picture, one senses his presence behind the lens, directing jokes to his favorites. Grandma stands off to the back, and Mother does too, her torso turned toward her mother in an oddly protective stance.

In this atmosphere, Mother's social awareness developed early. She massaged her mother's shoulders when no one was looking. She secretly threatened her half siblings when they misbehaved. She became a model student as well as a model daughter, thus depriving Grandpa Ichiro of any excuse to harass Grandma on her account.

In my mother, Grandma found an outlet for all the ardent romantic love she had felt for Yasunari. This child, she thought, is all I have left: of his genes, of his loyal, solicitous nature. Often Grandma left her chores and hurried over to the neighborhood playground where, using sleight of hand, she would slip a treat into Mother's pocket: a bit of baked potato in winter, to keep her warm; in hot weather, a tiny salted rice ball with a pinch of sour plum at its center. This was during the postwar days, in the midst of food rationing.

There just wasn't enough, she tells me now, for the other children.

Aunt Miho dropped by last week during O-bon, the Week of the Dead, bringing one of those seven-thousand yen gift melons that come in their own box. She sat alone at the dining room table, sipping cold wheat tea. All afternoon we had visitors: friends of Mother, dead thirteen years now; friends of Grandpa Ichiro, dead three years. They all trooped past her into the altar room, bowing politely as they passed. Aunt Miho listened from the dining room as they chanted sutras at the family altar and struck the miniature gong. Christians cannot acknowledge Buddhist holidays, much less pay homage to their ancestors.

I put the melon on a dish and took it to the altar room, placing it on the slide-out shelf among a clutter of orchids and boxed pastries. "Mother and Grandpa Ichiro used to love those melons," I told her, coming back into the dining room. "Auntie, you're the only one who remembered."

She smiled, with a warmth that her daughters rarely show me. She is still pretty. She now wears her hair swept back in a French twist, a style similar to my mother's.

This afternoon, Grandma and I discuss Aunt Miho's new hairstyle as we stroll to the open-air market to buy *hiramasa* sushi for supper. Our conversation has the same familiar rhythms I grew up listening to as a child. "She copies a lot of little things from your mother," Grandma says, amused. "She always denies it though. Between you and me, I think she honestly doesn't realize she's doing it."

"Mmm," I say. Unlike my mother, I am uncomfortable discussing Aunt Miho. It's bad enough that I, a mere grandchild, have usurped her rightful place as Grandma's only remaining daughter. "This heat!" I exclaim, adjusting our shared parasol so that it shades her more fully. This solicitousness is a habit I've developed since Mother's death, partly to carry on my mother's role but also, especially in those early days, to provide an outlet for all the tenderness I never gave my mother. It seems to impress the elderly neighbors. "What a comfort your granddaughter must be, in your old age!" they say wistfully. And Grandma replies, "She's just like her mother. Sometimes I actually forget who I'm talking to."

"A! A!" Grandma now exclaims. We have just crossed Shimbonmachi Boulevard and are entering the crowded open-air market. "Good thing I remembered! Remind me, after the fish store, to buy plum leaves for your dinner. To go with the sashimi."

Whenever I accompany Grandma to the open-air market, the fish vendor—a shrewd older woman—sidles up to us with her most expensive items. "Madam!" she greets Grandma today. "After she's back in America you'll be kicking yourself, with all due respect, for not letting her taste these highest-quality roe eggs! At their absolute prime, madam, this time of year!" She waits, with a complacent smile, as Grandma wavers. "Over in America," she informs my grandmother, as she wraps up our sashimi plus two other unbudgeted purchases, "those people eat their fish cooked in *butter*." She turns to me with an apologetic smile. "You sure have your granny's laugh, though," she says, exempting me from her earlier slur against Westerners. "Startles me every time, miss, coming from that American face."

It's true I bear little resemblence to anyone on my Japanese side. Sometimes I imagine Yasunari rising from the dead, and his shock and bewilderment upon seeing his own wife walking alongside a Caucasian, channeling to her all the love that was originally meant for him. But Grandma is adamant about our physical similarity. The way my thumb joins my hand, for instance, is the same as Yasunari's, and I have the same general "presence" he and my mother did. And she recently confessed that in the early days, whenever I said "moshi moshi" over the telephone, she would have a crazy lurch of hope that Mother's death had all been a big mistake. My voice, she insisted, was identical to my mother's.

We turn homeward onto Temple Alley, walking abreast. Three years ago this alley was gravel; now it is paved. Our summer sandals make flat, slapping sounds against the blacktop, and I miss the gentle *k'sha k'sha* that had reminded me of walking on new-fallen snow.

The houses have changed too, since my last visit: many have been rebuilt Western style, with white siding and brass doorknobs. Shiny red motor scooters are parked outside. In the middle of one door hangs a huge wooden cutout of a puppy, holding in its smiling mouth a name-plate spelling out THE MATSUDA'S in English letters. A bicycle bell tings behind us: we stand off to one side as a housewife rides past, straight-backed, her wire basket filled with newspaper-wrapped groceries for dinner.

"Where was that little alley that never changed?" I ask Grandma as we resume walking abreast. She gives a short, puzzled laugh as I describe the alley to her.

"I have no idea what you're talking about," she says. "Ginkgo tree? *Cicadas*? What kind of clue is that to go on?"

"There was an old-fashioned adobe wall," I say.

Grandma shakes her head, baffled. "They've torn a lot of those down." She stops short. "Meli-chan," she says, "did we remember to lock the back door when we left?"

Perhaps in the future when Grandma is gone, I will walk with my small daughter—who may have even less Japanese blood than I do—through these same neighborhood alleys. And a certain quality of reproach in the late-afternoon sunlight will remind me with a pang, as it does now, of my mother's confident voice saying, "I'm irreplaceable."

"Once, when I was a girl," I will tell my daughter, gripping her hand tightly, "I walked these alleys just like you, with my own mother." Saying these inadequate words, I will sense keenly how much falls away with time, how lives intersect but only briefly.

"Thank goodness I remembered the plum leaves," Grandma says now. She peers over into my shopping basket. "You're always so particular about wrapping them around your *hiramasa* sushi."

"That's not me, Grandma," I say. "That was Mother."

"Oh. Well . . ." She is silent for a moment. "That would make sense," she says. "Poor thing. It was never available during the postwar years, and she craved it for years after she moved away to . . ."

"Grandma," I interrupt gently. "It's too late for that now. It doesn't matter."

Grandma quickens her pace, as she sometimes does when she is annoyed. "One doesn't always get the luxury of timing," she says.

Crystal Wilkinson

The Fight

Before the fight, the house is swarming with Aunt Daphne and her three children. Girl, boy, boy. The girl is three years old and dumpling fat, like me and my sister, Candy. The boys are six and seven, skinny little things, wild as puppies. Aunt Daphne's husband, Leroy, is out in the backyard with my father. Through the side porch window I can see Daddy firing up the grill and Leroy's hands flying up in the air and his lips working ten miles a minute. Daddy's face looks like he's in some physical pain, like he's caught in a wrestler's headlock.

Leroy is not the kind of uncle you call uncle. He's just Leroy. He talks loud and nonstop about everything there ever was like a record player with no off button. The house and the yard are loud, loud, loud and me and Candy are like our father, quiet like birds.

My mother and I are at the kitchen counter, which still has white flour spots from this morning's biscuits. She is mixing the hamburger with chopped onion, spices, a bit of breadcrumbs, and an egg. I am patting out the hamburger meat, forming it into large, round patties and placing them on wax paper, which lines a big green serving platter. Our mother is a culinary magician. She has perfected the art of stretching food. She can feed twelve people with one pound of anything and a few odds and ends. But barbecuing is my father's specialty.

Candy and Aunt Daphne are at the kitchen table. Candy is shucking corn and placing the long blonde silks into a large piece of newspaper and Aunt Daphne is chopping cabbage for coleslaw and has just put the potatoes on the stove to boil.

The kitchen is a mess just like the rest of the house. Mama has never been one for appearances. There is no magic in her cleaning skills. The house is not filthy or nasty. It's just messy. Piles of paper in the corners—bills, articles torn from magazines, mimeographed copies of poems my mother liked in high school, old photographs of Grandpapa before he died, and Mama dressed in pleated, long skirts and sweaters when she was young. Our house is full of things like that, things my mother wants to keep.

There is clean, unfolded laundry on all the beds. All of our dirty clothes are still on the floor in the bathroom from our baths this morning. We are amazed when we visit other people's houses and see things neat and tidy behind closed pantries and shut closets and cabinet doors. Our house is not like that.

The boy cousins are running through the house playing cowboys and Indians. They are running from the living room to the kitchen over and over in a circle, yeehawing and grinning from cheek to cheek like it's the most fun they've ever had. I hear the coffee table being shifted from its spot. It makes a dragging sound across the hardwood floor in the living room like fingernails on a blackboard.

My mother and Aunt Daphne keep on talking as if they can't see the hooligans running through the house taking whatever's in their path with them. All this noise wakes the fat baby girl, Isella, who has been asleep on the couch. The toddler who looks so cute in the pictures that Aunt Daphne sends is suddenly transformed into a monster. Her hair is all over her head from her nap and her face has the nubby imprint from the couch fabric. Her face is so torn up that she looks like one of the Sleestacks off Saturday morning TV, her mouth is gaped open to holler. She is red and silent, but when she gasps for breath a blood-curdling scream comes out. Aunt Daphne grabs her up in her arms like she's a smaller baby than she really is and rocks her over her shoulder. "Yes· that's Mama's love. Shhh. Brothers waking the baby up." Our cousin is big for her age and looks like a six-year-old with her creased, plump legs sprawled across Aunt Daphne's lap. She goes from screaming to cooing like a dove under Aunt Daphne's open-palmed fingers rubbing her back in wide soothing circles.

"Bless her heart," Mama says and smiles that 'I remember when' smile.

Aunt Daphne and my mother are both slender as string beans. Only when they smile wide smiles and wrinkles form at the edge of their mouths, can you tell they are in their forties. They are close like me and Candy. The only difference is that me and Candy are more heavy set. Not fat, really but big boned. At least that's how our mother explains it. "Big boned from your father's side."

Late at night in the glow of the nightlight, in our room, we talk about all the things we could do if we could will ourselves skinny. "I'd be a model," Candy says. "Walk down the runway with my bony hips.

Cameras would flash and I would smile like this." Candy puts on a face that makes her teeth look false and ghostly under the glow of the orange bulb. We sputter and choke with laughter.

"I'd marry the finest thing walking," I say, recovering my breath. "I would live in a big house and I would cook and have babies and all that. I'd be a detective, too, like Christie Love but only I'd have a bigger Afro than hers, wear my Aigner boots and short shorts, have gold earrings big as coffee saucers." I scoop my hands up into the shape of a large circle. "And I'd grin at them, like this." I smiled too, wide enough to make Candy laugh. We laugh and try to keep it low because if we laugh too loudly Daddy knocks on the wall and threatens to come in and whip us. He never does, no matter what, but we keep it down anyway.

Me and Candy have bunk beds but when we are in the mood to gab we climb into one bed and whisper out our skinny futures into the dark. I wake up in the middle of the night and kiss Candy on the forehead. She wakes up and kisses me back too. She always thinks I'm asleep but I'm usually playing possum.

We both wish we were like Mama and Aunt Daphne, who don't dress in style any more but would look perfectly good in a mean pair of hip huggers or a body suit. No flab hanging over even with all these kids.

Sometimes me and Candy lie to each other and say, "You look like you lost some inches." We pinkie swear that we'll go on another diet soon but we were never serious about it before the fight.

By the time the sweet pickles are cut into the potato salad and the baked beans are removed from the oven, Daddy is stabbing the blackened meat with a fork and throwing it into a waiting pan. He is jabbing the steak, the hot dogs, the hamburgers and rubbing his head. Just from looking, from this distance between the backyard and the house, I know that Leroy is not only standing on my daddy's last nerve but jumping up and down on it. Daddy likes it quiet. I lean into Candy and whisper, "Time for a rescue mission," and we carry out the plastic utensils and plates to set the picnic table. Mama and Aunt Daphne are still talking in the living room and the baby is now rounded out in my mother's small lap, spilling over the edges like yeast bread rising.

"Daddy, we got the plates," Candy says as we leave the stuff on the table and head toward the men. Daddy's face is pinched up like he's at his maddest. And Leroy, whose back is slightly turned to us, seems oblivious that he is adding steam to Daddy's pressure cooker.

" . . . and so I told that fool, man. 'Fool if I ever catch you around my car again' and he shot off straight down the street like a bullet, lickety split. Like a God damn bullet. Like I was telling my friend, Petey, 'Petey, I said, I don't know what I'd do . . . all these years . . . '"

"Girls," Daddy turns to us like we're saviors. "Take over for a minute while I go in and use the restroom."

"I got it man."

"These ladies know what they're doing. Don't nobody live in my house and not learn how to cook especially as much as they eat. Now don't they look like they know how to cook?"

Daddy winks at us.

Leroy laughs like a crazy person and Candy don't say nothing. We are both mad. Well not really mad, but hurt. Everybody always has some little fat joke to tell. Seems like they all think it's okay. It's not. It still hurts just the same but we play like it doesn't stab us in the heart.

"Daddy, please," I holler back over my shoulder, keeping my smile in place. His belly is round as Buddha's and I say, "look at that" and point.

"I'ma remember that one girl," Daddy says and points his finger toward me. "I'ma get you for that one."

"You girls looking prettier and prettier every time I see you. You hitting them books like you sposed to?" Leroy asks.

"Yeah." We shrug our shoulders.

"You got boyfriends yet?"

"No." Candy looks at me with that he-is-so-yuck-look.

Through the back door we can see Daddy in the kitchen talking to Mama and this time he's the one with arms flailing in the air. We hear their voices rising but we can't hear exact words. Aunt Daphne is there too, the baby on her hip, playing mediator.

Leroy's tongue is a worm set loose, wiggling its way through all our business, asking so many questions that Candy and I are lost in his jabber. We try to keep our responses to head nods and three-word answers.

Daddy finally makes his way back and as Candy and I head for the picnic table Leroy gets in one last blow.

"Them girls so pretty. Just wait til they lose that baby fat and y'all gonna need a stick to beat off them wild boys."

"I got a shotgun if I need it," Daddy says. But even through his joking we can see that he is angered by something. Something is blowing in the wind.

We have crossed the yard and are about to shut the back door before we turn to see our father belly to belly with Leroy, his fist clinched down by his sides.

"Leroy, if you don't shut the hell up, I'm gonna give you something to talk about."

"Come on then, I know you don't want none of me."

"Mama, Leroy and Daddy are about to fight," Candy yells. "Right in the yard," I add knowing the words make no sense even as they are coming out.

"Lord, God, come on Daphne. They are so crazy."

"Stupid ass men all these years and they still can't get along for ten minutes."

Mama and Aunt Daphne are into the yard before we know it. Aunt Daphne has passed Isella to me. I am holding her with my hip jutted out, trying to balance the weight. Candy is talking to her and grabbing her chubby fingers into her hand.

"It's okay, Baby Isella," she coos, "Your Mama'll be back in a minute."

Isella's lips are puckering slightly, one of her arms reaching for her mother.

I shift my weight again and bounce. She's really a cute baby.

"Hi girly girl," I say. She seems to like the sound. "Hi girly, girly, girly." If that's what keeps her from crying, I'll do it until Aunt Daphne comes to get her.

"What in the hell is going on?" Aunt Daphne steps between Daddy and Leroy facing Leroy. Mama is in charge of Daddy.

"Y'all are too old to be acting this way."

"Don't he ever shut his damn mouth?"

"Man, I ain't done nothing to you. You better keep your hands to yourself. Daphne, you better tell this fool something."

"I'm going to tell you both something. The children are watching." All the grownups turn toward us. I am balancing Isella like a large box wedging her on my hip. Candy is standing with her arms folded, waiting to see what happens next. The boys are in the house doing God only knows what.

But it is over before it gets going too far. Daddy is back tending the food and Leroy is walking around in the yard a few feet from him cooling off.

⚜

At dinner, Leroy is back at full speed talking about nothing to nobody in particular and everybody at the same time.

"This potato salad is good. Y'all ever had that potato salad in the store. Now that is some awful mess, tastes like paste. No flavor. No salt. No mustard. We had this picnic at work and I was telling this guy

I work with, 'Man this tastes like glue.' It did too. Just like some paste or something. Awful." Leroy screws up his face just like Baby Isella had earlier.

Me and Candy are sitting by each other and just for that purpose, as a Leroy shield. We roll our eyes at each other. We communicate with our eyes and decide not to talk unless we have to.

Mama has Aunt Daphne. They are carrying on their own conversation about how long they were in labor, even while Leroy is talking.

"Lord, girl I thought Candy was never gonna make it out. I was in labor for forty-eight hours. I know you remember that. Probably got the scars still on your wrists to prove it." Mama laughs a cackly young laugh.

Daddy is putting all his energy into an ear of corn, concentrating on blocking out both conversations. At least that is what I think he's doing.

"And ain't nothing worse than bad potato salad or bad mashed potatoes. Now you would think folks couldn't mess up mashed potatoes but they can."

"And look at her now," Aunt Daphne says. "Look at both of them now. Wouldn't ever believe either of them started out this big." Aunt Daphne snaps her fingers. "No bigger than a minute." She looks at me and Candy like we're Mama's prizes. And Mama smiles at us like we are. Like she always does when she remembers us in plaits and baby walking shoes.

The boys have each other, fat Isella is pounced on Aunt Daphne's knee and has a long string of slobber slivering toward the table. Daddy is sulled up like a bullfrog.

"Good, God, Daphne do y'all have to talk about childbirth at the eatin table?" Leroy shakes his head. Aunt Daphne glares at him but acts like he hasn't spoken a word.

"She," Aunt Daphne nods toward Isella, "was my hardest. All back labor all up in here." She rubs the small of her back and makes a face like she's feeling the pain again.

"All that time," Mama says, "and you had only dilated four centimeters."

"Uh huh, exactly."

Mama and Aunt Daphne go back and forth like this and ooh and ahh like they are in a room full of women telling these birthing stories for the first time.

The boys are playing in their food.

"Mama, I don't like this it tastes like it's got dirt clods in it. See?" one of them says and spits the potato salad into his hand.

"Shit, Miles." Aunt Daphne tries to catch him before he rubs it into the picnic table and mixes it with the baby's slobber.

"Daphne, baby, get that boy. Damn it boy. Now why is he doing that, Daphne? Daphne get the boy. My God. I'll be damn. Ain't got a bit of table manners. I'll be damned."

"Leroy, please."

Daddy sucks air through his teeth and takes his frustration out on his hamburger. He bites it hard and shakes his head. Mama eyes Daddy but don't say nothing to him.

"I'll be damn, boy."

"Daddy, it tastes like dirt."

"Boy, you don't know good food when you see it. When I was a little boy like you I ate what was put before me. Didn't say a word." Aunt Daphne shakes her head, scowls, and keeps up with her conversation with Mama.

Leroy's diatribe is much more embarrassing than anything that little Miles has done.

Miles tucks his chin close to his chest.

Aunt Daphne is one of those mothers with octopus arms; she is cleaning up Miles' mess and doing all this while holding the giant baby and shushing the other boy, Marquez, before he does the same thing, all the while keeping a conversation going with Mama and occasionally glaring at Leroy.

"Good Lord," my mother says with a teenager's voice that we rarely witness. She and Aunt Daphne cup their hands around their mouths and giggle. They are wearing the same shade of brick-colored lipstick like thirteen-year-old girlfriends. My mother and Aunt Daphne whisper in each other's ears. They block the rest of us out and talk about people and things that only they can understand.

⚜

Mama becomes playful when Aunt Daphne is around. Aunt Daphne and Leroy come to visit from Cincinnati once or twice a year. It has always seemed to be a chore for my father. I look at these women and wonder what they were like when they were little. I can't see ever being away from Candy.

That night me and Candy settle into our beds and the day becomes a collection of memories to be stored away. The bad boys. Isella, the screaming baby girl. Leroy. The smell of my mother's baked beans and my father's secret sauce. Mama looking as though she was about to cry when she waved bye-bye to Aunt Daphne from the driveway. Daddy's discontent. With the memories stored away, all the world is right again. I feel the warmth of Candy's familiar body next to mine. We are bedtime-clean and donned in our favorite pink pajamas whispering quietly, not knowing that our lives are about to change. I cling to the memory of this moment even now because it is the last time I remember feeling totally certain about my place in the world.

In the moments that followed our parents voices grew from the familiar inaudible mumbles to full-fledged war words that left us all scarred.

"How am I sposed to feel?" My father's voice quivers with rage. "How in the fuck am I supposed to feel?"

"I don't know how you are supposed to feel," my mother screams, "What's done is done. It's been a long time ago. What can I do about it now?"

"Every time the son-of-a-bitch comes down here, he throws it in my face. Did you have to tell your sister everything? You told her and she told him. I don't want to hear his mouth every single Goddamn time."

"Bennie, what do you want me to do about it?"

"Janice, I don't know. All I know is that they are both my girls. They're my babies no matter what." We had never heard our father cry before.

"Bennie, they are always going to be your girls, both of them. You're *her* father too."

My sister and I grow cold underneath the covers and hug each other. We all cry together.

One of us is not our father's real child. We feel our parent's hearts breaking through the wall that separates us.

The next morning, a Sunday, Mama cooks breakfast. A mound of bacon, scrambled eggs, toast, buttered on both sides, bacon gravy and fried apples. Our mother cooks over the half-filled baked beans dish, the rank potato salad bowl, all the barbecue utensils from yesterday like they are not there at all. She is our regular mom, pleasant but yesterday's giddiness is drained. All the tears too. She's living life in neutral again. My father seems normal too. Nothing is spoken about last night's revelation and me and my sister watch our father place his arms around our mother's small waist and plant kisses in her neck. Candy and I are afraid to ask, hoping it's a dream that will float away. In the whiteness of daylight, last night seems surreal. I look at Candy and shrug my shoulders when nobody's looking. She is glassy-eyed and bewildered but we all hold up this farce through breakfast and seemingly, so far, for the rest of our lives.

By late summer, Candy and I grow tired of searching through our mother's old pictures and putting our ears up to the walls trying to seek more information. We even eavesdrop on the other line when Mama talks to Aunt Daphne. Still we know no more than we learned that night.

⚜

The second Saturday in August is back-to-school time. Me, Candy and my mother have sat on the porch all day long watching the other families and their kids carrying in bags loaded down with blue jeans, skirts, blouses and shirts, number two pencils, and reams and reams of notebook paper in bright pink, blue and green. It is one of the hottest days of the year and we are on the porch swing and our mother is rocking gently back and forth trying to make a breeze in this sweltering heat. We are each sipping a glass of fresh lemonade and waving at the neighbors as they arrive and depart from their houses. We watch the boys climb into cars with their parents with mad on their faces. Boys hate this time of year. We watch the girls and their mothers drive off together. We even see someone we don't know pick up Jeanette Stokes.

But this is a time of rest for us. Our dresses are already pressed and hanging ready for church. The house is clean, as clean as it gets around here, and Daddy is napping in a lawn chair in the backyard. The yard is mowed and we are all waiting for five o'clock when Daddy will fire up the grill and we'll bring the boiled meat from the kitchen, the hot dogs and the perfectly round beef patties that are waiting in the refrigerator. School is about to start but we are prepared. Our mother finished our shopping in June. Candy and I are two sizes smaller. When we tried on our new bras last night we both marveled at each other's smooth lines—not hardly any flab at all, only a tad bit on both of us around the middle.

While our parents dig into the heavy meal and make small talk about the weather, a neighborhood softball game and church, Candy and I nibble at our meat and fill our plates with salad. Neither of our parents notice who we've become. Tonight we sleep with the lamp on. It is our new normal. Our whispered conversations are inventions of what our mother's lover looks like. Tall, short, young, old.

Brown-skinned, light-skinned. We invent worlds where our mother engages with her man, the man that is one of our fathers.

"Maybe he is a poet from up in New York, who was a speaker at the library and she couldn't resist his love poems," Candy whispers.

"No, why would he be here in Kentucky at Stanford's library? No, he was her high-school sweetheart, you know, the one that Daddy used to tease her about."

A traveling preacher who gave a guest sermon at the church. Somebody Mama works with down at the creamery. The plumber from over in Crab Orchard who's tall and light and looks like a movie star. The truck driver who broke down at the bottom of the hill one time. We do this every night.

Sometimes we stare at each other without blinking to try and figure it out, trying to find the father in one of our faces. While she is sleeping, I look at Candy and wonder which of us is the real daughter. A flash of jealousy rises in me when I think I spot Daddy in her face but then I kiss her just the same. When I try to fall asleep, I can't. I lay awake and watch Candy sleeping like she's at peace, like she holds the real answer inside her like a secret. I want to shake her to wake her up and ask but I don't dare. Candy and I have always been the same, almost like twins but I can't help but think that somewhere inside our bodies, inside our hearts that something is growing and stretching out of shape between us like a rubber band, stressed and pulled so tight that there is nothing left to do but snap.

Silas House

SAINTS

Not long before her death, Mother Teresa visited the town of Hawk, Kentucky. She was there to open one of her charities on the outskirts of town, and a huge, churning crowd assembled to see her. They all pushed and were pushed as they tried to get close to the side of the road upon which she would reportedly pass, on foot.

There were very few Catholics in Hawk, but everyone in the county came to see her. People from other towns came, too. The scent of her celebrity had traveled to them and brought out those who thought she was a saint, those who thought she was someone it might be worthwhile to lay eyes upon, and those who waited for such things to happen just so they would have an excuse to get out of the house. Cars clogged the highway leading into town. People who lived nearest the charity house placed signs in their yards reading PARKING $4. News-vans with satellites attached to their roofs rolled in, as did the bishop from Louisville. Everyone felt pressed to dress up, and many of them wore hot suits and heavy dresses, even though honeysuckle dripped from the vine. Perfectly round circles of perspiration showed under the arms of the men's starched white shirts. Heat lay against the ridges like stripes of mist.

Among the people was Marcella Morgan, who was sixteen and about as pregnant as a girl can be. She had to walk two miles from her house to the town, since she wouldn't have dared told any of her family where she was going. Her people were both old-fashioned and religious and refused to support the actions of a Catholic—a religion that smelled strongly of blasphemy. Marcella's sister, who had the fieriest tongue of all, had spent the whole spring dreading the arrival of Mother Teresa, and nearly spat every time she fumed: "Them Catholics don't even worship God. They pray to *Mary*."

Marcella held both hands on either side of her round belly as if she was keeping the baby in balance and felt each muscle in her body move as she forced one leg in front of the other. People stepped back out of her way. She knew that most of them moved out of politeness to a woman carrying a child, but some of them parted the way because they frowned on her condition. These people glanced straight from her belly to her hand, where no wedding band graced her finger. They wondered who the father was—although she would tell no one, they all had a good idea—and if her mother would end up raising the poor baby. Most of them considered Marcella and concluded that nothing would ever become of her. Things seldom came of girls like her.

She too had dressed for the occasion. She worked at her sister's beauty shop, A Woman's Glory Salon (which specialized in Pentecostal hair—it was hard to find someone who knew how to do a bun just right these days), although her condition reduced her to answering the ever-ringing phones. She had saved up enough money to buy the best maternity dress they had at the Fashion Bug and had chosen it with great care. She had bought black because she thought it was a color that showed respect.

The saleswoman had asked her if she was going to a funeral. "You ought not, you know," the woman had said. "A pregnant woman ought never go to a laying-out. You'll mark the baby with grief."

It was very plain, which she thought a nun would appreciate, and fit snugly enough so that Mother Teresa would notice her belly right away.

Marcella managed to get right beside the road, where black-eyed Susans lay pitiful and broken beneath the trampling feet of onlookers. The high school band was marching by, playing "Ave Maria." She ran her hands over her abdomen so quick and deliberate that it looked like she was in pain, but she only feared the tubas and trumpets would startle the baby. She knew that the child was sound asleep because the doctor had told her that long walks would rock it into a state of content.

"Here, take this chair," a voice said. Marcella turned her head and saw that a teenaged boy was holding out a plastic folding chair. She didn't know him, although he looked about her age. He was a canepole of a boy, tall and straight in all respects, and his bangs needed trimming; they kept getting caught in his eyelashes and quivered every time he blinked. He was not even old enough to shave, but he stood like a man. His back was very straight and his hands were large. Marcella thought that he was somebody who had never even had a childhood. He looked at her without any expression on his face and she noticed how gray his eyes were. He looked worn out for his age.

"That's all right," she said. "Thanks, though."

"No, take it. You don't need to be standing up."

"All right," she said, and laughed nervously. Her feet were swollen and her shoes were too small and she had walked all that way, after all. The boy unfolded the chair for her and sat it below the bank of the grassy shoulder, right on the road. Relief spread up her legs when she sat, but she felt foolish, sitting down with everyone standing tall and close behind her. Further up the road, lots of old women were sitting in similar chairs, and on the mountainside people had spread out quilts and held straight hands to their brows so they could look below, but no one was sitting down here. The boy stood close to her side. Not knowing what else to say, she repeated: "Thanks."

The mayor rode by in a convertible. He sat on top of the back seat and waved as if everyone was here to see him. A piece of poster board reading WELCOME MOTHER was attached to the passenger door. Behind him came the guffawing men who made up the Lions' Club and members of the Women's Auxiliary, who were all very pale and skinny and wore nearly identical flowered dresses. The walk had managed to work half of the women's slips down, but they were too caught up in the adoring crowd to notice. Marcella wondered what the Women's Auxiliary did besides walk in parades. That was the only time she ever heard a peep from them.

"When is she coming?" A woman asked in a booming voice, as if someone nearby might know. Marcella had seen her before she had sat down and knew that it was Loma Sizemore, a woman who frequented A Woman's Glory. Loma never had a good word to say about anybody but Jesus. "I never came to see no parade."

"She'll be by directly," someone answered.

"I don't know why we came anyway. Could have watched it every bit on the news."

"She's a saint," a young woman said breathlessly. It sounded as if she had rehearsed this line and had been waiting a great while to say it. Marcella didn't look over her shoulder to see who was doing the talking, because she could picture each one of them. She didn't know everyone in Hawk, but she knew what everyone was like.

"A saint!" Loma snorted. "No such thing nowadays, honey. What's she done, is what I want to know. Helped people overseas is all."

The young woman sounded taken aback. Marcella thought that this girl had most likely worn a hat for the occasion, and she tried to picture what it looked like. She thought it would be flat and straw, covered in plastic flowers. "Why, she's opened a charity house right here in these mountains."

"That's the only time anybody comes to the mountains," a man said. He stood so close to Marcella that she couldn't help seeing him. He had a belly nearly as big as hers and a face so red that she thought he might blow up right there on the road. He hitched up his pants and coughed wetly into his hand. His chest rattled with black lung disease. "They come to hand out charity or talk about how poor we are."

The baby rolled over just as a fire engine went by. A crew of cheerleaders sat atop the truck, smiling with lipsticked mouths and teeth so white they caught the sunlight. Marcella could picture them getting ready for the parade, smoothing globs of Vaseline out across their teeth. She soothed her baby, whispered "Shh," just as she always did. The cheerleaders had always made her cringe, too.

"You all shouldn't talk about her. She's the best woman alive today."

Loma was getting angry. She let her temper flare whenever she had the opportunity. "You ought not believe everything you see on the news. You don't know her, do you?" Her voice took on a growling curl at the end of each sentence. "What's she done for you?"

The young woman sighed so loudly that Marcella could hear her, even over the murmuring crowd. A great buzz arose over them, the way it sounds in church just before the meeting starts.

The boy squatted down beside her and shook a cigarette out of his crumbled pack. "Smoke bother you?" he asked.

"Go ahead," Marcella said. She wondered why he was here. She tried to imagine what he hoped to learn today. He had a kind, square face with high cheekbones. She couldn't get over his eyes. They looked like they ought to be in an old man's face. They looked dead. "Sure you don't want your chair back?"

"No, no," he said. He exhaled the smoke through his nostrils in two blue lines. "I couldn't set and a pregnant woman having to stand. I was raised better than that."

A shadow spread itself out over the land and it seemed to silence the crowd. Instantly it was cooler, and a short breeze drifted over them, just enough wind to move dress-tails and set the lime-colored leaves to swinging. The mountainside was tinted lavender and the hush of the people moved down the road like a great wave until all of them were quiet. They had heard of miracles where Catholics were concerned.

There was a Catholic church up near Lexington where a statue cried and people claimed they were healed. But the shadow moved on and the sun was once again a white coin on the noon sky. Everyone started talking at once, no longer looking upward.

No sooner than the talking started back up, a row of nuns walked by. Their habits fluttered out behind their heads like the wings of blackbirds. They kept their hands inside the folds of their clothes and walked very stiffly, like bridesmaids. Their eyes watched the road in front of them, their necks slightly bent.

Marcella had studied the parade itinerary that had been printed in the newspaper and knew that these nuns were from the Louisville convent. She had decided long ago that these would be the first ones she would approach.

"Sister!" Marcella cried out, and jumped up from her chair. It fell over behind her and the boy fumbled to sit it upright.

Marcella ran out into the road and got hold of the nun closest to her. She was careful to not grab on too tightly. She didn't want the woman to think that she was a lunatic. She spoke as quickly as she could, knowing that she would be dragged away.

"I have to talk to Mother Teresa, please. You have to get me into see her."

The nun kept walking, as if nothing out of the ordinary had happened, as if this happened all the time. But she looked up. She looked straight into Marcella's eyes. "What it is, child?"

"I have to see her. Please. I want her to take my baby. I'm due in a week. I want her to have it."

Marcella felt hands on her, felt her heels scrape against the blacktop as she was pulled back. One of her shoes clattered away. She smelled musky colognes and hot breath played out across the side of her face. A police officer held her by both arms. She felt how large her eyes had become as she made her face plead to the nun she had spoken with.

"Wait!" the nun hollered, and stopped. The rest of them stopped walking at different times, so that their economical line became a jagged thing in the middle of the road. The nun ran to her. "Don't hurt her," she said. "Can't you see she's carrying a baby?"

Marcella felt all eyes upon her, burning into her back. The nun laid her hands atop those of the police offer and he loosened his grip.

"This is not the right way," the nun said to Marcella. "Mother Teresa is an old woman."

"I heard that she had never refused a child. Not one." Marcella spoke so quickly that she wasn't sure the nun could even understand her. She was suddenly aware that spittle from her fast lips was spraying the woman's smooth face. "Please. They'll never let me close to her. You have to talk to her for me."

The nun put her hands on Marcella's belly and closed her eyes. Her lips moved as she prayed, the way some people's trembled up and down when they read silently. Marcella felt electricity moving through her body. Light filled her, shooting out from her belly and into her extremities. She felt the baby curl up inside of her, pull its knees toward its chin. She was limp. For the first time in months, she didn't feel the tightening of every bone and muscle in her body. She felt made of water. She stood on her tiptoes. She held her arms out straight on either side of her. She sensed that God was about to swoop down, take her beneath each arm and fly her away.

"Go now," the nun said. "Everything will turn out well. It's not as bad as it seems."

Marcella began to scream as the nun walked away. "But I love my baby! I want what's best."

Again the cop tightened his grip on her. "Come on, I said." His voice was harsh in her ear.

She darted her head ferociously, like an animal that doesn't know which way to go. She saw another line of nuns coming up the road.

They wore white, they nodded to the crowd. Applause ran up the side of the road like a widening wave of salt-water. Police officers walked close behind them. She knew that the one in the middle was Mother Teresa. She managed to break away from the policeman's grasp.

She ran out in the middle of the road and fell down on the pavement. She sat on her haunches, supported herself with both hands on the road, and held her face very high. She wanted Mother Teresa to see the light that shone there. She felt black grit bite into her knees, could hear the cop's shoe-leather slapping against the asphalt, so hot that she thought it might melt and seep down the valley like a river of tar.

Closer they came, so slowly. People moved out onto the street, hoping to touch Mother Teresa. A teacher directed school children to throw flowers on the road in front of her. It made Marcella think of Palm Sunday, Christ entering Jerusalem. Some of the children crossed themselves, put their hands together as if praying, closed their eyes. Mother Teresa nodded, waved. She was so little. At first she looked like a little child, slightly bent.

"I need you!" Marcella screamed, although this was not what she intended to say at all. "Take my child away from here!"

Mother Teresa continued to acknowledge the crowd. She was too far away. Marcella knew that she did not even notice her. The men were behind her suddenly. Two of them.

They dragged her away, over into the crowd where Mother Teresa couldn't see her. People stepped out of the way as if she was something they did not want to be near. She could hear them all around her, putting hands to their throats in shock, staring down at her. She fought the cops, but didn't scream. She was silent, her face an open book. They laid her on the grass near the road and crouched over her.

One of them spoke loudly into her face. "Don't make me cuff you, girl."

She managed to sit up. She looked out onto the road, where Mother Teresa was passing. Marcella could see her through a fence of legs as the crowd moved forward. For a moment she thought that the old woman had seen her, that she paused and was about to walk over and ask what the trouble was. But she had not seen her at all. She was just scanning the crowd, trying to lock eyes with as many people as she could. Beside Marcella the cop spoke into a walkie-talkie and wrestled with her arms.

"Wait!" she cried. "Please don't leave me."

When Mother Teresa was out of sight, Marcella broke down. She shook with tears, weeping so violently that she could not catch her breath. She grabbed hold of the policeman's arm, stroking it, peering up into his eyes for a hint of compassion. If he had looked at her with anything but callousness, she might have been all right. She wished that he would just help her up. He could get her standing, spread his hand out on the small of her back and walk her away from this swimming crowd. Away from the people who now only wanted to look at her. She could hear people saying her name. Telling others who she was. "Faye's sister," "Down at the Woman's Glory Salon," "Marcella Morgan."

"Please," she said to the officer, but he didn't even ask what it was she wanted. His walkie-talkie sizzled in his hand and a dispatcher coughed out a string of indecipherable words. When she tried to talk, saliva caught between her teeth and formed a bubble in front of her mouth. Her face felt like it had been dashed with cold water, even though her tears were hot. They had been building up for some time.

"Please," she said again.

The boy came running up the road. He stopped in front of her, knelt down to smooth her hair out of her eyes. Still she shook with crying. She couldn't make her bottom lip stop shaking. It felt like an alive thing that squirmed beneath her nose. She looked into his eyes, let her face tell him to take her away from here.

He put one arm under her legs and wrapped the other around her neck. He did not weigh much more than her and had trouble lifting her. Once he straightened his legs and back once again, he held her with ease. He said something to the police that she couldn't understand. Everything was suddenly slurred, made blurry. She felt as if she saw and heard through a sheet of water. Her belly still crackled with the nun's touch. Light crept over her body, pulsating in her arms and legs, crawling along her scalp. She thought it might be shooting from the ends of her fingers.

The policeman nodded and cut the air with an outstretched arm so people would move aside.

The boy carried her up the side of the road as people stepped back to make way for them. She put her hand on his face for a moment, feeling of him the way a blind person might have. She put her thumb over one of his eyes very briefly, then let her hand slide down over his nose, his mouth. Her hand fell from the point of his chin like a bird that had been shot out of the sky. She laid her head against his chest and closed her eyes. She was exhausted from weeping and felt she might be lulled to sleep in his arms.

Creative Nonfiction

Dianne Aprile

from *The Eye Is Not Enough*

THE Y OF A TREE

When I was very young, I made friends of two sisters who lived next door to my grandmother. One sister was my age; the other, a year or two older. They knew their urban neighborhood the way I knew my suburban one: blind-folded, they could find their way, landmark by landmark, to any house or patch of grass they were seeking. I, on the other hand, was an outsider in their domain; a weekend tourist who fell in love with the sidewalked streets and tree-arched avenues of that city landscape but did not know its ins and outs by heart. That knowledge would come much later.

The two sisters took me under wing. They introduced me to places I am sure my grandmother never glimpsed, never knew existed. It doesn't take much for me to return to the scents and sights of those secret places of forty years ago. I can look away, toward the sunlit woods that fill the window frames where I sit now, and I am there again, poking down brick alleys, crawling between hedges, skipping through side-yard shortcuts and, most pertinent to this particular memory, stepping through the cleft trunk of a massive, branching, magical tree.

Most likely it was an oak, huge and handsome, the hardwood of choice in a neighborhood of elegantly placed trees that bordered a sprawling urban wood designed by none other than Frederick Olmsted, the visionary architect of America's finest city parks.

I don't know how old I was the day the two sisters took me to the tree. Solemnly, they warned me that this was no ordinary specimen. It was a tree like Alice's looking-glass: one step through its cloven trunk, and all would look different, changed, unlike what it had been before. I shuddered, wanting and at the same fearing what they offered. The older sister urged me not to be afraid: I could turn away from what I saw on the other side and step back through the opening at any time. *Do you wanna?* she asked. I nodded yes.

The sisters went first. We were standing near the edge of the park, as I recall; not far from a tot lot where we sometimes played. The tree's central trunk formed a Y at a spot about waist-high for me, where it diverged into two slightly smaller branches. I watched each sister extend a leg through the breach, then heave the rest of herself to the other side, landing with a little hop and an exclamation of unmuted joy. *Come on, Dianne!* I lifted my leg, pointed my foot tentatively through the opening, closed my eyes and leapt.

Everything was different on the other side. The houses perched on the hillside road were not the same as before. The lay of the land was not the same. The sky, the treeline, the clouds, the magical tree itself—none of it looked the same. It was a miracle! I had no other word for it. I don't know how long we lingered in that mysterious Other World, but I recall it was not without regret that I obeyed the sisters when they said we had to go back. One step, and we were home, seeing things as we had always seen them. The treetop archways along the parkside road again looked the way I had memorized them, lying in the back seat of my parents' car as we drove past them for as many years as I could remember, en route from our house to my grandmother's.

I never forgot the magic of that one-and-only trip through the tree. Later, as an adult, after putting down roots of my own in my grandmother's old neighborhood, I searched for the trunk with the Y, but never found it. A tornado had ravaged the park in the interim, snapping the trunks of enormous oaks and leaving them scattered like pick-up sticks. Perhaps the tree fell in that storm, a casualty of nature. I know it makes no sense: a tree that opens one's eyes to another dimension, a tree that invites a leap into a reality ordinarily hidden from view. But I experienced it. Or, at least I have always believed I did. I remember it. I've never forgotten it. I've searched for it, one way or another, since that day with the two sisters on the edge of the park.

Years and years later, I came upon a phrase written by the poet Theodore Roethke: The eye is not enough. A simple sentence on the surface, but sit with it a moment or two and it begs for completion, resolution, a personal response. *The eye is not enough* . . . that is, it takes more than the eye to see. *The eye is not enough* . . . in other words, the visible world alone will never reveal all we need to know. The 'aye' is not enough . . . the 'nay' is needed as well.

Each response, even the comic, provokes another line of questioning. If it takes more than vision to see, then what other gifts are required? If images are inadequate for illuminating our world, what else is needed? Poetry? Faith? Imagination? Friendship? And if the positive alone is not sufficient to give balance to our lives, then what is the purpose of negative experiences? To flesh out the story? To fill in the blank spaces? To make us whole again?

Roethke's Zen-like phrase has become my answer to the riddle of the looking-glass tree. How else to explain a mystery, an apparent impossibility, other than by accepting the hard truth that the eye is never enough. Worlds of reality exist outside our vision: atoms, stars, black holes, peace, love, the past. We cannot witness their presence from where we now stand but we know they exist.

I ask myself then: why not a tree that splits our perspective, that opens the mind to another way of seeing? Was the tree-leap my rite of initiation into the world of hidden reality, or my first conscious encounter with illusion? Was the sisters' suggestion enough to make me see what they wanted me to see, or was I already primed to reach that extraordinary destination and they just happened to accompany me the day I found it? No matter how these questions are answered, I know I was blessed to pass through the Y of that now-lost tree. The experience gave me a puzzle to contemplate in the hard years that followed: it became for me a sign; an adventure turned metaphor.

Tree of life. Tree of myth. Tree of mystery.

Roy Hoffman

WITNESS TO CHANGE: CHARLES MOORE, PHOTOGRAPHER OF THE CIVIL RIGHTS MOVEMENT

Pictures can and do make a difference. Strong images of historical events do have an impact on our society.

—CHARLES MOORE
from the preface of *Powerful Days: The Civil Rights Photography of Charles Moore*

FLORENCE, ALABAMA

Nearly forty years have passed since Charles Moore slung his Nikon camera over his shoulder and headed to Oxford, Miss., to chronicle for the nation what would be, by today's standards, a mundane event—the enrollment, in the University of Mississippi, of a young black man named James Meredith. A storm was brewing at Ole Miss—Mississippi Governor Ross Barnett had sworn defiance of desegregation—and Charles Moore was heading into that storm.

Moore, an Alabama photojournalist on assignment for *Life* magazine, had already experienced the turbulence of the early civil rights movement as chief photographer for the *Montgomery Advertiser*. He had snapped dramatic images of Martin Luther King, Jr., and memorable, sometimes harrowing street scenes.

One of the most unnerving, taken in 1960 in Montgomery the day after black students tried to desegregate the Capitol cafeteria, showed a white man about to crack a baseball bat over the head of a black woman — a split-second of rage captured forever by Moore's shutter. Moore says he made the picture in the midst of running down the street, which tilted the angle of the shot. The image created a sense of a moral universe turned on its side, dislocated from normal time and space.

Moore had also put himself, physically, on the line. He had been pushed, yanked, cursed at, and threatened with his life for the simple reason that his camera would not tell a lie.

The weekend of confrontations over James Meredith began not in Oxford, but in Jackson, Mississippi, during a rally downtown for the Ole Miss Rebels football team. An Ole Miss game was scheduled for that afternoon at Jackson's big stadium. As Moore remembers it, there were young men on the street waving Rebel flags and cheering on Ole Miss. But those chants soon changed to "Roll With Ross," an expression of support for the Mississippi governor.

When Moore had started taking photographs of the fans, one man with a flag had told him to stop. He then, according to Moore, began to jab Moore with the pole of the flag. Moore knocked the pole out of the young man's hand. The man swore revenge. That afternoon, while Moore was gathered with colleagues in a Jackson hotel room, the door burst open and the same young man, followed by his friends, came storming in.

The man who earlier had stuck Moore with the flagpole now grabbed him by the throat. "I ain't got nothin' against the niggers," he spat. "Every white man should own ten of them!"

Moore, now sixty-nine, trembles with anger as he recounts the story.

"He gripped me with his left hand so I could reach up like this"—he demonstrates for a visitor—"and grab hold of his left thumb. You can hurt a guy pretty bad if you turn back his thumb."

But Moore, who had learned self-defense as a combat photographer with the U.S. Marines, wanted to stay calm. "I knew if I took a swing at him we'd have chaos in that room . . . My right arm was free. It was like a coiled spring. Oh, I wanted so badly to let loose with that spring!" He shakes his head.

Moore had faced down bullies before while growing up in small-town Alabama, and he sensed the right strategy. "I told him, 'It's me you want! Forget about the rest of them. Send everybody out of the room—and it'll be just you and me.'"

The bully did not budge. Then he let go and backed away. "He'd lost face," Moore says.

Moore's photographs from Oxford tell the rest of the story: How the twenty-eight-year old Air Force veteran, James Meredith, walked into the university with federal guards to each side; how a local law enforcement officer stood with grinning men, slapping a billystick against his palm to show power; how the Mississippi National Guard was federalized and used tear gas to quell rioters opposed to the entrance of Meredith. In searing, now-classic photographs of the university's administration building, the Lyceum, under siege with tear gas, Moore put his viewfinder up to the goggle-eye of his own gas mask and snapped haunting images of the National Guardsmen looking like storm troopers, their otherworldly gas masks like haunting apparitions.

As Moore's first big assignment for *Life*, it was a journalistic triumph. But he was a native son of the South who says he recoiled from the very violence he captured.

Like it or not, Moore had become the young man who helped show, to the rest of the world, the anguish of his native region, and, as the civil rights movement unfolded, its sense of promise, too.

A gentle artist with an aggressive camera, Moore today is an energetic, compact man with silver hair and penetrating blue eyes. As a teenager, he boxed as a lightweight. He still betrays the instincts of a man who knew combat in the ring—quick on his feet, a little edgy, with a habit of pinning you with his gaze.

He moved back to Alabama only last spring after spending twenty-three years in California. He settled in Florence, a picturesque town on the banks of the Tennessee River in northwest Alabama, where the University of North Alabama lies close to downtown and his old hometown of Tuscumbia is a short drive away. His cozy house on a quiet block near the university—filled with art books and photographs—is one he inhabits alone. He is divorced, and his three children and their families live in southeast Alabama's Dothan and in Florida.

The heart of the house is the study where copies of his book of photographs about the civil rights movement, *Powerful Days*, lie among his landscape images of Sonora, California, where he once lived, an idyllic town just west of Yosemite National Park.

There are new images he's making, too—digital photographs of blues musicians, many from the Muscle Shoals area close by to Florence. As he talks with a visitor about his love of photography, he returns to certain words or phrases—the "excitement" of the picture; its sense of "feeling the action."

The feel of the action is dramatically evidenced in Moore's photographs of events in the civil rights movement:

- Martin Luther King Jr., on September 3, 1958, being arrested after trying to enter the Montgomery courthouse accompanying his friend, Ralph Abernathy, who was responding to a subpoena. King is being pushed against the police station counter, his arm twisted behind his back.

- Firemen turning the force of their hoses on black citizens in an effort to break up voting rights demonstrations. People huddle in doorways, cover their faces, sustain the rocket-impact of the water.
- White and black marchers, waving American flags, heading from Selma to the state Capitol in Montgomery. They are tired, resolute—exultant.

Many of these images in the day when *Life* magazine came out every week, brought the movement into American homes. The pictures, as the years wore on and the images deepened, pressed on the moral nerve of the nation.

As the journalist Michael S. Durham wrote in the text of *Powerful Days* about the passage of the Civil Rights Act of 1964: "By then Charles's Birmingham photographs had become so much a part of the public memory of those events that they even received some measure of credit for the passage of the legislation. As the historian Arthur Schlesinger, Jr., later said, 'The photographs of Bull Connor's police dogs lunging at the marchers in Birmingham did as much as anything to transform the national mood and make legislation not just necessary, which it had long been, but possible.'"

If there is a sense of destiny about Moore's photographs of the movement, though, he arrived at that destiny quite by chance.

After joining up at age seventeen for a stint with the Marines, he studied fashion photography at the Brooks Institute in California. Family responsibilities called him home and he returned to Tuscumbia to work for Olan Mills, the studio portrait chain.

Restless with studio work, he turned to photojournalism and applied for a job at the *Montgomery Advertiser*. He showed up only to be directed to the local country club, where the chief photographer was doing a shoot of models dressed in evening clothes.

"You take the rest of the roll," the photographer told Moore.

By the time Moore had rearranged the models, changed the lighting and snapped the remaining pictures, the chief photographer said, "You're hired."

It was 1957, and within the year Moore was chief photographer. By then, the world had taken note of a young minister, Martin Luther King Jr., who'd arrived at the Dexter Avenue Baptist Church in Montgomery two years earlier and had led the Montgomery Improvement Association during the Montgomery bus boycott.

"I was spellbound by his oratory," says Moore, remembering how he'd photograph King up on the altar of Dexter Avenue Baptist.

Moore found himself agreeing with King's positions, but had to be careful about what he said. "I was not on any pulpit preaching," Moore says of himself during those years. He was only serving as a witness to the drama breaking around him.

While crouching on the floor before King, taking photographs, he was exercising one of his principal philosophies of photography: Watch your subject, get to know him, be ready for the right moment to capture a sense of who he is.

"I project myself into a person," he says of his photographic technique. "I look at everything, the arms, the hands, the expression. I wait for the moment . . . I shoot."

One of Moore's famous pictures of King, in Dexter church with a cross behind him, served as the model for the Postal Service's August 1999 stamp honoring King on the thirty-sixth anniversary of the march on Washington, D.C., when King delivered his epic speech, "I Have a Dream."

⚜

On the outskirts of Tuscumbia is a community named Valdosta—railroad tracks, barns, modest one-story homes, and roads weaving off through the north Alabama hills. It is here, after being born in nearby Hackleburg, that Charles Moore spent his childhood.

Showing a visitor his boyhood home, he drives past familiar landscapes, remembering walking down the hill to home after school, crossing an old iron bridge that spans the creek, enjoying a carefree boyhood of baseball and bicycles.

The era of segregation is long over, but there are the vestiges of racial divide. "They said there was no Klan here," Moore says, pointing to a shed-like structure near the railroad tracks. "But everybody knew that's where they held their meetings."

Moore's trip to his boyhood locale evokes memories, as well, of his early rambles with his Brownie camera, a free sense of walking down lanes, and through woods, that he still enjoys.

It also brings back his father, the Rev. Charles Walker Moore, a Baptist minister, and, says his son, a teacher of important moral lessons. "Dad was invited by black ministers to visit their churches," he says. "He'd be the only white there, other than me."

One of his strongest images of his father was on Sunday afternoons. "On Sundays, after church, we'd go in to the jail and he'd give a pack of cigarettes to prisoners, and pray."

The white and black prisoners were kept separated in those days. Moore says his father distributed smokes to both races, a tiny gesture, but profound in its way in the segregated South. "Dad just accepted people, but he didn't go out and try to change the world."

Of his life as a photographer—and as a man—Moore says: "I wanted to look back and honor my Dad about being good to people."

To this day, Moore can hardly read aloud the dedication to his book,

Powerful Days, without having to stop to fight back tears: "To Dad, the Reverend Charles Walker Moore, in loving memory, for his gentleness and strength of faith . . . "

Moore drives up to a lane where he grew up as a boy. A white house sits back on a rise, with a bright maple tree nearby. Across the yard is a stone house where his best friend lived. He tells how he introduced that friend to the girl who'd become his wife. The couple went on to be married fifty years, and the man became Tuscumbia's mayor. Although Moore has been home in Alabama since last spring, he has not worked up the nerve to go knock on that door, to introduce himself to the people who now live where he grew up, to ask to walk across the floorboards.

He parks the car near the house. "You stay here," he tells his visitor. He gets out, goes to the front porch, up the steps. Knocks.

He knocks again.

The shades are drawn. The house is silent. He returns to the car.

"Maybe they recognize me and don't want to answer," he says, perhaps only half-joking, referring to his long-ago reputation, as a photographer, of being someone others might think wanted to paint them in an unflattering way.

Before he pulls away he tells the story of his mother, how she died from cancer when he was thirteen, and how it shattered his father. The Rev. Moore, still a young man, had grieved long after her passing, and never remarried.

"I can see him sitting there, crying, night after night," says Moore, a grandfather now remembering like a son.

He takes a long, silent look back at the porch, then drives on.

Behind Helen Keller's home in Tuscumbia there is a water pump where Helen, as recounted in the play, *The Miracle Worker*, first uttered the word, "water," after her teacher, Annie Sullivan wrote, "W-A-T-E-R" in the palm of her hand.

On a bright afternoon when the trees are turned to flame, Charles Moore shows his visitor the Helen Keller home, Ivy Green, a picturesque white house surrounded by green, and a sense of hush. In the back of the house he deftly lifts his camera and takes a picture of that pump. Inside he trains his lens on antique portraits of Helen made by photographers of yesteryear. Two of those photographs show Helen as a raven-haired, sensuous young woman with captivating, dark eyes. Moore says he knows of the artist who captured those images.

To travel the Tuscumbia area with Moore is to see northwest Alabama through the eyes of a native son come home, still trying, in his own restless way, to find the place he left. He carries his camera with him, but it is his camera that seems, ultimately, to lead the direction.

At the Alabama Music Hall of Fame in Tuscumbia, he takes photographs of one of the museum directors standing in the lobby talking with his visitor. He wanders through the galleries, praising the exploits of Alabama musicians, among them Percy Sledge, who grew up close to where Moore did.

Like a man discovering his home area anew, he reads aloud, to his visitor, information on the recording studios on Muscle Shoals, summoning great musicians who've recorded there—among them, Aretha Franklin, Greg Allman, the Oak Ridge Boys. The photographer once accused, by some Southerners, of portraying his homeland in a bad light, now wants to promote it, and "to help make it better," he says.

In downtown Tuscumbia he lunches in a cafe. Meeting up with a friend from high school, he ambles the familiar streets. The two men reminisce about how the town, in decades gone by, thrived with commerce on Saturday mornings; how the Tennessee Valley Authority had a research station in town, and Ford had a motor plant. The town, they say, is now quiet on weekend mornings, and the research station and Ford factory are gone.

In front of a store window they pause as Moore gazes with bemusement at a pair of thong panties on a mannequin torso. He shakes his head, lifts his camera. It is a changed South.

A lady who runs the store comes out, giggling, and invites Moore and the others in. She tells a story about a man who comes in sometimes asking for ladies underclothes—for himself. "He said, 'Why, I just want a change of lifestyle!'"

It is like a scene from a comic story by Eudora Welty.

As the woman talks, Moore is snapping her picture.

If the heart of Moore's house in Florence is his study, its soul is downstairs, in his darkroom. He leads his visitor down to a series of rooms where developing trays sit near a sink, and photographs are stacked up on counters. Stunning portraits of glamorous actresses, gritty photographs of boxers in reeking gyms, bucolic landscapes from California—the images captured by Charles Moore are everywhere.

What characterizes them all is an intimacy, an artist's eye engaged by beauty and drama.

After spending seven years of his career photographing the conflict of the civil rights movement, Moore explains, he turned his attention to the world of natural beauty around him. The youngster who'd loved to ramble back roads of Alabama became the grownup who relished the rolling hills of California. He took pictures of celebrities—Kim Novak and Raquel Welch, among them. He then turned his attention to Southeast Asia, going on photographic journeys for travel magazines.

"An artist," he says, "does not have to spend his entire life doing one kind of work."

During a later telephone conversation, Moore relates that he has not been to Oxford, Miss., since that tumultuous weekend in the fall of 1962. He sounds curious, perhaps a little surprised, at hearing how, today, Oxford's nineteenth century courthouse rises serenely in the square. There are cozy restaurants, sporty clothing shops, and a vast, yet homey, bookstore—all looking out to a town where students, black and white, mingle casually.

Moore, who describes himself as a modest man who does not like to trumpet his talents, said there is one accomplishment he is proud to claim.

"Had it not been for the photographs I made over there, that made so many people angry, it's possible that little town would not be that way now."

Luke Wallin

RIVER OF SILENCE

We slip our canoes into the Connecticut as clouds of spirit-mist rise from its cool surface. We are just below the Turners Falls dam, near the Massachusetts-Vermont line, and I am watching a strangely-alive formation of this surface fog. The Indians once saw in these whitish movements the ghostly residents of a place, and this morning as we slide past sandbar willows out into the current and the breeze, that vision feels true. But this site—Peskeompscut, to the local Pocumtucks—was the scene of a terrible massacre in 1676. The English colonials surprised sleeping villagers and destroyed one hundred women, children and "many old men and women." Another one hundred forty died leaping over the falls, or when their attackers followed along the shore and shot them as they swam. I wonder whether these are among the spirits rising from the river's silvery surface on this perfect fall morning.

I am here, in a way, on a mission from these ancient Indians. And I am hoping that before the day ends I will sense what I must do.

There are ten of us in four canoes. Nine are members of a University of Massachusetts Amherst team charged with preservation strategy and tactics. The tenth is our leader, Terry Blunt, a trim, quiet intense man of about thirty-five. Terry is a Senior Planner for the Commonwealth, and his first lesson to us was about language.

"Don't use the word 'preservation'," he said. "It makes people mad. More than mad, furious. 'Conservation' is all right, but the best word is 'protection'."

We have taken this deeply to heart. Our focus is formulation of a protection plan. Secret followers of John Muir and his great vision of leaving wild lands alone, we are now public workers for Gifford Pinchot, founder of the "wise use" approach to nature. This "wise use" is a catch-phrase popular with all sides, since its ambiguity leaves room for any particular use at all.

Our study area is Reach II of the Connecticut River in Massachusetts, stretching from the Vermont line down to Northampton. It is the last free-flowing section of the river within the Commonwealth, and Terry wants to preserve its quiet values before the region's development craze overwhelms them.

We make good easy speed over the water, and our bowman, John Bennett, maneuvers us closer to Terry's canoe to hear his soft commentary. Terry is pointing high above us as an elegant osprey, flashing its brown and white feathers, shoots upriver in the sunlight. A few years ago the river was terribly polluted and all the osprey had vanished. But new laws have brought better waste treatment plants to the river towns, and the fish are once again fit to eat. Osprey seem to have this news; they've returned in healthy numbers and become a symbol of valley pride. It is as if the river and its fish hawks have shown humans a small opening into an unexpected future. But there are new threats, too.

Terry indicates a pipe protruding from a high bank, streaming liquid down into the current. "That's why I'm here," John Bennett says to me as we paddle past. "I was working for the state as an inspector. I'd visit all these plants and they'd show me how they'd sealed off their pipes. They'd claim they were doing proper disposal, not dumping anymore. But you could look at the valves and tell. You could look in their eyes and tell. I knew they were lying and they knew I knew."

John is a powerful young man in his mid-twenties, he is handsome, self-contained and practical. He strikes me as someone here to learn the nuts and bolts of planning.

Terry motions us over to the east bank, where we hold all four canoes together, bobbing, as he shows us a deposit of thick blue clay. "The old Indians liked this," he says, "it works beautifully in pots." And then he gives us another warning: "Please don't anybody tell where this vein lies. We don't need people digging out the side of the bank, undercutting the ledge."

I look up to tall maples and oaks in fall colors, and at the steep eroded slope laced with poison ivy. It is amazing that people would destroy this bank, that we must hold the secret.

For the past few years I've researched and written books involving endangered species and Native American culture. I'm tired of my isolation, and my writerly role of documentary description. The aim of my books has been art, not action. Joining this project has given me a sense of how people can combine skills in environmental work, and make things happen. But the first lessons, it seems, are restraint, study, care, silence. I've been assigned the Native American "cultural resources" along the river reach, and I must find the path to their best protection.

The man in the middle of my canoe is Chris Ryan. He learned to make maps in the army, and now specializes in limited editions for conservation groups. His work is first-rate, and I have proposed to him that we collaborate on a book which would identify all the ancient tribal territories in the Commonwealth, together with maps and directions to each. When the traveller arrives, there would be a local path to a special place—an overlook, a grove, a waterfall. Each spot would express our sense of a sacred space, and would give the visitor a chance to experience what the old tribes might have most appreciated.

Toward this end, as well as the Reach II project, I've been visiting with Bob Paynter, archaeologist at the university, and he has been considering my request for tribal site information.

But he has slowed me down with a story.

"Look," he says, "there's a man in Greenfield who specializes in looting Indian graves and middens. He absorbs discovery rumors if we leak them, and he'll bore like a coal miner, like a human mole. Once he went underground from a neighbor's property, and tunneled all the way into an incredible site. He looted it, broke pots, took the bones of the dead. This man is the link between an international artifact-trading network, and the actual, physical locations we want to protect."

As the canoes bob in the current and Terry reminds us of our duty to silence about the vein of blue clay, I wonder how we're going to accomplish anything at all. Perhaps my idea for the sacred-places book would only invite the least spiritual among us.

But when we slide into the current again, and the wind picks up, clean fresh air drives some of my doubts away. Whether it's negative ions or benevolent spirits, I believe in our mission.

We paddle a long, lazy curve and the steep banks are timbered with thick beeches and maples. Straight, impressive hemlocks rise in a shadow-wall on the bluff. There is no sign of humanity, of farming or building, though this wildness is a sustained illusion of the river. The entire valley is intensely farmed, has been for centuries, and only a narrow band of forest follows the banks. But these enclosing trees and bluffs give a sense of timeless peace. It is a quality we can claim in our report as a rare cultural memory: we are experiencing what New

England river valleys were like five hundred years ago. Emerson declared that Smith and Jones may own their farms, but the view encompassing them both belongs to everyone. And since Lady Bird Johnson's White House conference on Scenic Beauty, back in 1969, planners have been able to articulate vistas like this one as "resources." There are even systems of comparison, rank-ordering, quantification.

We come into sight of a pair of black cormorants, and one of them dives deep. The ancient Dutch and Chinese trained these birds to retrieve fish from the sea, and ensured their return by placing brass rings around their necks. Only by returning could they earn an occasional fish, and be allowed to swallow. Such an old interaction between humans and birds brings to mind our mission here. Our team is not outside the ecosystem of the river, far from it. What we accomplish may determine the fate of these birds, certainly of the ospreys and bald eagles. This winding, riverine landscape is both a centuries-old, humanized site, a kind of grand public garden, and also a bit of wild nature in the midst of intense farming. I dip my fingers into the cold water as we shoot past the cormorants. A cluster of gray and white gulls bobs closer to shore.

After an hour Terry motions for us to beach our canoes on a big sandbar up ahead, and soon we are walking around and stretching our backs. He gathers us and we pull driftwood and stones into a rough circle. When we are settled on dry seats over the damp sand he shows us silver maples and a tall cottonwood on the bank. Here beside us grow limber saplings of sandbar cherry.

"Since the river cleanup, fish populations have become more stable," Terry says. "All year you have walleye, channel cat, northern pike, small and largemouth bass, rainbow trout, and pickerel. Anadromous, or migrating, fish include sea lamprey, blueback herring, American shad, Atlantic salmon and short-nosed sturgeon. That last one's on the federally endangered list, and there's a $20,000 fine for possession.

"Now the water flow is a big factor for all these fish, especially herring and shad, and especially during spawning. Large fluctuations can sweep away fish eggs and larvae, or kill them through lack of oxygen. To keep things even, the Cabot Station hydro plant is required to release 14,000 cubic feet of water per second at all times."

This information stuns me. It brings home how utterly dependent all this river life is upon constant human monitoring and care. We literally have this reach of the Connecticut in our hands; and I pray that some dial-watcher won't nod off, some midnight.

Terry wants to limit powerboats to ten miles per hour. This would give the shad better protection, and it's the sort of regulation the six river towns might agree to. He says commonsense would tell us this is a sound idea, yet he can't get a biologist to testify seriously: there are no data, no way to get any. The biologists, who met with us a few days ago, were chagrined by their professional codes. They didn't want motors in the reach at all, because oil and gas spills, and props churning up shallow bottom near the sandbars, can't possibly be good for spawning fish. Yet they don't know how to close the gap between their concern and their science.

It is time for another secret. "Right up there," Terry says, "is an endangered-species habitat. Whatever you do, don't reveal this." We are alert. "*Crotalus horridus*," he says, "the timber rattlesnake."

There are cries of *uuuuu*.

"It seems strange," he says, "but some folks would hunt them down, if they knew.

"The old males turn almost black. They're in demand in carnivals, zoos. Just for bands around cowboy hats."

We talk a while longer, then fall silent and listen to the river. It speaks strongly and softly, flowing within its frame of banks and timber, carrying its strange mixture of wildlife and culture. It seems a long time before Terry rises and says, "Well." And I am beginning to feel a belonging here, even to my team members, these recent strangers. Our task together seems less important than our canoe trip, at least right now. Yet I also feel that this "river effect," this possibility for quiet transit and learning, is precisely what we must protect.

Soon we see a site where Terry is on the brink of closing a deal to buy development rights. This is one of his—and our—most valuable preservation tools. Farmers who want to protect the scenic or wildlife or cultural values of their land, but who need cash and must face exaggerated land prices, can sell development rights but retain ownership. Many don't know how this works, and publicizing the process will be one of our tasks. But we mustn't get too close to an actual deal: not a word about this site, please. Not only because of the farmer's uncertain feelings, but because this is a small, fragile landscape of rare plants. And again, there are those who, if they knew . . .

The more I learn of the threats the more amazed I am at the river's intact richness, its wealth of life and history, its unspoiled timber and sandbars and long thin islands. Hedged in by the development boom in the valley, assaulted by looters, the river itself is coming to seem an island of sacred space in an urbanizing world.

We pass the spectacular Sunderland Cascades, huge water-worn boulders on the river's east bank, across which thin, glassy sheets and rivulets of spring water pour. This is another site targeted for special protection, another in-process deal of which we team members should not speak. We glide past in admiration, and soon come into sight of our landing beneath the Sunderland bridge.

Our trip is over. There are good feelings as we drag the canoes up the muddy bank, and carry them to cartop racks and pickup beds. I am tired, and wave goodbye to my new colleagues. My house is only one mile away, and in a few minutes I am home with my family, filled with images and sounds from the river.

My little boy, three-and-one-half, asks, "Did you save the river, Dad?"

I smile and meet his mother's eyes and we laugh.

"Yes," I say, "I saved it."

"Good," he smiles.

I drive them back down the road to the water's edge in the falling light, and we stand beside the empty landing. A kingfisher scoots upriver in its dipping pattern of flight, and a bat skims narrowly past my head.

I know my task is to write the section of our report on Native American "cultural resources." Archaeologist Paynter seems close to showing me the site files. But he has almost begged me not to reveal where the best deposits of arrowheads, pottery, and especially human bones might be found. I began this assignment eagerly, thinking the best argument for protection would be a clear designation of the values at risk, of what could be lost without strong action. But I know now that my writing task will be different. I must convey a sense of the whole reach's historic worth, without compromising the choice locations. It cannot be a lyrical, emotional appeal, but will skirt code and jargon, relying on Commonwealth statutes that protect archaeological sites. But why are we protecting them? Can I formulate an answer to that? Is there an answer related to my feelings about the river itself?

When the first English settlers arrived in the Connecticut Valley in the early seventeenth century, they happened to find it almost vacant. This was because of a recent massacre of the Pocumtucks by the Mohegans from what would later become New York state. The accident of timing led the English to believe God had prepared a fabulous landscape especially for them.

But after an Indian confederation destroyed settlers near Pocumtuck in 1675, Increase Mather explained it as "the sinful Degenerate Estate of the present Generation in New-England." The General Court designated October 7, 1675, a "day of Humiliation," and it declared that lack of proper religious practices, the wearing of long hair and new fashions in clothing, and excessive drinking in taverns had led God to punish and "heighten our calamity."

Interactions with Native Americans and nature have always been the occasion for soul-searching, and for projecting upon other people and the natural world our interpretations of ourselves.

So, what do the Indian sites mean now? How might they appeal to a public harrassed by development pressures and containing pot-hunting looters? My own view of history is a revisionist one. The Native Americans were done wrong, and we need to collectively recognize that. My recent book on the Creek tribe displayed its Trail of Tears history and sorrow. But books with backward-looking sentiment are always welcome, probably because they distract us from ongoing crimes and real solutions. The time is never right for such statements in action plans, in public appeals for restraint in overbuilding gravesites or removing "artifacts." The best we can do now is protect such places for future interpretation by a more enlightened citizenry. We especially need to protect graves; there is a gathering storm of native demand for the return of their ancestral remains. Many Native Americans today maintain that their ancestors' ghosts must walk the landscape, restless and weary, until their bones are finally consecrated in the proper ground.

I believe I can articulate now what the spirit-mist beings were telling me this morning. It is all right to know of the ancient riverside camps and middens and graves, and Bob Paynter will tell me in time. He will unlock a dusty, unused room and show me the eyes-only site files. Some of these places were indeed sacred ones, and if I visited the tribal regions I would be able to feel, immediately, where they lie. But such things have no place in my report, nor in a book of maps and directions. I wanted to know how to work within a group, to devise actual environmental protection at the expense of my private flights, my own writing. I see now, at least in this case, the path of silence.

Charles Gaines

Wendell Berry Profile and Interview

If you have never heard of Wendell Berry, it is probably as much his fault as yours, but it is clearly more your loss. At a time when the nation and its men citizens (not least our political leaders) critically need to grow up, Berry may own the most fully adult male voice in America. It is the stern but good father's voice—a wise, learned, compassionate if occasionally hectoring one that tells us, unquestionably for our own good, that we shouldn't take the car out until we know how to drive it, shouldn't think only of ourselves, and can't have our cake and eat it too.

You may think you no longer need to hear all this, but friend, trust me: from Wendell Berry you do, and after you have heard it, you will be quoting it to everyone you know. You may even come to believe, with me, that Berry has more to say and says it more compellingly to the points of our life-threatening national malaise, of who we have become, the nature of the abyss we are headed for pedal to the metal, and how we might yet swerve off, than anyone around.

It has been said that truly brilliant and inspiring individuals simply incorporate more people under their skins than the rest of us do. Under Berry's skin is a clamorously debating and proclaiming convocation of Milton, Blake, Jesus, Shakespeare, the prophet Jeremiah, Jefferson, Yeats, the Southern Agrarians, and Thoreau—to name a few. It is one thing (though a rare one nowadays) to be fully and vitally erudite; it is quite another, one rather on the order of magic, to cause so many of history's most redoubtable and urgent voices to seem to speak through you as they do in Berry, in prose that is appropriately eloquent, charged and clarified.

Despite his having taught English and Creative Writing off and on from 1957 until 1993 at a number of universities, despite his eight Honorary Doctorate degrees and twenty-five literary fellowships and awards, the seventy-year-old Berry is in no sense an academic writer. He is a sixth-generation farmer, a poet, a novelist and short story writer, and an essayist, whose more than forty muscular books have not a whiff about them of the Ivory Tower. That his readership is largely an academic one and does not at this point much include the businessmen and housewives, the farmers and foresters and construction workers and, most importantly, the politicians that it should include, is partially a function of our regrettable national reading habits, but also of Berry's intense disliking for self-promotion, for playing to the limelight of the culture, and for anything that might impinge on his privacy and work. This aloofness, which can be misunderstood as insouciance, stamps his essays with a slightly frosty caveat emptor that some readers find annoyingly Olympian. Not me: I admire people resolutely wanting nothing to do with efforts to bring them attention, even when they are my own efforts.

Since Berry will not use a computer and does not like the telephone, I spent months exchanging with him handwritten notes, addressed "Dear Mr. Berry" and "Dear Mr. Gaines," negotiating for a few hours in which to interview him. When at last, after the intercession of a mutual friend, he agreed to see me, I suggested that those few hours might be four or five. He answered, "Dear Mr. Gaines, No. If you come at three o'clock, that will give us two hours to talk and that ought to be enough. More than that would be too long for a conversation, let alone an interview."

The fact that there is no interview (with anyone alive) for which I would work half as hard as I did for this one put even this missive in a rosy light: it seemed a pure channeling of Jeremiah.

Since 1965 Berry has lived with his wife of forty-seven years, Tanya, on 125 acres of hilly land in the Kentucky River Valley near

Port Royal, Kentucky. In the fullest sense of the term, the area is his native land—farmed by both his grandfathers, by his father, by him, and now by his son, his daughter and her husband—and virtually all of his work springs from a relationship to that land as deep and complex as Faulkner's to his "postage stamp" of Mississippi.

Berry's white farmhouse sits on a verdant hillside overlooking the Kentucky River. There are ewes and lambs in a pasture by the river, chickens in a wire pen, and, on this sunny day in May, the cabbages are well up in a half-acre vegetable garden. After Tanya makes us tea, he tells me that the garden also yields peas, potatoes, onions, broccoli, cauliflower, beets, carrots, squash, lettuce, beans, sweet corn, tomatoes, peppers, eggplants, and herbs. From it and from his livestock and forests, he and Tanya produce most of the food and fuel they need to live. What they do not produce, they buy or barter for in their local community, of which they are wholeheartedly a part and where they have built themselves what Berry referred to in our interview as a "known life"— "a life in a known place among known people where associations and memories collect and become a guide to the proper use and care, the proper love for the place."

Berry is 6'4", gangly, white-haired and blue-eyed. He often seems to grieve as he speaks, but then suddenly he will laugh and his whole face seems to blow open like a wind-caught door. And what speech it is—vivid, passionate, elegantly-turned sentences as symmetrically punctuated as a ham with cloves by quotes from Shakespeare, Milton and the Bible, whole stanzas of Yeats and Shelly, paragraphs from obscure British agronomists and modern economists: in a lifetime of acquaintance with well-schooled and articulate people, I have never met its match.

Throughout our interview I was gripped by the same slightly eerie but exhilarating sense I get from his writing of being in the presence of a medium: of actually hearing Yeats on the subject of the bridal bed, for example, and Shakespeare on atonement. It was nothing less than what you wait all your life for intellectual talk to be; and when after almost four hours (we both forgot about my time limit) I told Wendell Berry goodbye, I did so with a grieving of my own.

"When I came back here in '64 with the intention of staying, after a long time away, I saw this place open-eyed in a way I hadn't seen it before, and I understood that this rural community of which I was a hereditary member, as well as everything I had been taught to value, was under threat. So I began to try to understand that threat, what its origins were in character and culture, and also to try to do something about it. I began to write about it with the hope that eventually I might be able to help other people who wanted to do something about it."

The nature of the threat to his community and values, Berry discovered, was failing health. He set about to identify and help treat on a local level the pervasive disease he found around him, and then—rather like a country doctor extrapolating from his family practice the pathology of a culture-wide epidemic—to describe and prescribe at large. His diagnosis? "The disease of modern character is specialization."

Berry believes we have become a nation of specialists, "People elaborately and expensively trained to do one thing," and in so doing have been forced to abdicate to other specialists "various competencies and responsibilities that were once personal and universal," and that once contributed to the integrity and health of our lives, our communities, and the planet. The diseased result of this specialization for individuals is a virtually total helplessness and alienation from the earth. "We cannot feed or clothe ourselves, or entertain ourselves, or communicate with each other, or be charitable or neighborly or loving, or even respect ourselves, without recourse to a merchant or a corporation or public-service organization or an agency of the government or a style-setter or an expert . . . In this state of total consumerism—which is to say a state of helpless dependence on things and services and ideas and motives that we have forgotten how to provide ourselves—all meaningful contact between ourselves and the earth is broken . . . Our model citizen is a sophisticate who before puberty understands how to produce a baby, but who at the age of thirty will not know how to produce a potato."

And for the national culture, the rule of specialization is equally disastrous—"though society becomes more and more intricate, it has less and less structure. It becomes more and more organized, but less and less orderly. The community disintegrates because it loses the necessary understandings, forms, and enactments of the relations among materials and processes, principles and actions, ideals and realities, past and present, present and future, men and women, body and spirit, city and country, civilization and wilderness, growth and decay, life and death—just as individual character loses the sense of responsible involvement in these relations."

Ultimately, of course, the largely corporate entities to which we have given our individual proxies to do for us what we can or will no longer do for ourselves operate out of one motive only, to make a profit. And without the checks and balances to that motive provided by an engaged, broadly competent and interested citizenry, those entities are free to pursue profit at any cost and to practice what Berry calls "an economy of ruin"—one "founded on the seven deadly sins and the breaking of all ten of the Ten Commandments" that has brought us "the spectacle of unprecedented 'prosperity' and 'economic growth' in a land of degraded farms, forests, ecosystems, and watersheds, polluted air, failing families, and perishing communities."

Berry believes that our paradoxical and poisonous industrial economy, with its global aspirations to allow "developed nations to subsidize their over-consumption, their idiot luxury, by depleting the production capacity of the third world," is one of utter and naked exploitation; and to the vast extent that that economy holds our individuals proxies, we become—by ignorant and/or lazy complicity, or by active partnership—ourselves exploiters.

It is exactly here that his diagnosis of the culture's disease gets uncomfortably up-close and personal.

"The growth of the exploiters revolution on this continent has been accompanied by the growth of the idea that work is beneath human dignity, particularly any form of hard work. We have made it our overriding ambition to escape work, and as a consequence have debased work until it is only fit to escape from . . . Out of this contempt for work arose the idea of a nigger: at first some person, and later some thing, to be used to relieve us of the burden of work. If we began by making a nigger people, we have ended by making a nigger of the world."

The world we have made a nigger of, according to Wendell Berry, is populated by two groups or classes: the aforementioned exploiters and nurturers (or in the parallel terminology of his friend and mentor, the late Wallace Stegner, "boomers and stickers").

"The exploiter is a specialist, an expert; the nurturer is not. The standard of the exploiter is efficiency; the nurturer's goal is health—his land's health, his own, his family's, his community's, his country's . . . The exploiter thinks in terms of numbers, quantities, 'hard facts'; the nurturer in terms of character, condition, quality, kind . . . The exploiter is clearly the prototype of the 'masculine' man—the wheeler-dealer whose 'practical' goals require the sacrifice of flesh, feeling and principle. The nurturer, on the other hand, has always passed with ease across the boundaries of so-called sexual roles." Whereas the mental habits of the nurturer are cultivation and restraint, the mind of the exploiter/boomer, says Berry, "operates outside all restraints of culture and principle. Just as tragically, it operates outside history; it does not remember experience. It deals with all its subjects on the basis of the crudest sort of economic metaphor. Any person, place, or thing is understood as a mine having a limited 'yield'; when the yield falls below expectation, it is time to move on."

Berry profoundly believes that just as surely as nurturing leads to wholeness and health (those two words, along with "holy," he points out, have a common root) in both the nurtured and the nurturer, so does exploitation lead both its victims and its perpetrators to division and disease. If you are an open, self-acknowledged exploiter, more poxes on you. If you are one of the rare and endangered American Nurturers, God bless you, and avoid flying low. For the rest of you, here is a list of exploiter symptoms for home diagnosis and early detection.

- **Carelessness.** Use without care is Berry's definition of exploitation. Active exploiters consciously use without caring what or how they use, blithely making niggers wherever they go (look to our current Presidential Administration for a terminal case in point). Passive exploiters (the majority of us) are simply too otherwise-occupied to care about what use is made of the proxies we give out—the rivers that are niggered to carry our wastes; the strip mines and clear-cut forests; the seas and wilderness areas plundered for oil; the farmlands raped by the agribusinessmen, to whom Berry refers as "the pornographers of farming." To be careless, whether actively or passively, in Berry's view, is to despise the object of your carelessness; and the ultimate and most unhealthy carelessness is that that despises our home and comforter the earth, and thus ourselves.

- **Pride.** The habit of carelessness and despite leads to pride, as nausea does to vomiting. And pride's separation and glorification of self, its blinding of empathy (St. Augustine likened it to a "spiritual wound to the face, swelling shut the eyes of understanding") locks us into armor that turns all the outside world into the enemy knight or serf. Pray you are without this symptom.
- **Avarice.** Pride asked the question "What can't I have?" Avarice answers, "Nothing, baby." The epigraph that begins Berry's book, *The Unsettling of America*, is this quote from Montaigne: "Who so hath his mind on taking, hath it no more on what he hath taken." So does avarice cheapen and diminish everything it acquires; as both a sin and a symptom of exploitation, Berry says, "it makes division within unity, disorder within order, and discord within harmony." Avarice also leads directly to what he calls "the pragmatization of feeling," a belittling if not outright renunciation of all emotions and attitudes that do not contribute to acquisition and profit; of leisure, art, mystery, awe . . .
- **Faithlessness.** As is suggested in the Montaigne quote above, avarice engenders first dissatisfaction and then faithlessness toward what we already have. It is no wonder that "Our age could be characterized as a manifold experiment in faithlessness," and that "The dominant story of our age, undoubtedly, is that of adultery (carnal avarice) and divorce"—divorce in both the literal sense of the word and in the figurative sense of separating things that once were joined. Accordingly, we should not be at all surprised to find the prevalence in our culture of "marriage without love; sex without joy; drink without conviviality; birth, celebration, and death without adequate ceremony; faith without doubt or trial; belief without deeds; manners without generosity . . . "

The progression of the disease that is not so slowly killing us, our culture and the planet, is division, Berry believes. Faithlessness, avarice, pride and carelessness are both the tools and the symptoms of the countless separations—of use from care; of ourselves from responsibility for ourselves, as well as from other human beings, other creatures, the earth, God—that contribute to our disintegration from the wholeness of good health. His good news is, there is a cure—one that must ultimately extend into our practices of wholeness, to what Christians call our "works," if the culture is to be healed, but that has to begin in our minds and hearts.

"To grow up is to go beyond our inborn selfishness and arrogance; to be grown up is to know that the self is not a place to live."

The first steps toward good health are first to pack up and move out of the self-realizing with Milton's Satan that "Myself is Hell"—and to begin to care about something, anything, other than the rock star posters and floor length mirrors in that cramped, adolescent room.

Once out of the self, care becomes the natural and necessary response (in fact, a sort of survival strategy) to the freshly-emerged realization that it is a different ball game out here, and that the two cardinal rules—Berry calls them "absolute laws"—are these: 1) "As we cannot exempt ourselves from living in this world, then if we wish to live, we cannot exempt ourselves from using the world," and 2) "if we cannot exempt ourselves from use . . . if we want to continue living, we cannot exempt ourselves from care."

With those twin realizations, metabolized and put into action, you're on the other side of the fence from exploitation and now under the nurturer's "cultural imperative to be caretakers, good neighbors to one another and to other creatures," and to clear the carelessness out of your life according to this ultimate sticker/nurturer understanding: "There is simply nothing in creation the does not matter."

Now you have the wind at your back.

"Once we have understood that we cannot exempt from our care anything at all that we have the power to damage—which now means everything in the world—then we face yet another startling realization: we have reclaimed and revalidated the ground of our moral and religious tradition. We now can see that what we have traditionally called 'sins' are wrong not because they are forbidden but because they divide us from our neighbors, from the world, and ultimately from God."

Faithlessness and carelessness are defeated symptoms in that sea-change of mind and heart. Avarice seems simply obscene in its benign light. And pride? At this stage of the cure, you may want to shout from the rooftops Pound's great injunction to "Pull down thy vanity, it is not man / Made courage, or made order, or made grace, / Pull down thy vanity, I say pull down. / Learn of the green world what can by thy place. / In scaled invention or true artistry." The division of disintegration that is the progress of our disease is itself defeated by this at-one-ment, this reentry into partnership with our pasts, with our moral traditions, with our brotherhood and creaturehood on the earth, with the earth itself, and with the eternal mysteries that surround us.

Erwin Chargaff has written that "Life is the continual intervention of the inexplicable." When I asked Berry what the thought, quoted in Berry book *Life is a Miracle*, meant to him, he paused for a moment. " . . . To say something like that, you've got to be awake and alert and very careful and thoughtful and even gentle for a long time."

Berry holds that "We are alive within mystery, by miracle," and that the only adequate, the only possible right responses to that fact are joy, gratitude, and the daily practiced carefulness of good husbandry and nurture. Finally, it is in that practice, and in it alone, that good health for ourselves and our culture is reclaimable.

⚜

"My daughter has three daughters, and the two oldest can gut a chicken a minute. Two chickens a minute, I think it is now."

Berry has written that "No matter how much one may love the world as a whole, one can live fully in it only by living responsibly in some small part of it . . . one can become whole only by the responsible acceptance of one's partiality." And he believes that living responsibly in your part of the world means reclaiming as many as possible of the proxies you have given away for that responsibility. Over and over again, he counsels us to pay attention to how natural and human resources are being used on our behalf, and to renounce misuse or use without care on every level we can: to rail against it, vote against it, lobby against it, and most important, to communitize against it.

At this critical point in the history of western culture, he insists, it is too late to sit on the fence—you are either them or us. The "them" belong to the party of the "global economy," the party of the boom, profit, and exploitation. Berry's "us" belong to the "party of local community."

"They are people who take a generous and neighborly view of self preservation; they do not believe that they can survive and flourish by the rule of dog eat dog; they do not believe that they can succeed by defeating or destroying or selling or using up everything but themselves. They doubt that good solutions can be produced by violence. They want to preserve the precious things of nature and of human culture and pass them on to their children . . . They see that no commonwealth or community of interests can be defined by greed. They know that things connect—that farming, for example, is connected to nature, and food to farming, and health to food—and they want to preserve the connections. They know that a healthy local community cannot be replaced by a market or an entertainment industry or an information highway . . . The aims of this party really are only two: the preservation of ecological diversity and integrity, and the renewal, on sound cultural and ecological principles of local economies and local communities."

And just exactly how are local communities renewed and sustained? In his small, invaluable book of essays, *Another Turn of the Crank*, Berry gives seventeen concrete suggestions. Among them:

- Always ask of any proposed change or innovation: what will this do to our community? How will this affect our common wealth?
- Always include local nature—the land, the water, the air, the native creatures—within the membership of the community.
- Always ask how local needs might be supplied from local sources, including the mutual help of neighbors.
- Develop properly scaled value-adding industries for local products to ensure that the community does not become merely a colony of the national or global economy.
- Strive to produce as much of the community's own energy as possible.
- See that the old and the young take care of one another . . . There must be no institutionalized "child care" and "homes for the aged."

If these guidelines seem radical to you, Berry suggests it is because our national and global economies "have been formed in almost perfect disregard of community and ecological interests." And if they seem to you—as they do to some of his detractors—laughably impractical, agrarian pie-in-the-sky nonsense, go look up the Amish—who in almost every important way live better lives than you and I do by cleaving to "outdated" principles like the ones above.

You say you don't want to become Amish and don't live in a rural community? Fine. What Berry is talking about here is living your life according to the conviction that your own good health and security, as well as your children's, are inextricably tied to the good health and security of the planet and all its creatures. He would have you care about that conviction, and actuate it in your life in as many ways as possible. Make yourself an enemy of avarice, pride, and any mechanistic definition of life; or violence, and cultural and economic imperialism. Make yourself the champion of the small, the handmade, the cooperative; of neighborhood and patience; of Jeffersonian reasonableness and propriety. Take back a few proxies: learn to gut a chicken, or at least how to cook one: plant and nurture a garden, and while you're at it, ponder this Berry jeremiad: "A man who understands the weather only in terms of gold is participating in a public insanity that either he or his descendants will be bound to realize as suffering. I believe that the death of the world is breeding in such minds with much more certainty and much faster than in any political capital or atomic arsenal." At the very least: pay attention; be careful and responsible; get out of yourself; keep faith and pull down your vanity; say your prayers . . . Just like your father told you.

And do it as if everything depended on it.

> "We have lived by the assumption that what was good for us would be good for the world. And this has been based on the even flimsier assumption that we could know with any certainty what was good even for us. We have fulfilled the danger of this by making our personal pride and greed the standard of our behavior toward the world—to the incalculable disadvantage to the world and every living thing in it. And now, perhaps very close to too late, our great error has become clear . . . We have been wrong. We must change our lives, so that it will be possible to live by the contrary assumption that what is good for the world will be good for

us. And that requires that we make the effort to know the world and to learn what is good for it. We must learn to cooperate in its processes and yield to its limits. But even more important, we must learn to acknowledge that the creation is full of mystery; we will never entirely understand it. We must abandon arrogance and stand in awe. We must recover the sense of the majesty of creation, and the ability to be worshipful in its presence. For I do not doubt that it is only on the condition of humility and reverence before the world that our species will be able to remain in it."

Molly Peacock

from *Paradise, Piece by Piece*
TWO SHORT EXCERPTS

How do you grow up if you don't have children? How do you remake the original love—mother love—into a mature love? Becoming a parent provokes this conversion, but the transformation into adulthood without the bearing of children means metamorphosis. The change is not instant and permanent like parenthood. It is a surfacing into adulthood and a diving down into childhood, and a poking into sharp air again, then a plunge into watery warmth, gradually converting your gills to lungs. After a time, you breathe in air exclusively, just as all adults do.

But birth is not the only event that propels us into adulthood. Death does, too. Any sharp change that brings us face to face with what we thought life was but now must revise instigates the entree into maturity. So the childfree grow up, either by evolution or by the swift witchcraft of event—or both. Gradually the childhood world vanishes into its own reflection and we look back from the other side of the mirror. To consciously refuse to be a parent and yet consciously to grow, to determine both to love and to understand love, is a project big as any in life. It is not necessary to originate a child to discover your origins—though it takes longer if you do it on your own.

If I could have told that girl, who waited to hear her father's car crawl up in the driveway, that things would never be as bad as they were at that moment, I think she would not have believed me. I imagine whispering into her ear, a skinny little shrimp with lank hair wearing a soiled blouse, her face at once both horrified and grim, that her life will be an adventure and that she will become a poet and live in two countries with a boy she would meet very soon. I see her turn her head a little bit on her neck, straightening her slump just a bit, and watch a slow, noncommittal sort of astonishment begin in her spine, delight moving up her vertebrae till it hits the top of her head and moves her shoulders back. I tell her—she is fourteen years old—that if she holds on for thirty years she's going to love her life. This girl does not say, "Thirty years! How will I hold on?" She does not dare complain or hope; instead, she walks. She walks across the empty plain, requiring that emptiness completely. Paradoxically, for her it will become full of creativity.

When I said No to having children, I felt as if I went to some viscerally interior place, the place of recognition. I'd always thought that the positive, the embracing, the Yes that is so characteristic of women's assumed responses, would let me affirm who I am. But it was a refusal that led me to understand my own nature. It was the saving No. The saving No seemed to emerge from the ready emptiness that is required for all creativity, not just for the making of art. That No can't be confused with loss, or the painful emptiness of not having what you need. Like a well-proportioned, unfinished room with open windows, the affirming refusal invites life. It's a room, not a womb. Like a womb, it harbors life, but unlike a womb, it *leaves room* to create the rest of life.

Robert Finch

SOMETIMES I LIVE IN TOWN

Sometimes I like to pretend I live in town. I almost did once, or like to think I did. It was several years ago, when K. and I were looking around for a year-round place to rent or buy. Shortly after Christmas, a friend mentioned an old house in the center of town that might be for sale. We went to look at it. It was on a narrow side street just off Main Street, and I fell in love with it at once. It was a vintage three-quarter Cape, a sweet old house on a quiet cross street of sweet old houses, with a central chimney, a large yard, and a large Norway maple tree shading the house. It sat at the top of a low arch that the street makes, facing towards town, and to its immediate right was a large old full Cape that someone told me used to be the summer home of one of my old college professors. It seemed propitious.

The owner used to live here, but had remarried and moved to the West Coast a few years ago. Our friend knew him and mentioned an asking figure that was at the outer edge of, and probably a little over, our financial limits. When we contacted the owner, he was initially non-committal, but arranged for us to get the key to the presently vacant house. It was even better inside than out. The interior architecture was largely unaltered, retaining much of its original paneling and trim, and had a large bright front room, an open keeping room, a kitchen-bedroom ell with wonderful wooden counters painted by the famous folk—artist Peter Hunt, two downstairs fireplaces, and a pair of capacious rooms upstairs that had never been finished.

K. also liked the house immediately, but wondered if we could afford it. For one thing, it had never been properly insulated and the only source of heat was a coal stove. In all likelihood it would require a new septic system. The exterior had been sadly neglected and would need a new shingle roof, clapboard siding, some new windows, and possibly some sill work. The front steps were completely missing, and several piles of bricks, which looked like they had sat there for years, were piled up in front of the door in anticipation of a restoration project that had never gotten under way. A friend who had bought another old house just a few doors down from this one some fifteen years ago warned me, "You want to continue being a writer? Then don't buy an old house. You can't serve two masters."

But all these potential problems and drawbacks, not to mention the owner's diffidence, were minor details in the face of a sudden overwhelming conviction that this was the house that I wanted to live in. I had never really lived in an old house, certainly not a vintage Cape Cod house, and had not known before that I wanted to live in one, but I did. Suddenly I knew that this was the house I was meant to live in, that I would live in. Like a love affair where a part of you suspects the outcome will be hopeless, even disastrous, I nonetheless yielded to my imagination's desire to project our future in it. The small front room could be K.'s study. I would turn one of the upstairs rooms into a temporary shop while I finished off the other gable room into my study. I would make the deep kneewalls into closets, plant the garden at the back of the yard, set up a hammock under the maple tree . . . all this before I had even left the house during that first January visit.

I wrote again immediately to the owner, asking him what he wanted for it, prepared to put myself in debt up to my ears for this house, if necessary. I did not hear from him over the next several weeks, but in the meantime I began to haunt that house and that street, visiting it at all times of the day and night, peering through its windows, daring a neighbor to call and have a policeman show up to ask me what I was doing there. I would simply reply, "Why, I"m going to live here!"

I began driving into town early in the morning, parking in the side yard, and walking down Main Street, just to know what it would feel like to walk into town every day for coffee and a paper. I parked in town at night, strolling slowly up the street on which the house sat, passing beneath the single street lamp across from it. It was a motion-activated lamp that switched on as I came within its charmed circle, as if it were lighting up just for me. I began to observe my future neighbors, smiling at them as I passed and thinking how I would get to know them intimately, their quirks and habits, over the years. There was one elderly couple whose bedroom was in the front of their house on the ground floor; each night they fell asleep, bathed in the blue glow of their television, for any passerby to see through the uncurtained window. I thought, I will grow old here, and eccentric, just like them.

Even then, however, in the initial throes of my passion for the house, I was aware that it was its location as much as the house itself that fed my imagination and enticed me to recklessly project my life and my future there. The house was in town, less than a minute's walk from Main Street, yet on one of those quiet, little-used side streets and dirt lanes that vein the town's center and which the waves of summer traffic and tourists largely bypass.

As with the house itself, I had not realized before that I wanted to live in town. I had spent my first quarter-century on Cape Cod living as far from other people and other houses as I could, yet now I found myself increasingly drawn to the idea of village life. I did not know why, but the desire was so strong I had no need to understand it then. And it was not just any town, either, but this one. If this was the right house, then Wellfleet was the right town. I recognized this at once, although it took me a while to understand this as well.

Some of the reasons seemed obvious and generic. Wellfleet has one of the most visually attractive town centers I know. Its major streets, radiating out from the center, are lined with old Capes, substantial Greek-revivals, a few old captain's mansions, and some gingerbready and apricot-colored summer cottages with blue shutters and spare and white interiors.

But many other towns on the Cape have preserved their visual charm. Wellfleet is unusual in that it still has a real town center, fully-functioning rather than a mere historical facade. During the summer its main street is, like many others, fluffed out with a number of art galleries, trendy clothing stores, ice cream shops, restaurants, and other seasonal enterprises, including occasional short-lived absurdities such as a new woodcraft shop that calls itself "I Used To Be A Tree."

But between Labor Day and Columbus Day these estival accretions gradually wither and blow away, leaving an almost Norman Rockwell Main Street of basic year-round small town businesses and civic buildings: the library, a florist shop, two book stores, a small auto garage, a funeral home, three churches, a year-round restaurant, a liquor store, a pharmacy, a family grocery store, a real estate office, the local historical society, the Town Hall, and a husband-wife cello duo with an instrument-shaped sign outside their house offering "LESSONS-WEDDINGS-RECEPTIONS."

Moreover, Wellfleet has largely kept the physical template of the classic New England village: a compact cluster of houses and buildings surrounded by open fields and pastures. Our agricultural landscape disappeared decades ago, but two other factors have protected the town from the unlimited residential and commercial sprawl that has blighted so many other communities. First, the town center is built on a series of glacial mounds and hills separated and surrounded on three sides by a complex network of wetlands and open water. It has expanded somewhat to the east and along the state highway, but here too its growth has been limited, in this direction by the establishment of the Cape Cod National Seashore in 1961, whose boundaries protect 70 percent of the town's land mass from further development.

But these are only abstract, if fundamental, characteristics of the town, ones that anyone might soon come to notice and appreciate, but which hardly accounted for the kind of passion I felt to live Here. As I sauntered its streets and explored its byways, I realized that what I was drawn by was its unique character, its specific identity, those elements, personalities, details and idiosyncrasies that could only be truly perceived, or in some cases even understood, by a genuine resident.

One of the things that appealed to me was that, although most of the establishments along Main and Commercial Streets kept up a well-maintained and freshly-painted face for the tourists, the town had not yet become so self-conscious a resort community that it could not tolerate a certain run-down and unkempt element. Especially on the side streets many of the houses sported peeling paint, deteriorating porches, rotting trellises, and worse. There was at least one true derelict off West Main Street, and I was gratified to see a genuine trailer home bordering one of the church parking lots—a rarity under current local zoning laws. My house (as I had already begun thinking of it) would fit right in—at least until I got around to fixing it up.

One of the secrets of Wellfleet Center is Squires Pond, a small lake that sits right in the middle of the town, but which is hidden from the sight of summer visitors, becoming visible only after the leaves have fallen. There is a narrow public lane that provides access to its edge, where I sometimes went skating during hard freezes, or collected the ripe seedheads of cattails, or "punks," as we called them when I was a kid, drying and "smoking" them for their pungent scent and the appearance of delinquent behavior.

One of the more baffling sounds in town is that of the church bells of the Congregational church, which ring the hours and half hours in a code indecipherable to newcomers. When it is one o'clock, they ring two. When it is seven o'clock, they ring four. When it is noon, they ring eight. I have seen visitors stopped by their sound, looking at their own watches, first in puzzlement, then with a dismissive expression for yet another small town that can't keep its clocks running properly—unaware that they are listening to the only public clock in the world that rings ship's time.

I found that I even took a perverse pleasure in the town's reputation for eccentricity. During the nineteenth century Wellfleetians were referred to by other Cape Codders as "Bible-faces," for their excessive devotion to reading Scripture, particularly among the Methodists. Early in this century the town had a reputation for inbreeding, though it probably had no more than other rural towns. When I told an old friend, who had lived on her own Main Street in a neighboring town for nearly ninety years, that I was moving to Wellfleet, she said, "Oh, that's where all the idiots come from. It's improved some lately, I guess, with all those artists moving there. But it was always a backwards town." Yes—backwards. Different. Peculiar. I wanted my town to be a bit crazy, crooked in its nature, like its old lanes and wildly curving streets.

As the winter wore on, I had received no definite reply from the house's owner. Moreover, we had been notified that the house we were renting would only be available for one more year, adding an urgency to finding a permanent location. Still, my faith that we would eventually possess the house on Cross Street was unshaken. I had already taken up residence there in my mind, and physical occupation would follow shortly. I had the faith of a true lover who knows that it is only a matter of time before he wears away the obstacles and objections of his beloved and the world.

So I continued my regular walks around the town, imagining, or even acting out what it would be like to be an actual town resident. I established a charge account at Lema's Grocery and got to know Charlie, the singing butcher. Charlie sings pop standards constantly with his Scotch burr, Sinatra and Tony Bennett, sometimes synchronized with the radio going at the back of the meat department, sometimes not. He flirts openly with all the woman customers, who seem to love it. I think some of them come in for it.

I began filling my prescriptions at the Wellfleet Pharmacy, whose windows are decorated with changing seasonal scenes. One time, when I bought a memo pad, the tall, gangly, curly-headed boy behind the cash register took my money and said, "Is that all, sir? That'll be 72 cents, sir—which means you get three shiny new pennies back! Have a good day, sir!" I smiled at his extravagant courtesy and put one of those three shiny pennies into the old weight machine that stands by the door.

I bought occasional hardware supplies at Nickerson Lumber Company on Commercial Street down by the harbor. The lumber yard fronts Duck Creek, and on moon tides the water floods the marshes and rises a few inches around the base of the open lumber piles, threatening to float them off. At such times one could almost believe that they had been unloaded by there by an old packet schooner that morning. It is the most beautiful setting of any lumber yard I know, and I gladly pay a few cents more per board foot to get my wood against such a backdrop.

One of my favorite walks, when doing errands in town, was to saunter down to the foot of Bank Street and walk across Duck Creek on Uncle Tim's Bridge to Cannon Hill, a small mound of glacial debris surrounded by marshes that serves as an informal public park. The vegetation of this marsh island is sparse and fragile, and the hill has a worn and overused look, with several severely eroded gullies scarring its sides. Its lasting value, however, is the prospect it offers on the town itself, the opportunity to hold it all in one's eye—a view common enough to attain in mountain valley towns, but rare in a landscape as flat as the Cape's.

From its modest forty-foot summit one can look from Cannon Hill south to the broken causeway of the Old Colony Railroad at the mouth of Duck Creek, whose construction in 1872 effectively cut off the creek as a working inner harbor. For decades abandoned and rotting wooden ship hulls have lined the muddy banks of the shoreline, a practice which gave rise to the local saying that "Old oyster boats never die, they just lie around Wellfleet Harbor."

To the west, back across the bridge, stretches the meandering shoreline of the old harbor, fronted by Commercial Street, which, during the early nineteenth century, was, as its name suggests, the town's center of commerce. The great red barn of Moody's Fuel and Grain and its large cylindrical oil tanks still stand on the inner shore beside the vanished railroad siding that served it, though the tanks are empty and the building itself now houses a local artists' cooperative.

To the north a jumble of houses climbs up the hill from East Commercial street to East Main street, the piled roofs and gables rising like a New England version of some Italian hill town, culminating in the graceful, blue-green, bell-shaped steeple of the Congregational Church. From here the whole town looks, as Tracy Kidder said about his hometown of Northhampton seen from the summit of Mt. Holyoke, as though "if you shook it, it would snow."

All this, however aesthetically or imaginatively pleasing, still did not explain to me why I had such a visceral passion to live within the confines of this town. Was it just a reaction against twenty-five years of trying to escape the human landscape and forge my own personal vision of where I lived? Perhaps I was tired of making clearings and paths for myself in life's "pathless woods," and simply longed for settled streets and known neighbors at this point in my life.

Or was it my urban background reasserting itself and a long-buried need for communal life? Besides pure desire, I recognized a strong feeling of nostalgia for a past, a childhood, I had never had here. On the surface, of course, comparisons between my real home town and this one were ludicrous. North Arlington, New Jersey, was a working class suburb of Newark, whose smokestacks and huge gas tanks I could see from my bedroom window. It comprised a grid of two-and-three story frame houses and bungalows built in the 1920s and 30s, occupied primarily by a potpourri of first-and-second generation European immigrants—Scotch, Hungarian, Polish, German, Jewish, Italian, Swedish. It was bounded on one side by the heavily-polluted marshes of the Hackensack River, which seemed to be perpetually on fire, and on the other side by the oil-fouled and glass-littered shores of the Passaic River, which at the time had the distinction of being one of the ten dirtiest rivers in the country. The only open spaces in town were the cemeteries.

And yet, I came to realize, those were only superficial differences. I recognized, along Wellfleet's narrow Yankee streets, the same old trees, the same old houses, the same old garages and cluttered yards, the same density of settled human community on a modest scale, and that constant daily platter of human interaction that I had known in childhood and, without realizing it, had come to long for again.

But the longing, I began to suspect, was deeper, more subjective, more complex than that. I knew it had something to do with the breakup of a thirty-year marriage and the subsequent uprooting from a house I had built and lived in for two decades, the profound physical and psychological dislocation of the next several years, and the growing need to be settled again, unnomadic, in a structure made by others, for I had come to deeply distrust the ones of my own creation.

Or was it simply a growing sense of mortality and an accompanying need to place myself within a human community that had predated and would outlast me—a secular version of a religious impulse, perhaps? Surely it was the element of ritual in town life that seemed at the heart of its attraction, the opportunity to participate and submerge the individual personality in the established liturgy of the town, in its comings and goings, its stations and responses, the daily and generational passing of its human life.

Once I spent a month in a small medieval town on the coast of Tuscany. Each morning I walked into the paved square and had espresso under the awnings of an outside cafe table. It was the best part of the trip. Since the fourteenth century the lives of the people in that town had been marked and regulated by the tolling of the ancient bell tower. Every hour, the ringing of the bells scattered hundreds of pigeons out of the tower crevices and over the square, casting a momentary fluttering shadow of wings over the people and the old buildings until the bells stopped and the birds flew back into the tower and perched there until the next hour when they would scatter again as they had for six hundred years. That was it. That was what I wanted, to live the rest of my life beneath the shadow of the Congo Church, walking the village streets to the rhythm of its ship's bells like some Yankee monk as it tolled out the canonical hours.

I loved to watch the local teenagers hanging out in the parking lot or on the small green before Town Hall, beneath the shade of a large maple to which a local woman had chained herself a few years ago when the selectman proposed cutting down the tree to create a pullover space for the daily bus which stops there on its way to Provincetown. The younger kids would sit on the benches or play hackysack on the grass, while a somewhat older group of teenagers assembled in the parking lot, mostly boys dressed in black with reversed caps, and a few girls, all gathered around a battered black sedan whose boomboxes pumped out rap and hip\hop in a town whose black youth population hovers somewhere between two and none. When they do this they are full of townie energy, all arms flailing and mock fighting, a bit of noise and display expressing that mildly rebellious, small-town camaraderie of limited options, limited ambition, as if they were taking their inarticulate grievances to the municipal authorities.

One day, on the other side of the street, in front of the Lighthouse Restaurant, a gaggle of three or four men, one of whom I recognized as a selectmen, stood looking across at the kids. "Oh yes," one remarked with jocular sarcasm, "that's the new Town Recreation Area, don't you know?"

I loitered in the periphery of their group, mentally rehearsing for the time when I would become An Official Main Street Observer, espousing different attitudes or politics, perhaps, but standing with my group of cronies, one of the ole farts of the town, expounding on what was right and wrong with this microcosm of the universe.

One afternoon in late winter I drove into town to get something at the lumber yard. It was an unusually warm day and the town was enveloped in fog, the tide out, and the sere marshes and dark gray mudflats of Duck Creek exposed and redolent. I walked across Uncle Tim's Bridge up the scarred and tattered flanks of Cannon Hill. From the top the outline of the town was obscured in the middle distance. This time of year the pleasure-boat moorings and wharf fingers are hauled out, and with its small fleet of weathered draggers, trawlers and oyster boats, the harbor has a pleasing working look. The long sheds of the lumber yard stretch out along the shore. A fast tide was beginning to course through the bridgeless railroad dike, and the invisible copper-domed steeple of the Congo church chimed seven bells: 3:30.

To the north I could make out a flock of some larger and smaller ducks paddling and feeding at a bend in the creek. A large bird flew from the east over the trees and marsh toward the church which I recognized as a harrier, not from any visible markings or even its shape, which was obscured, but from its wavering, feathery flight, so seemingly unstable, so unlike the steady, imperturbable flight of gulls, who always seem in perfect agreement with the winds they fly through. The harrier's flight by contrast appears nervous, uncertain, as if the hawk were about to be overturned by each slight shift in wind or position, though in fact it is superbly fashioned for shifting, low flight and gliding among the dunes and marsh grass—like the Jedi rebels' fighters threading their way through the labyrinthine surface of the Empire's Death Star—and must therefore fly that way, no matter where it is, never having learned or needed to soar.

So, too, I recognized the ducks as black ducks and smaller buffleheads by the intermittent wink of silver wing-linings as the black ducks flapped over the water, their manner of congregating like sheep, all beaks tending to point to a common center—as opposed to the smaller buffleheads, which tend to pair off, even in winter, or gather in fours or fives at the most.

I thought, I know these birds, not by appearance or field marks so much as by gestalt, by long acquaintance and frequent meetings over many years, so that the recognition is a fitting together of memory and image. This is the advantage of growing old in a place we know, with familiar surroundings: as our senses falter and dim, we continue to recognize the things we have come to know by their more general form and motion, their distilled essence combined with our memory, just as we recognize instantly the rhythm and inflection of an old friend's voice, or her posture and walking gait, even when we can no longer make out her features at a distance.

⚜

In the end we did not get the house, though at the time I had resolved to mortgage my life to do so. But I did not count on an equally stubborn irresolution on the part of the absentee owner. When I eventually pushed him for a decision, he proved terminally ambivalent. Just as I had developed an irresistible need to establish ties in the town, so he, too, it seems, had an immovable reluctance to sever his own. In both cases it was a matter of subjective and irrational need, but his was rooted in an existing reality, and in the end I had to give it up.

The following fall, while I was out of town, K. found a small, quirky, fairly new, and quite lovely house in good repair that we could comfortably afford. It was situated about a mile north of the center, on the boundary of the National Seashore, and about a twenty-minute walk into town. It is a good house, layered with the creative and off-beat character of the two artists who built it, and we have grown to love it.

I have even come to accept that buying the house in town would probably have been a practical and financial disaster. Aside from its obvious needs, I would no doubt have had to contend with a myriad other concealed ills that old and unmaintained houses are heir to. Just the other day I spoke to a woman who is now renting the house year round. Her husband, she says, spends nearly all his spare time cutting and chopping wood to avoid the expense of the coal it takes to keep the house heated. "And even then" she said, "it's almost always cold in winter." In the end I told myself that my friend had surely been right, that the old house, had we bought it, would have become not my home but my master, one that would have left me little time to enjoy it and a life "in town."

Still, every now and then, I experience deep pangs of regret—for the house, yes, but even more, I think, for the missed chance of living in town. I find I am most vulnerable to these feelings in the fall, perhaps because it has always been for me the season of loss and regret as well as new beginnings. Perhaps it is also because the town—the center, that is—is always at its best this time of the year, especially in October, after the last real summer weekend has come and gone. The crowds have left, the frivolous shops are all closed, the clear light gives everything a more vivid edge, a deeper dimension of reality. As the leaves come down various aspects of the town, hidden all summer, are revealed: old houses down long curving driveways, the deep cut of the old railroad right-of-way running right through the middle of town, and Squire's Pond, suddenly reflecting the steeples of the two churches in its still waters. If September is the smoking of the punk, its pungent aroma awakening memory, October is the sweet juices being forced up the stem by the last of the glowing stub, the distilled essence of desire.

It was on such a day, the year after we moved into our present house, that I went into town and was walking between the bank and the library. It was a soft and warm late autumn afternoon, and yellow maple leaves were pasted to the wet sidewalks. It was a day I longed to live in town again. The light slanted on the old houses, a man sat on a front step rubbing his dog like a scene from an Edward Hopper painting, two young women passed me, talking about—what were they talking about? If I lived here, walked by this spot every day, I would know.

I passed Cross Street on my left and looked up the lane. There was the house, crouched beneath its tall, defoliating maple, its beige gable peering out from behind the dark red clapboards of the house in front of it. I was suddenly struck by such unexpected regret, such longing, such a sense of missed rightness, that it was like being punched in the stomach without warning. It was desire thwarted that pushed through all the barriers of knowledge of why we could and should not have had it: its indecisive owner, all the necessary expenses, constant upkeep, etc. All these seemed like fleas on a dog in heat. Once again it was a place I felt I would have killed for: the right house on the right part of the right road in the right town at the right time of my life. There was no other like it. It was, simply, the right place, and we had lost it.

Of course I did not think those words then. What I actually thought was that I could spend years just learning to paint that view from Main Street up the gentle arching rise of the road toward the house peeking out from behind its neighbor. But that is always the keenest form of regret, when it takes the shape of sharp, specific, even trivial, unlived possibilities: watching snow softly limning the trees that line the street, or raindrops dancing on the asphalt just outside our front bedroom window, or the yard maple beginning to leaf out once again, seen through the small upstairs gable window partially blocked by the ell roof . . .

Over the past five years, as K. and I have settled into our new life in our new house with a new dog, the sharpness of the regret has become blunted, or taken new forms; but like all profound desires, it abides and, whatever path our actual life takes, is part of who we are. And so, every fall, it seems, there comes a day—when the sky turns a deep blue-blue, the Norway and sugar maples along Main Street catch red and yellow fire, the white clapboards of the old houses all seem freshly painted, the Congo Church's copper-green cupola seems to rise fifty feet higher above the town, the first brown fugitive herds of cottonwood, maple and locust leaves begin to scuttle across the streets, and small clumps of old men stand outside the Lighthouse Restaurant talking about town matters—when the life I think I might have had suddenly becomes more real than the one I do have, and for a few hours I walk about the center of town, pretending I belong there.

Richard Goodman

Wings of Maine: Three Journal Entries

My wife and I began spending summer weeks on a small island off the coast of Maine when our daughter was just two years old. We rented the same house each year, a large, old, wide-porched glory that faces the sea. The island, a place outside of time with no stores and a mere forty houses, had many lessons to teach all of us, and they have been rich and unforgettable. Since we began coming to the island, my wife and I have divorced. The island, though, remains steadfastly there for our daughter.

Sweetwater Island. August 19

I did the wash today. Not an extraordinary event these days—even for a male. Afterwards, I hung the wash out to dry, which was unusual for me. That's something I can't do in the heart of New York City where I live. I wouldn't, even if I could: the metropolitan air. I could have used the clothes dryer, but the dryer at the cottage we rent here on Sweetwater Island in southeastern Maine is too noisy; it goes on forever, a sixty-minute hyper-buzz that smothers the quiet of this most serene point on the island. I hesitated, though, I have to admit. Hanging out the wash takes time. With the dryer, you just push a button, and you walk away. But the desire for stillness prevailed over laziness. I took the heavy, damp, clothes to the back porch and began pinning them to the line. The line climbs about thirty feet on a slant, nearly touching some rocks along the way, until it reaches its twin pole on a rise. As I hung out the clothes, one by one, the line became bowed as a pregnant cat. I had previously used it only to hang a bathing suit or two to dry, nothing more.

What this did, this hanging out of the wash, was give me the sheer satisfaction of completing a domestic task, a satisfaction similar to that Thoreau describes in *Walden* after sweeping out his house. It is a domestic task still performed in many parts of the world, if not here, and one that connects you to the old, simple pattern of life. But this did something else, something unexpected. It opened a chest-full—or rather a hamper-full—of memories that had been in profoundly deep storage in my heart. It took me back to Virginia Beach, Virginia where I grew up. More specifically, it took me to 1955, and to my back yard. And in this backyard, my mother was hanging out the wash, and I was there, watching her. My mother, dead these five years now.

Yes, suddenly, there she was. I was, too. I was myself as a boy. I was watching my mother work. I was watching her doing something she had to do at least three or four times a week. She was hanging out the wash to dry: providing clean clothes for her three children, and for her husband, and for herself. She worked efficiently, reaching above her and pinning the edges of the garments to the clothesline. She had two or three wooden pins in her mouth at the ready, replenished steadily from an arsenal in her apron pockets.

She must be thirty-five or thirty-six. She is energetic and real and beautiful. I want to speak to her, but she doesn't like talking when she is hanging out the wash. She doesn't like doing the wash, period. I remember her telling me so, and she wants to finish it as quickly as possible.

Everything about washing clothes and hanging them out to dry in Virginia Beach in 1955 comes back to me on that Maine hill. I know there is a big difference between my hanging out the wash here in Maine and my mother's inescapable routine of long long ago. I remember driving in the car with her, and seeing it start to rain, and she, full of things in her head, slapping the wheel and saying, "Oh, God, the wash!" She knew the distance between her and the clothes was too great to retrieve them before it poured. So she knew the clothes were out there, getting soaked, getting heavier and heavier, even dragging themselves to the earth and into pools of water made by the rain. No dryers then—at least not for us. What should have been a sure thing was not, and had to be done all over again, with the added work of wringing out the drenched clothes, piece by piece.

I watched her as long as I could today, my Mommy, so alive before me I could hardly believe it. I continued watching her as I pinned my clothes to the more deeply bowing line. I pinned shirts, socks, towels and jeans for my own six-year-old daughter, for my wife and for me. But even then I could see my mother turn and look at me as I extravagantly used two, sometimes three, clothespins for each piece of laundry. "Double up on those clothespins, Richie!" She meant that two pieces of laundry could share the same pin. You get more on the line then, and the hanging will be over faster.

So there she was, my mother, my faraway gone mother. I could see her again as I had as a ten year old: my coping—not always coping—mother. She who was to have so many problems and pains later, whose heart was broken and who attempted to repair it with drink. She was mine, and I was hers, for a moment—for an eternity. I think that could only have happened to me here, on Sweetwater Island, where the old verities of life are championed. These are the things which link us to the past and to people who, though dead and far gone, we will always love and try very hard never to forget. And I won't forget you, Mommy.

Sweetwater Island. August 20

The house we rent has a two-sided, expansive porch. We spend a good deal of time on that porch. It faces an exposed eastern point of Sweetwater Island, and so we and the island's weather—which is the fullest here—are pretty well acquainted. Near the house is a small cluster of pine trees. Sometimes for shade, and for peace, I walk into these woods. They are quite different from the dark, Frostian woods that take up most of the center of Sweetwater Island. While there is indeed shade, there is space and light, too, and soft brown pine needles underfoot. These pines remind me of the wind-shaped pine trees I used to walk among in France, near the Mediterranean.

On the edge of this little cluster of trees, my brother-in-law put up a hammock between two crabapple trees last year. He can lay there, a concave lump, happily reading his French books for hours.

I don't always get the peace I'm after, however. I keep forgetting that in this little woods reside a small, secretive band of crows. When I walk among the trees, more often than not three or four crows suddenly alight, cawing an alert. I jump—their actions are so abrupt. They, of course, notice me immediately through the branches. When I come too close for comfort, they start crying bloody murder. If that weren't enough, two or three crows typically remain behind. Without warning, there is a second explosive fleeing and cawing. I jump again. Do they think this is funny? Through the branches, I see the second cluster fly away. They are large birds. I can even hear their wings wafting the air. No creature can expose you like a crow. They expose you so blatantly that you feel totally isolated, as if a large circle had been drawn around you. Their caws sound as if they are communicating precisely what color your hair is, how tall you are, how much you weigh, exactly where you are standing, and why you are here. How obvious you are, they seem to say.

You cannot, on the other hand, surprise a crow.

As long as I've been coming to Sweetwater Island, these crows—or a similar group—have resided here. A few years ago, they were extremely loud in the early morning. Their *caw caw caw* has the insistence and penetratingness of a car alarm. They woke us with their 5 am bickering and squawking, and I began to have detailed poisoning fantasies. Given half the chance, I would have carried them out. But that would have been very un-Sweetwater Island.

This year, thankfully, they seem to be doing their dawn cawing elsewhere—specifically, a few houses down, in front of a new insomniac's cottage. They still have retreats in our little woods, though.

Crows are the most inscrutable of birds, maybe of all animals. They are aloof and secretive, and they exist in their aloof secretiveness almost everywhere on the earth. Crows will be on Sweetwater Island as long as we are, long after, and probably forever. They are so common, and so mysterious. They are the part of a world we will never know, and will never have dominion over. There is contentment in that.

New York City, May 23

I won't be going to Maine this year. My ex-wife and my daughter will. In the aftermath of divorce, I drifted away from the island, like a boat untied. This always seems to happen after the sundering of a marriage. Those common friends are no longer common. Who was originally whose friend becomes clear again through what was once the opaqueness of joint living. Maine was not mine first. It was my wife's. It was she who introduced me to Sweetwater Island. She had gone to college with a woman whose family owns a house—three houses, in fact—on SI, as they call it. She has been going to the island for twenty years, since her college days, and it is part of her. It's part of my daughter, now, too, and I am grateful for that. Maine, especially the islands of Maine, is about as timeless a place you can find.

I'll miss the island, that goes without saying. I'll especially miss those things my daughter and I would do together—our things. When she was three, I began taking her out to look for blackberries. I would hold her in one arm as we went from bush to bush searching for the berries, which were often in lovely clusters. Few things are as nourishing to the soul as a Maine-grown blackberry. For us, the renowned blueberries are a distant second. I remember the time my girl took her first bite. She had a look on her face that you could only describe as an exclamation mark. Customarily, whenever we would get anything to eat, she would say, sometimes sternly, "Save some for Mommy!" After we had gathered a handful of the black treasures, I said, "Let's save these for Mommy."

"No," she said unemotionally, gathering blackberries from my palm.

I won't be collecting mussels with her, either. When the tide waned, baring great stretches of soggy land, we would set out on our hunt. There were so many mussels! She loved ripping them from their rocky declivities, running to toss them into a bucket and dashing back for more. She was unquenchable.

"Look, Daddy!" She rushed up with a clump of the black bearded shells in her two hands, held them up before me, then tossed them into the bucket and ran back to her spot. I have had few moments as a father as intense. Seeing my girl there, her hands and feet slathered in mud, her legs streaking with Maine water, her hair a windy mess, I knew she was fully in her childhood. I knew this was childhood as it's supposed to be. We gathered mussels and gathered. We never fatigued.

"Look, Daddy, over here!" she cried to me. I had to come. We covered the whole mudflat, and then we branched out this way and that. No mussel escaped our relentless pursuit. We were mussel bloodhounds. The good thing about mussels is that you need a lot of them if you're going to cook them. And we were. That means you have to collect a lot. One person can easily eat twenty. The meat itself, just a bite, really, is oh so good. I like the taste of Maine mussels better than lobster, better than clams, better than scallops, even better than oysters.

So, we kept looking, the two of us. We got maybe fifty, sixty—even seventy who knows? It was only the clock that stopped us. We had to take them up to the house, clean them, and cook them. People were coming over to eat them. Cleaning mussels takes forever, and my girl is not interested in something that takes forever. So, she left the task to me. She doesn't much like eating mussels, either. Never mind. Now my daughter, New York City born and bred, knows what a mussel in the wild looks like, where it comes from, how it lives. She has seen its habitat, and the strength such a small thing can summon to remain fixed there. She has witnessed how a creature so small has adapted itself to this difficult environment. She has seen how suited mussels are to being where they are. Seeing this amazing compatibility, she will learn to respect that. She will realize how much wiser it is than the things we humans engineer and boast so about.

I taught her to climb the rough rocks that jut out from much of the island. I taught her to scamper, to pull, to leap goat-like, and, trickiest of all, to descend. She fell once, in her arrogance. My heart leapt, but she escaped with tears and a little blood. She is daring, and passionately self-sufficient, and you can't stop her. You just pray she won't break her neck. But the island provides risk; it provides an opportunity for my daughter to test herself; to discover that she has power within her to surmount difficulties of a physical nature. She is aware now that nature will never go easy on her, just because she is who she is. She is learning that nature is democratic in its indifference. This lesson, and others about the sanctity of our earth, will help connect her with the rest of the world.

She leaves in just a few weeks. I feel a lump in my throat already. I'll find it very hard to say goodbye to her this time.

Maine, as she learns to fly, watch over her.

Elaine Neil Orr

from *Gods of Noonday: A White Girl's African Life*

GREEN LIKE THE GREEN MAMBA

The Ethiope River is where I swam as a girl. It was cold enough to knock you silly when you jumped in, but then you swam for the opposite shore, crazily, your eyes open so you could mark your progress against the current, and below you could see logs like huge fallen monuments and greenery on the white river bottom twenty-five feet below and a school of fish parting at your approach and veering off at forty-five degree angles and all the while you pulled for your life against the river that would not let you alone and when you kicked finally that last time, you lifted your arms and grabbed hold of the mossy tree trunk that leaned out over the water, and came up spouting and spraying. Afternoons at the river were the happiest I have ever been in my life—in the company of the people I loved the most—and I believed, when I was young, that I would live by this river forever, that I would learn to breathe underwater, that I would build a hut by its side, that I would never let it go.

I was born to southern Nigeria, and, for several years, I lived on the Eku Baptist Hospital compound with my medical missionary parents, Anne and Lloyd Neil, and my sister, Becky, until she was sent to boarding school, and then I lived there with my parents and prayed to Jesus that we would never part, not the three of us and not the three of us and this land and the Ethiope River and the Urhobo people surrounding us.

The river passed not far from our front yard but was separated from us by a rubber plantation so that we had to drive up the Sapele-Obiaruku road about nine miles to Abraka where there was a Western-style landing with piers and diving boards. Like a huge tendril, the Ethiope wound through the neighboring countryside until it reached Sapele and the estuary called the Benin River and eventually the Atlantic Ocean. It was named after one of the first successful trading ships to find its way into the Nigerian interior. Given how I grew up, with few playmates on the compound and comings and leavings all the time, I learned to cling to the steady objects of my material world: a guava tree in the side yard, the gravel path that ran in front of our house, a cluster of squat palm trees, the compound drive, the yellow hibiscus outside my bedroom window, the river.

I did have one close companion in Eku, a young boy my age who lived next door. His name was David Gaultney. He was generous and he admired me and I didn't have to be as generous but I admired him too. I liked the way he smiled out of one corner of his mouth and the way his brown eyes gathered in the noonday sun as if he were serious and laughing at the same time, and the way when he walked, he sort of leaned to one side as if he were listening to some distant music, and his olive brown skin, so unlike mine, which was fair and freckled. The best thing that happened to us on any given day was a trip to the river. We two, muffled in sweat and dust from playing knights of the roundtable, would be down by the compound's eroding tennis courts when my father came looking for me on his black Raleigh bicycle after his day at the hospital. The sun would be coasting over the compound's towering palms by now. "Would you like to go to the river?" he would coyly inquire, still crisp as the morning and perfectly balanced on the cycle.

David and I would throw up our swords—really the long pods that fell from the flamboyant tree—and race down the path to our houses to change into swimming clothes.

With our legs sticking to the protective plastic that covered the seats of my family's 1957 sierra gold Chevrolet station wagon, David and I called off the names of the villages as we passed through them: Okorori Sanubi Oria Erho Urhovia. Our car was tailed by a band of young children, waving furiously and calling "oyinbo, oyinbo, oyinbo": white person. As a girl, I thought they were telling me I was special, but now I realize they were pointing out my foreign nature. Sometimes a young boy would have a stick and a large thin metal cylinder and he could keep the thing rolling alongside the car all the way through the village, his eyes always on the cylinder because he was performing for us. This was his magic. But the older youth held back, like elders who have seen through the trick or who never let themselves be lured to the show.

Sharing the road with goats, bicycles, lorries, and walkers, it took us awhile to get to the Abraka landing. We might be slowed by a tilting lorry overloaded with bundles of raw rubber, its bulky odor entering our open windows. In such a "go slow," David and I would sometimes spy a line of people just appearing through the bush carrying loads of firewood and water and cassava and, of course, we just hadn't seen the path but it was there and so they had been walking perhaps many miles before coming out of the dense forest and into our line of sight. A mysterious world of interaction was occurring beyond what we could see or beyond what we could comprehend. Take the Mamy Wata devotees, for example. These were women doused from head to foot with white powder and carrying white basins on their heads filled with cowrie shells and kola nuts and other treasures, who were on their way to make sacrificial gifts to the goddess of the water. I see those women now, right this minute, standing up on a little brown hill casting their look at us momentarily as we passed, their breasts chalked and gleaming. I had nothing in my own world with which to compare them, certainly not the women at the local Baptist churches who were members of the

Women's Missionary Union and who dressed in elegant wraps and smelled like starched fabric.

After such a sight, you would look back at your legs and hands to be sure you were there. Our car, of course, was not air-conditioned and my father had to swerve to miss the potholes or hit them, all of which made us anxious to reach the cool buoyancy of the river. Finally, we would reach Abraka, turning left off of the paved road at what appeared to be a post office, though there was never any activity around the building, down a white sandy road that was gutted in the middle so that the car bounced wildly from side to side. The land on the right had been converted to a large sandlot, but just next to the road tall grasses grew so close that if you stuck your hand out the window, you could feel the slender stalks hit against your skin. I submitted to this pain as a girl because there is something sweet about such a slender hurt.

Near the river, palms and hardwoods and thick forest undergrowth returned, and we would round a curve, pass through the gate, and drive the car nearly into the river before stopping. The old man who guarded the landing was like a chameleon. At first you would not see him but then he would stand up under the towering tree that sheltered his seat and begin a measured approach into the sunlight, as if to say: "Remember, I am watching." Never had he the hint of a smile. Looking back, I think the Ethiope was the laughter of Urhobo divinities. It was cold enough to have been spent snow instead of tropical water. Coming into view, it appeared as if the upper currents were racing the bottom ones, as if it were overtaking itself. It was absolutely, purely, spectacularly clear, singing down its white sandy bed, but because of the surrounding vegetation and the sky above and the river grass, it wore many colors: a fluffy white like cotton from the kapok tree, the blue of the woodland kingfisher, or granite beneath a threatening sky. Yet the chief color of the river was green, green like the green mamba, like grass-green garnet and just as shimmering, or, in the shade, green like the glossy leaves of palm trees.

Whatever the color, it was honest, like colors after a rain: deep and true, distinct and fluid at the same time, fresh as if newly created.

I should have fallen on my knees every time I stepped out of that station wagon and found the Ethiope still there. Always I was stunned to see that any earthly thing could be so constantly new, so fresh, so gorgeous. This was a river beyond poetry, lovelier than the diamonds of Sierra Leone, lovelier than the gold of this country Nigeria, lovelier than the young women and men who bathed in it. Nothing you could tell me about Jehovah was equal to the proof of divinity provided by the mere existence of so lovely a river. And so I worshipped it.

But entering this bright church was a challenge. Sometimes, David and I would let ourselves down slowly on one of the white ladders descending from the piers; this was trial by ice. On other occasions, however, when we were feeling daring—or especially in need of salvation—we would jump from the car and run straight down the longest pier and veer out over the water, taking on the river all at once. This was the wiser approach, believe me; the other was torturous, especially when you reached your regions of privacy. If you jumped, however, you were acclimated by the time you swam back to the pier and lifted yourself for another dive. David and I loved to cross the current, pull ourselves up on an overhanging tree, and launch ourselves with a rope swing out over the water. You could lean back and let the top of your head tunnel through the river's surface. Sometimes when the swing was high in its arc, you let go and fell into the Ethiope, your feet going so far down they might touch the green weeds that grew on the river bed. Occasionally, a Nigerian boy from the local school joined us and he would climb farther up in the overhanging tree than we and rather than swing out on the rope, he dove straight down into the water, entering the Ethiope neatly as a spear. We might have said to him: "Brother, like the lizard that fell from the top of the iroko tree without hurting itself, you deserve praise," but we did not. We felt tongueless in the presence of such a feat. Our own courage was exposed as timidity. One landing up or down from where we entered the river and you were swimming in the midst of whole villages of folk washing their clothes and taking their baths. Even from where we swam you could hear the voices, at least the ones upstream, which must have been carried down on that swift current. We were hearing Nigerian speech as it might have sounded if white people had never come here. The villagers were not speaking for us or to us but for and to one another. The voices were high and low, like musical scales, full of mothers' commands and young men's jokes and children's games, vibrant splashing mixed with agile voices, all of the medley hugely harmonious.

Occasionally, a great raft of mahogany or iroko trees banded together and engineered by a lone driver would come into view. David and I would swim out midstream, hoist ourselves onto the barge, and, saluting the mariner, catch a lift to the next landing. Floating down the river like that, you could catch a glimpse of monkeys blazing through the trees, or an opalescent snake shining on a log, or a shrine up in the bush overlooking the bank, a small hut with a thatched roof and an open door and in some cases a totem; there was always something bright white at these shrines, maybe a white enamel bowl or maybe the devotees of the Mamy Wata sprinkled the shrine with white powder. The current would carry you down before you could really see what it was you were seeing; it was like a glimpse into somebody's intimate chamber. David and I deboarded at the next landing and walked back to our accustomed spot. The sandy road was flaming hot so we jumped from one clump of grass to another, speeding across the sand when we had to, then ran like crazy when we got close to the river and careened out over the current like madmen. I experienced my first orgasm in the Ethiope, lying on an inner tube in a small inlet where the current pressed gently against my body. It felt as if a spirit were stirring between my legs and then there flowered between them a feeling as red and frilled and elegant as the flower of the gloriosa lily.

⚜

There was a permanent red raft in the middle of the river, kept in place by a chain attached to a log on the river bottom. We spent a good deal of time swimming out to it and diving off and you could get under it because it floated on large drums filled with air. I have pictures taken of me standing on that raft, my legs long and lean, my hair short and slicked back from the river, a girlish manner in the casual sway of my body. I had not yet learned to be looked at; I was not yet posing. In her black one-piece bathing suit, my mother would swim upstream to the raft as a form of exercise and then she would hold on and kick her legs, always with her head aloft.

One day, we discovered a snail on that raft and some adult thought it should be sent off for testing; it might be a carrier of schistosomiasis. The precaution seemed silly to me then. The river was large and long and adjacent to swampland and full of all sorts of animals. At that stage in my life, I didn't even know the name of the disease my parents suspected. What I have since learned is that the Ethiope was too swift and too cold to be host to the snail that carries that dreaded illness and so the facts correspond to my youthful perception that our fair river could not harm. I will admit, however, that on the day a pearly pink snake crossed from the opposite bank to our landing, taking refuge under the red raft, I joined the crowd as we lifted from the river like a covey of birds from a field. Once David and I determined to "hike" up the edge of the river, in the shallows, to the landing that lay above us. I don't know how exactly this idea came to us, and it surprises me now that my parents let us undertake this venture since it took us well out of their sight. In any case, we set out, pulling ourselves against that zealous spring. We could not possibly have made this journey swimming; the current was much too powerful. Even walking upstream required determination: you had to keep your head down, learning the floor of the river rather than looking ahead.

At that moment I was at one with the river, amazed at its beauty, the patterns of submerged greenery and sand like small compounds underwater. I have never felt less alone than I did then, with David, headed upstream. Above my head, a canopy of trees and a family of monkeys, those swift noisy foragers who love the oil palm nut. I suppose David and I were friends in that short moment between early childhood and adolescence when you don't really think about gender yet. It is perhaps the only real time in which males and females are absolutely true to each other. During those Eku years, we were in a budding period. We didn't realize the delight we took in each other's difference but surely the competitions were sweeter because we weren't quite alike. I was charmed by his ease and his loyalty and his eternal availability in our collaborations. He was quietly there, which was all I needed. I guess we were like young growing trees, still in the shade of elders and before the distinctive marks of our genus were upon us. Or I suppose David was my Adam whether or not I was Eve. I never liked anything better than solitude and one close companion with whom to spend part of the day. I never ran with the pack. I never lived in the city. I never liked a band better than one lone pianist even if it was just my mother playing old hymns, whose theology, if I had considered it, I would have rejected. Certainly the River Ethiope was my Eden; the snakes never tempted, no one sinned here.

During my years in Eku, a new high dive was constructed at the Abraka landing. It probably was not that high, but it looked high to me, especially standing at the tip end of the board. From where I was standing, looking down to the bottom of the river, it was a high dive indeed. Its appearance coincided with the arrival at the Eku hospital of a new missionary doctor, Uncle Jack Toler, who was a skilled diver and could turn flips and everything before entering the river. The rumor was that he had performed for Vice President Johnson. Uncle Jack's prowess, like the Urhobo boy's diving, raised the stakes for David and me.

Jumping from the high board was one thing, but diving was another. One day, I told my Daddy to watch as I ascended the ladder. But once up there, I had second and third thoughts. I would lift my arms obediently, making a little arrow out of the palms of my hands and leaning over, but nothing would happen. Though my father stood patiently, holding his towel, his long thin legs slightly bent at the knees like they always were, clapping his hands both to encourage and as a push, David seemed hardly to notice my brave heart. He had gathered his things as if ready to leave and appeared only dimly aware of my presence. His head was at a three-quarters turn as he gazed across the river, his eyes narrowed. Finally, I leaned over and fell into the water head first as if I'd been shot. During my last Christmas in Eku some sinners did arrive at the Abraka landing, a band of British businessmen and their wives. It seemed to me they ignored our river etiquette. The men were loud and wore brief swimming suits and their stomachs were large, almost like beach balls. They wore gaudy gold wristwatches and drank Star beer and said Bloody this and Bloody that. Passing by one of the men standing on the pier, David and I smelled his warm yeasty breath and it seemed to me the man's eyes were like hands that could touch. I dove alone and headed at an angle across the current, trying to cleanse myself of that look. I can't even remember the British women; there was no room for them in my vision after I had taken in those men. Always I thought of the British in Nigeria as foreigners whereas we Southern Baptist Americans belonged. After all, I was born here.

More often than not, David and I drove back to Eku with my father, riding in the back of the station wagon with the gate up but the glass down. My fingertips were shriveled from swimming, and the evening air gave me goose bumps. Passing the farm planted in maize as we left the river, my father occasionally stopped and bought us a roasted ear.

The kernels were so hard and blackened you could really only suck on them, which was why, I guess, my father thought the purchase less than worthwhile, but the plush dusky smell of the corn was so enticing you believed you were partaking of a delicacy. Returning through the villages, we saw the orange moon come up. At this hour there were no children running by the car calling "oyinbo." They were, instead, obediently gathered with their clan, waiting for the soup to pass. You might catch a glimpse of a lonely figure with a load returning from the farm or an old man still sitting in the open air of the evening, under a canopy of hibiscus.

As much as I loved the river, I always felt it a homecoming when we got close to our Eku compound. The car would slow down like an animal finding its way home and we would turn in through the gate. Oh joy, the crunch of tires on gravel as we eased into our drive. By now, my hair was dry except for the very back. On these evenings, I didn't have to bathe. I would eat like a soldier home from war and fall into bed still drowning into the pull of the river.

During my last year in Eku, two new missionary families appeared on the compound. First came the Pitmans and then the Normans, or it may have been the other way around. Both families, however, had a daughter David's and my age, so our little classroom was suddenly bursting: where there had been two of us, now there were three and four.

Having other girls around meant I had to think more critically about myself as a girl, which was a subject I had been avoiding. Now I saw that one might prefer to be petite or to have dimples or to pull one's hair back in a ponytail. All of these choices complicated my outlook. I began to doubt myself.

One afternoon, I was with David along with Julie Pitman in his side yard. Here was a tree that produced prodigious leaves and the stems of these, once they dried, were almost like African drumsticks. We used them in all sorts of play. But Julie-of-the-long-dark-hair was not interested in the sticks; she had another agenda. Standing in her blue jeans with her weight on one leg and her hips slanted provocatively, she asked David who his girlfriend was. I had never imagined such a question and it frightened me. David said nothing for a long time but walked about with his head to one side, dragging one of those drumsticks in the grass. But Julie kept insisting: he must have a girlfriend. So she proposed an answer: Is it Elaine? And then after pacing a bit more and ignoring Julie further, David whispered in a low voice, as if his answer was coming to him from a distance or maybe he was just making it up: It used to be.

Gulf Oil arrived in the region at about the same time as these missionary outsiders. Seismographers came onto our compound one day to explore the possibility of oil deposits. Our parents just laughed at this preposterous idea though they should have known; major oil finds had been made a year or two earlier at Ughelli in the western delta, about forty-five miles from Eku, twenty-five miles as the crow flies. Production was due to start in the Greater Ughelli area in June of 1965, when the trans-Niger pipeline system linking the Midwest fields to the Bonny Terminal was completed. Great trucks and rigs began to move down the road like a column of war. To the left and the right of the one-lane highway, expanses of land were cleared, the smaller trees looking as if they had been chewed by some prehistoric predator. Stretches of the shadowy drive to the river were fully exposed to the sun. Rigs were erected at some distance from the road, though we could see one at least on our drive back and forth from Abraka. Returning from swimming in the evening, you could spot oil flares spewing black smoke and flames on the seaward horizon.

When I was eight, I read about how the Romans could make a knife so sharp that it would cut a hair on water. At age twenty-three, living in Louisville, Kentucky, and attending graduate school, I wrote this poem:

Our cook sharpened knives
fit to kill
So I tucked one between the folds
of my towel
and carried it to the river

But the water only bled
and the fish only died
and the eel only choked on my hair

Dear God, damn the Romans
and send me a needle to sew up the water
and send me a spell to chant over the fish
and send me a language to comfort the eel.

Today there is a hotel at the landing where I swam as a girl; during the Nigerian civil war, people died violent deaths on the banks of that river, notwithstanding that the Mamy Wata is a goddess of peace; the oil has brought prosperity to very few.

During the summer of 1964, we began to prepare for furlough. Every day at the river, someone would ask me how many more days it was until I went to America, and I would answer cavalierly, "fourteen," "thirteen," "twelve." I was anxious and excited. Maybe something better lay around the corner. But I wasn't sure. I remember one particular moment when this question was put to me. I was standing in the shallows at the upper end of our landing, preparing to swim across. I remember looking around me at the tadpoles and small minnows that swam in that cove and at the soft green weeds that bent eternally in the direction of the current and the white sand comforting my feet. The feeling I had at that moment was what you must feel if a twin were dying. A part of my life was over. One evening in preparation for the transcontinental journey, I sat on the floor in the living room, in the middle of the sisal rug, and studied a Sears catalog. I was trying to get a picture of myself in America when my eyes came to rest on a girl like me. Except that she was not me; she was better. Her neatly combed blond hair fell to her shoulders where it turned back up in a perfect half circle, like the letter "C" on its back. She wore a navy blue headband and though her blue eyes were not quite so large as mine, her nose was more obedient, her lips redder, and her teeth neatly hidden. The clothes she wore were both familiar and impossible: a trim white shirt buttoned to the very top, tucked into a pleated navy blue skirt. I did not think I was going to pass.

A few days before we left, housecleaning and packing began in earnest. My sister, home from boarding school, was helping my mother go through my things. But she should not have been so bold. When I discovered that she had dispensed with some of my least prized but nonetheless most familiar possessions, I was overcome with grief and, with my mother trailing behind me, I undertook a hasty reconnaissance effort down at the koto, in the far reaches of the front yard. But the cherished items were too soiled and too polluted to retrieve. So I left them there to rot among the orange peel and old shoes. Some time that summer, Dad drove the sierra gold Chevrolet station wagon down by the back steps where he washed and waxed it and took pictures of it and then sold it off to the highest bidder. On the day we left, an unfamiliar van drove up. David was standing there, his back pressed into a red hibiscus bush, his eyes held in that sideways look he had begun to practice. I got into the transport without giving him a hug or even a proper good-bye, closed the door, and, looking straight ahead, determined to take on the dark continent of America.

Writing for Children

Louella Bryant

ages 4-8

Great Gobs of Goose Grease

Tully Bartholomew Juniper was extra-ordinary—or so he said. One summer he visited his Aunt Helen and Uncle Leroy, who had a regular dog and a regular cat. They ate regular food, wore regular hats, and they lived in a very dull house.

From morning to night Tully Bartholomew Juniper lent spice to the day with the marvelous, magical, mystical, fabulous, simply fantastical things he would say, like:

"I have a pet lion escaped from the zoo—He sleeps on my bed and does math homework, too."

"Heavens to Betsy!" cried Aunt Helen.

"Blather!" bellowed Uncle Leroy.

"A zebra named Humphrey is munching my lawn—He starts in at bedtime and eats until dawn."

"Mercy!" murmured Aunt Helen.

"Bawlderdash!" pouted Uncle Leroy.

"The man in the moon has sent me a letter—He said that come autumn he'd knit me a sweater."

"My stars and garters!" yelped Aunt Helen.

"Hooey!" scoffed Uncle Leroy.

"My brown cow Mathilde gives chocolate milk while wearing a nightgown of clover and silk."

"Great gobs of goose grease!" gulped Aunt Helen.

"I'll be a monkey's uncle!" mocked Uncle Leroy.

"My garden is growing unusual fruit—cream covered suckers, a horn and a boot."

"Good night nurse!" hooted Aunt Helen.

"Beans!" balked Uncle Leroy.

"I caught me a rainbow the last time it rained—It sits by my window; I have it well trained."

"Pshaw," hissed Aunt Helen.

"Hogwash!" chuckled Uncle Leroy.

"If you don't believe that, I've got one more to try—Come close and I'll whisper: Did you know I can fly?"

"For Pete's sake," sputtered Aunt Helen.

"In a pig's eye!" bellowed Uncle Leroy.

And with that Tully held out his skinny brown arms and waved them and flapped them and recited three charms:

"Goose grease and garters and golden pig's eye."

And to their astonishment, he started to . . . fly!

"I never saw the like!" gasped Uncle Leroy.

"Why I'm tickled pink!" giggled Aunt Helen.

The cat barked, the dog meowed, and they all had a splendid, wonderful, anything but dull-i-ful time.

Luke Wallin

from *Ceremony of the Panther*

GRANDFATHER RATTLESNAKE

The weeks became months, and John heard nothing from his father. Sometimes Sedie Jumper, his cousin who ran the little store by the airboat dock, came to visit, and once she brought John a letter from his mother. It was just a note, with a clipping from the tribal newspaper, about a woman from an Alaskan tribe who had come through, visiting.

She had given a talk at the youth center, telling about the history of alcohol and Native Americans, and she had finished up with saying, "For one of us to stay sober is a revolutionary act." That was her message, and it was Anna's, too. John had expected a long letter saying how much she missed him.

After that, he began to really wonder how long they might leave him in the swamp.

Then one day Sedie came by to say Moses would be out to the res the next afternoon; he wanted John to meet him at the store.

"You want me to come and get you?" she asked John.

"No!" Mary said, "We don't need that air boat out here again tomorrow. He can take the canoe in."

They looked at John, as if to test him.

"Sure," he said. "I don't care."

He tried not to think about seeing his father, and he got away by himself as soon as he could. It was hard to get to sleep that night. After midnight a storm blew in, and it rained for hours, on into the morning. John waited it out, with nothing but worry on his mind. When it finally slacked off and quit, he still couldn't figure out how he would feel when he actually set eyes on Papa again. And he wondered, Is this it? Is he going to bring me home with him now?

It seemed years later when John finally eased the long dugout canoe into the weedy bank behind Sedie's little store. His father's air boat was in the willows, and John's stomach turned in anticipation.

An old refrigerator lay on its back with its door gone, and inside a big gopher turtle crawled in a slow circle; it would be Sedie's supper tonight. John walked into the rear of the store, where the air was still and tense. Silently, Sedie handed him a soda and a Twinkie, and her eyes told him not to speak.

Moses Raincrow stood by the broken jukebox with his powerful arms crossed and his wide, serious face focused on the man he was talking to. Moses nodded at his son and returned to his conversation, and John saw at once why he was so formal. The tall, bony white man in the khaki uniform, standing with his back to John, was Mr. Crane. He had red hair and thickly spread freckles over his skin, and not much humor about him at all.

"We know they're in the area," he said. "Don't try to fool me about that."

A dark blush of anger passed across Moses' face, and he looked out the open front door toward the old highway that cut through the reservation.

"We have a pretty good idea you could help us on this pair, Mr. Raincrow."

"Look," Moses said quickly. "I just got here. I been working all week on a gladiola farm. How do you expect me to know where two panthers are in this whole swamp, huh? Even if I knew last week—you think they haven't moved since I was out here? You think panthers don't move?"

Sedie Jumper began to laugh. John started in, too, then finally Moses. All of them together made a soft, musical sound. Even Mr. Crane closed his eyes and smiled.

"All right, Mr. Raincrow. You got me there," he said. "But you could help me look around, couldn't you? You could save me a lot of time."

Moses turned to his son and with a straight face said, "John, this is Mr. Ron Crane, of the state's Task Force. You ever met him before?"

"No!" Crane said loudly, reaching for John's hand over the counter.

"My son," Moses said. Crane pumped John's hand up and down.

John had been about to say yes, he had met this man at school last year, when Crane had come to talk about saving the panthers because they were an endangered species. How could the man not remember him?

"He's a fine boy!" Crane said, releasing his hand. How does he know if I'm fine? John wondered.

Moses gazed out the door.

"Look," Crane said, "the pair I'm after . . . the big male's radio collar has gone dead on us. Shoulda been good another six months. Anyway, they were seen crossing the road up by Blackwater Creek, just last night. Heading east. 'Course, rain's washed out all their tracks by now. That's why I need you. Everybody out here, when I ask them, they say wait till you come. Ask you. So, I'm asking."

Moses glanced at Crane and returned to studying the palm trees beside the roadway.

"Well?" Crane said in exasperation.

Moses turned to him, jarred and frowning.

"Are you going to help me or not?"

Moses said quietly, "I don't know where those two panthers went, Mr. Crane. But if I did, I wouldn't tell you."

Now Crane stiffened up. "You know, sir, it's not me personally that's benefiting from all this work. Whatever you do . . . whatever effort you put yourself to . . . it's for the good of the animals out there."

"Oh?" Moses whispered.

"Yes!" Crane continued. "Do you think I like tracking panthers through this swamp? Do you think I enjoy climbing up in trees and lowering them to the ground? You may not know what this is all about, Mr. Raincrow, but someday your children might. This boy here"—he pointed directly into John's face—"he might appreciate it some day. There are only thirty of them left, Mr. Raincrow. Thirty. This boy's children might thank you someday for what you did—away back when he was young. It's like I tell the schoolchildren when I give programs, this is really important! You can make a difference! This is the hunt of a lifetime!"

Moses and Sedie and John were all turned away from the loud white man. Then there was the sound of tires in gravel out front, and they saw Max Poor Bear's camo-painted jeep pulling in. His tape deck was turned up loud, playing the Rolling Stones.

"Here's you man to help you!" Moses said, moving for the door. "Come on, son." They left Crane with his hands in his pockets and walked out the door. Max was leaning against his jeep, smiling.

"Look, here!" Max said. "Moses and John together. Don't see that every day, now!"

"Hello," Moses said. "What are you doing out here?"

"Come out to the swamp, man. Get away from the Trail for a night. What else, huh?" Max laughed. His big semiautomatic rifle lay on the seat of his jeep. And beneath the roll bar, in the back, there was a washtub loaded with ice and beer.

Moses looked glum, nodding. "You're out here to get drunk and then go spotlighting. You'll shoot a few deer, and if the heat doesn't spoil them, you'll sell them in Miami. Am I right?"

"What an imagination," Max said.

"It's thanks to you," Moses said, "that the tribal council may have to pass some hunting laws."

"I'm scared to death," Max said lightly, smiling at John. "Whatever you boys are up to," Max said as he stepped away from his jeep, "best of luck to you."

He headed into the store, and Moses got into his pickup and crashed the door shut.

They pulled out and started down the road, neither wanting to talk about Max. They had driven only half a mile and John was about to ask where they were going, when they saw a small crowd in the schoolyard. The children and Ellen Cypress, their teacher, were standing close together pointing at something, and they began to wave Moses down.

John could see the rattlesnake beside the soft pine stump on the grass as he opened his door.

"It won't go away!" one of the children cried out. Others laughed, and they all squeezed together.

"It's an old one," Moses said, easing close to the snake. It was about six feet long, thick, with the sharp black diamondback pattern, and it had a lot of rattles. "Does it live in there?" He pointed to the stump.

Ellen nodded. "It's been coming out every day." She spoke with deliberate calmness. "The children and I have been talking to it, haven't we, children?"

"Yes, Ellen!" they said. "But it doesn't listen."

"No," she agreed. "Any ideas, Moses?"

He squatted near the snake's head and said nothing. John knew he was trying to tune into it, setting the tone for a talk. Slowly, he took a little pouch of tobacco from his shirt pocket, worked a pinch of it between his thumb and forefinger, and sprinkled it on the ground beside the snake.

"Grandfather," Moses said to it, "we don't want to harm you, you know that."

The snake backed up a little; it was very sluggish.

"But each day you insist on coming out of your hole, and being near the children." He paused and looked at the sky, a clean blue with scattered white clouds.

"Now . . . that's no good. You might hurt one of them, even though you don't mean to."

Moses cocked his head and looked more closely at the rattlesnake.

Then he stood up and faced the children, who were perfectly quiet, their dark eyes very round and wide. "I'm afraid there's something wrong with our friend," he said. "I believe he's very old, maybe sick, and it's time we sent his soul on its way."

There was a sound of the children drawing their breaths.

"Now, I know Ellen is a good teacher, and she's spoken to you about the souls of four-leggeds." They nodded. "And you know that the old people, going far, far back into time, they never would kill a rattlesnake. They didn't want his shadow after them!"

"No!" the children said.

"Of course not. And they especially didn't want the Sky Rattlesnakes mad at them, did they?"

"Noooooooooo!"

"That's right. Because if that happened, then next time you went anywhere—out for a walk, over to the store—anywhere you pick up you foot, you're going to put it down on a . . . what?"

"Rattlesnake!" they cried together. "Rattlesnake!"

"Shhhhh . . ." Moses glanced at the snake, moving off toward its stump hole. "That's right, children. But let's not yell." He picked up a stick from the grass and blocked the snake's way.

"That's why, every fall at the Hunt Dance, we always do the Snake Dance, don't we?"

"Yesssss!" they hissed together.

"Uh-huh. We always do that dance . . . to let the Sky Rattlesnakes know we mean no harm to the great tribe of snakes. No harm at all."

The big snake began to coil up.

"Our grandfathers, in the old days of our tribe, they knew better than to get the spirits mad at them . . . they were pretty smart. Do you know what they did in a case like this, when a snake needed to be sent on to the other world?"

"Nooooo," the children whispered, shaking their heads.

"Well, they went out and got a white man to kill it for them! That's right! If they could find one. Because he doesn't believe in the Sky Rattlesnakes, did you know that?"

Some of them nodded their heads, some shook them. John knew that they agreed, that they were listening to their medicine man.

"Well, we're lucky today," Moses said. "Because we've got John here with us." He looked up and smiled. "And John, the keys are in the truck. Do you think you could find us a white man, right quick?"

John turned to the children with the most worried face he could imagine.

"I'll see what I can do," he said. "I'll go look for one."

"Good," Moses said. "You will be the medicine man's ceremonial assistant in this matter. While you find us a white man, who knows nothing of the snake's shadow or its master spirits up above, we will make our apologies to this Grandfather. Are you with me, children?"

"Yesssssssss!" they cried, studying the snake for a sign that he understood, too.

John drove off in the pickup and returned within a few minutes, followed by Crane in his government tuck and Max Poor Bear in his jeep.

"Hello, ma'am." Crane said to Ellen Cypress. "The boy here says you've got a rattler bothering these children—is that so?"

"Yes," she said, holding back a smile. She pointed to the coiled snake.

"Good night!" Crane said. "Look at the size of him. Get back everybody!" He got his revolver from his truck and stood very importantly over the snake. Moses had moved away to the school's doorway and waited with his arms crossed, amused.

Crane started shooting with his .38 Special, and the snake made a half-hearted strike in his direction, falling just short of the man's leather boot. Crane yelled something at the rattlesnake and fired five more quick shots, two of which actually hit their target and finished it off.

"Sheeehew!" Crane said, wiping his forehead with the back of his revolver hand. "That was a bad one! Did you see how he came for me?"

He turned to the children and their teacher, then to John. But everybody was watching the dead rattlesnake, and none of them said a word.

Crane put his handgun away. He seemed a little shaken. "Good thing you came and got me," he called out to John. "That one there was deadly!"

"Thank you, Mr. Crane," John said.

"Don't mention it!"

The white man climbed into his truck, waved at everybody, and drove away.

Max Poor Bear put his arm around John's neck and pulled him to his side.

"Come with me tonight, cousin, and we'll kill four hundred frogs!"

"No thanks, Max."

"I'll split the cash with you."

"Where were you all this time, man?"

"Water under the bridge, little buddy. The important thing is, I'm out here now. I got you a taste of something nice, too." He tightened his arm around John's neck, bending him sharply over. "Whaddya say to that, huh?"

"Let me up, Max."

"You gonna come out with us and shoot deer tonight?"

"Just let me go, creep!"

"Hold it! Hold it right there, kid. You owe me money, and I'm offering you a chance to get even. Listen, that guy Crane? I know where those panthers like to lay up. I told him where to run his dogs in the morning, and he's gonna do it. Now, that'll set us up with the best deer drive you ever saw! Get me? He' gonna run everything in those thickets right out on top of us! And I know exactly where we need to be. You listenin', cuz?"

"You're chokin' me, man!"

Suddenly Max let him go. As John coughed and drew his fist, he saw that Max was paying no attention but was staring across the yard at Moses and the children.

"What's that?" Max asked. "What's he doin' now?"

Moses had draped the long broken body of the snake over the pine stump, and he was leading the children in a chanted apology to its shadow spirit and to the Sky Spirits of all rattlesnakes.

"Is he kidding?"

"No, 'course not, Max. He's teaching them."

Max watched in silence, rubbing his palms up and down on his jeans. All at once he pulled a can of beer from the tub of ice in his jeep, popped it open as loudly as he could, and drank with the foam pouring out over his hand. He climbed in and drove away without a word.

Susan Campbell Bartoletti

No Man's Land

Chapter One

All that remained of Miss Bessie was her head.

Thrasher Magee and his pap stood along the edge of the swamp. Miss Bessie's eyes were still open and surprised-looking.

Pap fingered his bushy growth of beard. "I'm right sorry to see that," he said. "She was a fine cow. Real good milker."

Fourteen-year-old Thrasher was sorry to see it, too. He liked squatting on the milking stool beside Miss Bessie, talking soft, while the cow stood sleepily, chewing cud.

Chum sniffed at the head and whined softly as Pop spat out a long stream of tobacco juice.

"Time we settle the score. Tomorrow we find where that gator holes up, and we get him. A man don't let something take away what's his." Pap's eyes bored into Thrasher's. "If he's man enough, that is."

Pap spat again, then started back to the path that led through the piney woods to their cabin. The golden glow of his torch danced like a firefly.

Thrasher knew it wasn't his business to condemn his own father, but under his breath he cussed him anyway. "I'm man enough," he added quietly. "Just you wait and see."

⚜

Early the next morning, Pap and Thrasher poled through the swamp. Thrasher guided the punt, and his forked pole made a flat, gurgly sound each time he pushed off against the swamp bottom.

They floated past white and yellow water lilies, huckleberry high-holders, thick beds of maiden cane and purple bladderwort, and then a telltale mound of branches. An alligator nest. Thrasher and Pap eyed the bank carefully, knowing a she-gator would charge if they came too close to her eggs.

Thrasher pushed the pole harder now. A short distance farther, they reached the bank where they'd found Miss Bessie's head the night before. Pap grunted and pointed a finger. "There, boy."

Along the bank, Thrasher noted the drag marks that led to a black pool surrounded by blue-flowered pickerelweed. A gator hole. He was ready to draw that gator out and hack its spine, the only way a swamper could be sure he had himself a dead gator. Pap would be bragging on Thrasher at the Frables' next cornhusking party.

Thrasher eased over to the bank, and Pap climbed out to pull the punt ashore. Still grasping the pole, Thrasher climbed out, then made his way to the edge of the black pool. He smacked his lips loudly, the call to bring up a gator.

Nothing.

Disappointed, he jabbed the pole into the hole, once, twice. Still nothing.

"Smack on that pole," said Pap. "That gator's hard-of-hearing."

Thrasher grasped the pole tighter. He stuck the pole end between his teeth and smacked some more. His hands tingled as the sound traveled down the pole, into the murky water.

This time, the gator floated soundlessly to the surface, with barely a ripple, and its filmy lids transformed into hard, gleaming black eyes.

Pap's eyes gleamed hard and black as the gator's. With his spear, he pierced the gator's side where the tough armor turned to soft belly. The gator hissed and slapped its head. Its tail lashed. Its jaws snapped, and it bellowed.

Thrasher pulled his knife from its sheath and raised it over his head. But before the knife could fall, another roar sounded from the rushes. Out charged a female gator. The she-gator hissed, and interest flickered in Pap's eyes, a sort of amusement that now they'd have two gators to reckon with.

Thrasher gripped his knife tighter, ready to kill the gator, to hack through its spine, to be a man, but his feet wouldn't move. He stood transfixed, his feet planted as if mired in mud.

Then the she-gator rammed Pap, pushing him into the water.

Thrasher wasn't sure how long it had taken him to start screaming. Vaguely, he remembered Baylor Frable and his daddy gathering him up, as if he were a sack of corn. They put him in the punt and carried him back to the cabin.

The next thing he knew, evening had come. He was sitting in a chair. M'am's yellow patchwork quilt lay in folds on his lap. His sisters Mabel and Rebecca sat across from him, their faces squinched in concern. Little Rosalie sat on Mabel's lap, and her head was cocked to one side, as if to get a closer look at him. Chum lay at his feet.

The reality of it cut deep inside Thrasher. He tried to remember one of the prayers M'am had taught him so long ago, but all he could think of was "Honor thy mother and father." The words formed a hard ball in his throat. He remembered how he had stood on the bank the night before and cussed his own father.

Somewhere outside the log cabin, a hog began to squeal, begging for its life from some unknown swamp creature. Pap's scream came to Thrasher, over and over again. He couldn't stop seeing Pap's eyes, full of disappointment.

Thrasher pressed his back against the slats of the wooden chair. The cabin air was suffocating him. He reached down to touch Chum. Chum licked his hand.

M'am put her hand on Thrasher's shoulder. At her touch, Thrasher lost all control. He didn't deserve her concern, her kindness. His tears came in great heaves.

"There, there." said M'am. She stood behind him. Her strong fingers kneaded his shoulders. "Sometimes it feels better out than in."

Thrasher gulped. He didn't feel better. He felt weak.

M'am stopped kneading. She stood in front of him now. She was a tiny woman, with russet hair and a sensible face. Her belly, large with child, pushed out the front of her dress. She pressed her hand against the small of her back. He could tell her back was paining her, but she never complained.

"You ready to see your pap?" she asked.

The words rattled Thrasher. See Pap? But Pap was dead.

Then he remembered how it was. Womenfolk always washed the body before the burial. He tried not to think of how Pap must look.

M'am patted Thrasher's hand, urging him to his feet. "Come along. But be quiet about it. A man in his chewed-up condition needs all the rest he can get."

Chewed-up? Rest? Thrasher's confusion grew.

M'am led him to the tiny lean-to bedroom and pushed the curtain aside. There, on the rush bed, lay Pap, his left leg enormous beneath a wad of bloody wrappings.

Thrasher blinked and tried to take everything in: Pap's wrapped leg. M'am's chair drawn close to the bed. A pan of red-tinged water. A needle and thread. The lines on Pap's face were smooth. He looked dead.

"Your pap's one lucky man," said M'am. "You both lucky them Frables come along when they did."

Thrasher started as he remembered—the gators, Baylor and his daddy, a crack of rifles, the thud of knives.

Pap's eyes barely opened. "That you, boy?"

"Yes, sir."

"Been waiting on you."

Thrasher felt a rush of panic. Waiting on him? No doubt to cuss him good and tell him how soft he was.

Pap's fingers motioned to Thrasher. "Come here, boy, so I can get a look at you."

Thrasher stood at the bedside. Even in the yellow light of the grease lamp, Pap's skin looked unnaturally white.

"I'll leave y'all be," said M'am quietly. "Just for a minute. Your pap's plumb wore out."

No, Thrasher wanted to cry out. Don't leave me. But M'am whisked past and into the outer room.

"You look sick, boy," said Pap. His words were strained.

"Sick" didn't near describe how Thrasher felt. It was far worse than sickness. Pap reached for him, but Thrasher flinched. He couldn't bear for Pap to touch him.

Thrasher licked his lips nervously. "You remember what all happened?"

Pap winced. "No. But you must've tried to . . . 'Course you—" There was a hopeful tone, a pause in Pap's voice, as if he were waiting for Thrasher to say something. His eyes closed.

He knows, thought Thrasher, and he struggled to find words to make everything all right. But he couldn't. He was grateful to M'am, who had returned to his side. "Let Pap be now. He needs his rest."

She guided him by the elbow to the outer room and looked sorry-eyed at him. "I reckon it's hard, seeing your pap tore up like that."

Does M'am know? He forced himself to look M'am square in the eye. Her face was puffy, her eyes red-rimmed.

'Course she does, he realized. M'am always had people sense. She understood the spaces between words. No shifty peddler could cheat her on a fair price for her beeswax or Pap's pelts.

"I—I got to go," he said. The words felt fuzzy. He took his knife off the wall and slipped it into its sheath at his waist. He slung his gun over his shoulder. He had to get away. Somewhere. Anywhere.

M'am reached for him, and for a second, he thought she was going to draw him close, the way she did when he was little. But she didn't. Instead, she pulled Pap's chair out from the table. "Set a spell," she said, holding on to the back of the chair. "Baylor left some bowfin that I'm going to fry up with pork and biscuits."

Any other day, Thrasher would have jumped at M'am's cooking. But today, this morning, he couldn't bring himself to sit in Pap's chair.

"I—I'm sorry, M'am," he said. "But I can't. I—I just can't." He didn't want her reading the spaces between his words.

He slid past her and out the door, not stopping until he reached the water's edge. He knelt and cupped his hand to make a little whirlpool to draw cooler water from some deep hole—the way Pap had taught him when Thrasher was a little boy.

His stomach growled, sassing him about M'am's pork and bowfin, but he saw himself in the water, and he knew: Ain't no place for me at Pap's table now.

Playwriting
& Screenwriting

Sam Zalutsky

SuperStore

INT SUV—LATE AFTERNOON

The SUV darts along a large highway, moving quickly to the outside lane.

The car quickly exits off the highway and onto a suburban road lined with strip malls and gas stations.

A cell phone RINGS inside the car.

JOAN
(O.S.)
Hi. Yes. About 20 minutes. Uh-huh. My clothes are all out, I just have to—.

INT CAR—CONTINUOUS

JOAN, 31, an attractive, conservatively-dressed woman, focuses on the road while talking. She pulls up to a stop light.

JOAN
Yes. It's all ready. A new slicker . . . No. It's falling apart.

She looks in the rearview mirror to see STACY, 7, her daughter, dressed in a prim blue dress and sucking a lollipop.

JOAN (cont'd)
(growing irritated)
No. It'll rain. She needs a new one. It's fine. Relax. We're already there. Fifteen minutes. Love you.

Joan turns back and holds out her phone.

JOAN (cont'd)
Say hi to Daddy.

STACEY
Hi Daddy!

Joan smiles and snaps the phone closed.

JOAN
Daddy's worried we'll miss our plane. But we have plenty of time.

Stacey nods enthusiastically.

JOAN (cont'd)
We want to look beautiful for Nonna and Poppa, don't we?

Stacey nods enthusiastically.

JOAN (cont'd)
Yellow would be really pretty, don't you think?

STACEY

Yes, Mommy.

EXT COSTCO PARKING LOT—MOMENTS LATER

Joan turns into an almost empty parking lot and pulls up to the looming Costco Superstore.

Joan opens the back door as Stacey jumps out. She aims the key chain. BEEP BEEP. Car secure.

Joan whips out a wet wipe from her purse, grabs Stacey's lollipop, and wipes her daughter's face.

STACEY

Mommy!

JOAN

Honey, we don't want to get any on your new slicker, do we?

Joan takes Stacey's hand, and walks her quickly towards the store, tossing the lollipop and wipe into the garbage.

INT COSTCO ENTRANCE—CONTINUOUS

A giant warehouse with floor to ceiling rows of merchandise.

Joan pulls Stacey by two teenage GIRLS looking at digital cameras. She pauses before proceeding down the wide center aisle towards the escalator.

INT TOP OF ESCALATOR—MOMENTS LATER

Joan and Stacey move up the escalator. At the top, a young clerk, 19, MARCO, waits to greet them. His slacks dragging on the floor. He is gorgeous and knows it.

MARCO

We're closing soon, ma'am.

JOAN

(dismissive)

Thank you. We'll be quick.

Joan strides energetically down a long aisle and towards the clothing area.

STACEY

Baaarbieee!

Stacey pulls away and sprints off, shouting with glee.

Joan sees Stacey duck behind a mountainous Barbie display.

MANAGER'S VOICE

(cheery)

Valued Costco customers, we will be closing in five minutes. Please bring your merchandise to the register at your earliest convenience.

As Joan stands there, Marco approaches.

MARCO

Ma'am, you need anything?

JOAN

(startled)

No, thank you. I'm fine.

MARCO

Let me know if you do. I'm Marco.

Joan dismisses him with a glare and strides off to retrieve Stacey.

MARCO (cont'd)

Thank you for shopping at Costco.

INT LARGE BARBIE DISPLAY—MOMENTS LATER

Joan walks around the Barbie display, almost running into a YOUNG GIRL, 8.

Stacey stares at the Girl, who is talking to herself and grabbing as many Barbies as she can. Joan sizes her up.

One shoelace is untied; the other knotted. The lace on the bottom of her dress is frayed. It's been restitched before.

GIRL

(sing song)

Puerto Rican Barbie. Paris Barbie. That hat's a beret. Last time, they had Arctic Barbie in a fur-lined parka, but I couldn't get her. Too expensive. Real fur my Mom told me.

JOAN

Stacey?

STACEY

(doesn't look away)

What Mommy?

GIRL

Wedding Barbie ooh. I love her dress.
Simple, yet elegant . . .

Joan steps around the Girl to Stacey.

JOAN

Honey, remember?

Stacey doesn't flinch, staring enviously at the boxes in the Girl's arms.

GIRL

Do you have that dress? My dad bought me Made-in-the-Shade Barbie and Surgery Barbie. Do you have Surgery Barbie?

Stacey barely turns her head "NO."

MANAGER'S VOICE

(enthusiastic)

Valued Costco customers, please proceed with your purchases to the cashier as we will be closing soon. Thank you for shopping at Costco.

JOAN

We're not buying Barbie's today. We've discussed this already. Let's go.

Joan impatiently looks around the store. An elderly couple steps on the escalator with a large cart.

Joan rests her hand on Stacey's shoulder, gently tugging.

Stacey moves towards the girl.

JOAN (cont'd)

(enthusiastically)

Stace, we need to help Daddy finish packing. Let's get your slicker . . . We can match.

The Girl reaches up and pulls another pink box off the shelf.

GIRL

I gotta get a new Mermaid Barbie too . . . I wouldn't be caught dead without her. My last one, her hair turned green from the chlorine. My mom says that's what happens to hair like that unless you wash it every day.

JOAN

Remember which one you want. We can put it on your birthday list.

STACEY

But Mommy, you said we had plenty of time.

JOAN

Yes, but—

The store is almost deserted. Joan looks around and sees a disheveled WOMAN, 48, pushing a cart to the escalator.

Two female CASHIERS, 19 and 22, walk past with their till drawers.

JOAN (cont'd)

Sweetheart, I think your mommy is leaving. Maybe you should go.

The Girl flips a look at the woman.

GIRL

(indignant)

That's not my mommy.

Joan checks back. The woman is gone. The Girl gives Stacey one of her Barbies.

Joan is startled by a FINGER tap on her shoulder: Marco.

MARCO

Ma'am, need some help? Were closin' in a few.

JOAN

We were just saying goodbye to our new friend.

GIRL

Great Date Ken. Oooh. I had Earring Magic Ken, but my brother flushed him down the toilet.

Joan grabs Stacey's hand and walks off towards the clothes area. Stacey tries to pull away.

STACEY

Let me go, Mommy.

JOAN

Don't you want a new slicker?

STACEY

Yes.

Joan's cell phone RINGS.

JOAN

Can you act like a lady?

STACEY

Yes.

It RINGS again. Joan stops at the table of jackets and fingers through them as she answers the phone.

JOAN

This will take two minutes . . .

(overly enthusiastic)
Hi. Almost done. I know! Yes! Ten minutes.
This is cute.

Joan holds up a pink rubber slicker to Stacey but NO STACEY. Joan is pissed.

MANAGER'S VOICE
(sincere)
Dear Valued Costco Customers, we are now closed. Please proceed to the nearest exit. Thank you for shopping at Costco.

JOAN
Stacey?

(back to phone)
No. Want to show her something . . . Oh, here she is. She's right here. See you soon. Love you.

She snaps the phone shut and looks down the aisle towards the Barbies. Still no Stacey, only Barbie boxes on the floor. She marches over with the slicker.

FOOTSTEPS shuffle off in the distance.

Joan hustles towards the sound. She tiptoes to the end of the aisle and cranes her neck around.

But it's Marco, restocking a shelf of food from a large cart. He eyes her quizzically, a seductive smile in his eyes.

Joan lets out a stale breath. She laughs, embarrassed.

JOAN (cont'd)

Have you seen my daughter?

MARCO

No, ma'am. We're closed now. Do you
want me to help find her?

MANAGER'S VOICE

(authoritative)

All Costco Colleagues please report
immediately to the office with your drawers
and cash out.

JOAN

(growing more anxious)

She was playing with the other little girl at
the Barbie display. You saw her, didn't
you? When we came in?

MARCO

No. I'm sorry, ma'am.

JOAN

I'll find her.

Joan walks away, her stride revealing her growing anxiety.

MARCO

(by rote)

Thank you for shopping at Costco.

JOAN

Stacey? Honey, we have to go.

The Cashiers laugh and compare their manicures as they walk down the aisle towards Joan.

JOAN (cont'd)

Have you seen my little girl? Golden hair?
A blue dress with lace?

CASHIERS

No ma'am. I'm sorry.

They walk away, quickly returning to their conversation.

Joan runs over and peers through a large aisle of food.

Two sets of little legs run down the aisle, their hands clenched together. Joan follows, hunched over.

She reaches the end of the aisle and peers down another long aisle. Nothing. Four little feet SCAMPER off behind her in the distance.

The overhead lights begin to shut off. Joan spins around.

JOAN

Stacey?! Come out now!

The sound of GIGGLING drifts towards her. She looks back at the Cashiers but they are gone.

JOAN (cont'd)

Daddy's waiting. Did you hear me?!

(more sweetly)

If you come out now we can go get ice cream. Stacey.

GIGGLES emerge from another direction. Joan strides towards the noise. The Cashiers emerge from behind a display of frozen food. Joan stops abruptly, still holding the jacket. They are taken aback by her harried look.

CASHIERS

Ma'am, did you want to buy that?

JOAN

Yes! . . . No!

Joan throws it at the cashiers, turns and runs back the other way. She is seriously panicked now. The cashiers give each other a look: Crazy.

JOAN (cont'd)

I need to find my daughter . . . I need to find my daughter . . . I need to find my daughter. Stacey, your friend can come with us if you want. We can get the Barbie. Is that what you want?

Joan runs up and down the aisles. Different CLERKS sweeping and arranging items watch her run by, stunned.

JOAN (cont'd)

(shouting)

Honey! Why are you doing this? Daddy will be very angry!

Joan turns and runs down another aisle, barrelling straight into the Manager, CONRAD, 40.

CONRAD

Ma'am. We're closed. Can I help you find something before you leave?

Joan falls back silent, stunned by his patronizing calm.

JOAN

Yes, my daughter. And you better help me find her or I'll sue you straight to Topeka.

The Manager is stunned as Joan takes off again on her search.

JOAN

Stacey?

Joan stops briefly and gets down real low. She looks all around and listens. The Manager runs up behind her and after a moment squats down next to her.

CONRAD

Where did you see—?

JOAN

SHHH!

Joan listens. Light GIGGLES float towards her and she takes off, crawling between the boxes of Spam. She finds a Barbie box ripped open on the floor as Conrad runs around the displays, trying to keep up.

When Marco walks by, Conrad subtly steers Marco away by the upper arm.

CONRAD

Did you see her daughter?

MARCO

I never saw her daughter. I didn't do anything!

Joan's head pops out from inside the aisle.

JOAN

Yes, he did. He saw her when we came in. He was looking at us.

Joan returns to crawling. Conrad holds onto Marco's shirt. Marco vigorously nods his head "No."

CONRAD

(whispering)

We could get in a lot of shit for this if you're wrong.

JOAN

(O.S.)

Stacey!

Marco hurries off towards the back while Conrad runs after Joan again.

He sees her crawling from afar. He runs the other way and cuts her off in an aisle.

CONRAD

Ma'am. This happens all the time. We have a procedure for this.

JOAN

You're right! You'd better find her.

CONRAD

Let's go check the security cameras. Please come with me.

Conrad offers Joan his hand to help her up.

Joan pushes his arm off abruptly and turns on him, getting right up in his face, about to tear into him again.

RING. She groans, frustrated. She opens her phone, still right in Conrad's face.

JOAN

(almost yelling)

Hi! No. Nothing! I'm not angry. Hiding! Who knows? Ten minutes. Love you too!

She shoves the phone back in her purse.

Marco wheels by a cart loaded with restock toys. Conrad shoots daggers at him to get out of sight.

INT CONRAD'S OFFICE—MOMENTS LATER

Conrad leads Joan to a seat facing a large window overlooking the main floor and a TV monitor showing additional aisles.

CONRAD

Here, please sit down.

Joan sits down, staring in disbelief. She watches as each clerk, including Marco, line up at the head of each row.

Conrad speaks into a PA microphone.

CONRAD (cont'd)

Ready? Begin search.

Joan watches the clerks walk up and down the row, glancing between the monitor and the large window, while Conrad mimics her frantic glances.

JOAN

Tell them to hurry up.

CONRAD

They are following procedure, ma'am.

JOAN

(over PA system)

Stacey! Where are you? Mommy needs to see you.

CONRAD

Ma'am, we'll find her. I promise. Just calm down.

JOAN

Don't patronize me! I am not some crazy woman who just wandered into your store.

Crying, Joan runs out, pushing Conrad out of the way.

INT END OF AISLE—MOMENTS LATER

Joan runs onto the floor and staggers down the aisle. She looks around and sees the vastness of the Superstore, dark and quiet.

She hesitates, overwhelmed, and falls into a vat of bras.

Her head falls into her hands and she cries.

INT FLOOR OF STORE—SAME TIME

Joan's SOBS can be heard throughout the store. Conrad and the cashiers each stop where they are and listen.

Marco walks up and watches awkwardly a few feet away.

Joan can feel his presence. She slowly looks up.

CONRAD
(O.S.)
I found her!

Marco is relieved. He walks over and offers her his hand.

Joan takes it and he pulls her up. She tries to control herself.

JOAN
Thank you.

MARCO
Somebody's in big trouble, huh?

JOAN

No. No. It's OK. It's OK.

Joan wipes her eyes and fixes her hair, calming herself down.

CONRAD

(O.S.)

Here she is. You sure scared us, sweetheart.

Marco leads Joan over to the Cashiers as Conrad walks around the corner. Joan takes one more deep breath and smiles big. She turns around and sees Conrad leading the GIRL, dressed in Stacey's blue dress, and dragging a Barbie behind her. She is surrounded by Conrad, the Cashiers, and Marco, who are all smiling. The Girl runs at Joan.

GIRL

Mommy! Mommy!

Joan can't believe her eyes.

CUT TO BLACK

Claudia Johnson

first commissioned and produced by Actor's Theatre of Louisville

PROPINQUITY

Characters

DALE

ROO

ALEXIS

MARSHALL

The action occurs on and around a university campus.

(Lights up. A dorm room.)

DALE: Roo?

ROO: *(Absorbed in a magazine.)* Hmm.

DALE: Should I tell her I love her?

ROO: Who?

DALE: My T.A. in English is the most beautiful, warm, sensitive woman in the entire world.

(ROO lets the centerfold drop.)

ROO: No, *that* is the most beautiful, warm, sensitive—

DALE: C'mon, Roo. You know about these things.

ROO: Tell her, tell her.

DALE: I can't.

ROO: Why?

DALE: She's living with someone else.

ROO: Who?

DALE: Your T.A. in English.

ROO: Mr. Marshall?

DALE: Miss Saunders and Mr. Marshall, living in sin. Imagine living in sin with her.

ROO: There's no such thing as sin. Only what feels bad and feels good.

DALE: She's too good for him. She doesn't treat undergraduates like dirt.

ROO: And you wonder, should you tell her you love her?

DALE: Right.

ROO: Tell her? Simply come out and say it?

(DALE nods.)

No no no no no no no. A picture speaks a thousand words.

DALE: I should send her a picture?

ROO: Yes, yes! Do like the perverts do!

DALE: What perverts?

ROO: In the library!

DALE: Look, Roo, I'm serious—

ROO: *(Overlapping.)* A girl in my comp class works as a stacker—

she's also stacked, but that's beside the point—she stacks books in the stacks and she sometimes finds a picture.

DALE: Of what?

ROO: Of the pervert! He leaves her these little surprises.

DALE: Just a picture?

ROO: Would a pervert send just a picture? No, he waits until his love is at its height, then he snaps a pic.

DALE: Isn't that illegal? How does he get it past the developer?

ROO: Polaroid, Dalebird, Polaroid!

DALE: Aw, no, man.

ROO: It happens, once, twice a week, and my friend slips the pic into a campus mail envelope and sends it to the head librarian.

DALE: No.

ROO: The librarian loves it!

DALE: Miss Saunders wouldn't.

ROO: And you are not a pervert.

(He returns to his magazine.)

DALE: Maybe I should tell her in the essay I got to write on Poe.

ROO: *House of Usher*?

(DALE nods.)

Listen, I got a great angle on the *House of Usher*.

(DALE looks at him. Lights fade down as they rise on ALEXIS' office. MARSHALL paces around with a batch of blue books in his hand.)

MARSHALL: How the hell do they expect us to write a dissertation with this crap coming at us all the time?

ALEX: It's not crap.

MARSHALL: They can't write! *(Reads one.)* "Edgar Allen Poe should've went to college." That boy should've went to the army!

ALEX: That's why they're taking your class.

MARSHALL: You can martyr yourself to the cause. Not me!

ALEX: Not I.

MARSHALL: It's a conspiracy, that's what it is. They got it all worked out so you have to teach their shit courses to get experience so you can go out and get a job teaching, but in order to get a job you have to write a dissertation which you've shelved so you can get teaching experience, so you hang around longer to finish the dissertation and since you're hanging around anyway, why not teach? That way they keep a cheap labor supply on hand and don't have to hire real faculty which further reduces the number of jobs for people like me who want to get out and teach.

(He sits, exhausted. ALEX strokes his hair.)

ALEX: Marshall . . .

MARSHALL: Do you realize we handle over six thousand students and English is a requirement? If we struck the whole place would go down the tubes!

ALEX: Why don't you strike?

MARSHALL: I don't have time. *(Beat.)* You know what grad school is like? Five or six years, they put your life on hold.

ALEX: If you'd just enjoy life. You're turning into a greasy grind—

MARSHALL: Fifty fucking essays on Poe!

ALEX: Marshall, forget the Ph.D. tonight. One night, that's all I ask. I'm an emotional camel. I can go for weeks on one night. We'll cook steaks, get all dolled up—

(DALE walks in, turns to go out.)

DALE: I'll come back.

ALEX: No, no. Come in, Mr. Bender.

MARSHALL: I was just leaving.

ALEX: Wait outside, we can start the party early.

MARSHALL: I got a book on three hour reserve.

ALEX: When will you be home?

MARSHALL: Three hours!

(He's gone.)

DALE: If I'm interrupting—

ALEX: No, you're not. Sit down, Mr. Bender.

DALE: Dale. Or I think you're talking to my father.

ALEX: All right, Dale.

DALE: You're sure I'm not interrupting.

ALEX: No.

DALE: No, you're not sure, or no, I'm not interrupting.

ALEX: The latter.

DALE: The latter. I like that. Guess all English teachers talk like that. The latter.

ALEX: Does my vocabulary disturb you?

DALE: Me? Oh, no. No. My God, no.

ALEX: Good. *(Beat.)* I wanted to discuss your last essay on *The Fall of the House of Usher*.

DALE: Like it?

ALEX: No, not really. Some of the points are well taken, but your argument that Poe's rich red décor was really vagina imagery—

DALE: Oh.

ALEX: —and what passed through it, sperm . . . It's what we call an extended metaphor.

DALE: *(Hopeful.)* Yes?

ALEX: I hate extended metaphors.

(Slight pause.)

DALE: Look, I know, it was high school, juvenile, not entirely my own idea, sex obsessive, and I love you.

(Pause.)

ALEX: The extended metaphor's not my complaint, really.

DALE: No?

ALEX: No. The essay has no climax.

(Beat. Lights down, up on MARSHALL in bathrobe. ALEX walks into the area brushing her hair.)

MARSHALL: What makes you say that?

ALEX: He told me.

MARSHALL: I love you? Flat out?

ALEX: At the end of a long sentence, remarks about himself.

MARSHALL: How terrific he is?

ALEX: He's very self-effacing. He admitted to being sophomoric, high-school, juvenile—

MARSHALL: Redundant.

ALEX: Yes. Anyway, I like him.

MARSHALL: And he told you he loved you. Amazing.

ALEX: It happens, Marshall. All over the world. People fall in love and they tell each other.

MARSHALL: Only one reason why he fell for you, why anyone falls for anyone else.

ALEX: What?

MARSHALL: Propinquity.

ALEX: Propinquity of natures?

MARSHALL: Just proximity. Animal contact.

ALEX: No sparks?

MARSHALL: Just those made by rubbing two bodies together.

ALEX: Marshall!

MARSHALL: It's true.

ALEX: Is this what you tell your students? That Romeo loved Juliet, Tristan loved Isolde, because of proximity? You'll ruin them forever.

MARSHALL: Think of the disappointments I spare them.

ALEX: I can hear it now, all over the world: *Propinquito, propinquitas, propinquita—*

MARSHALL: Aren't you going to ask about my job interview?

ALEX: —and what about Elizabeth Barret Browning? She loved Robert Browning long before she met him—What interview?

MARSHALL: Colorado. Where I've been the past two days.

ALEX: How was the interview, Marshall?

MARSHALL: They loved me.

ALEX: Enough to offer you the job?

MARSHALL: They said I'd be hearing—

ALEX: Standard put-off.

MARSHALL: —this week.

(Pause.)

ALEX: What happens to lovers when they lose their propinquity?

(Beat.)

MARSHALL: Share a shower?

(Lights down, up on office. DALE sits. ALEX walks in with a white rose in her hand.)

ALEX: Thank you for waiting, Dale.

DALE: Sure. No sweat.

(Pause.)

ALEX: Did you bring me this rose?

DALE: Me? No.

ALEX: Are you sure?

DALE: Yes, I'm sure. No, I did not bring you that rose, though I might possibly have been responsible for having it brought.

(Pause.)

ALEX: Dale, are you in love with me?

DALE: What makes you say that?

ALEX: You said you were.

DALE: Ah. Then I guess I am.

(Pause.)

ALEX: My roommate says people fall in love because of propinquity. Do you believe that?

(Beat.)

DALE: What's propinquity?

(Lights down, up on MARSHALL, a suitcase open nearby. ALEX walks in.)

MARSHALL: So, how'd it go?

ALEX: What?

MARSHALL: The session with Romeo. Still carrying the torch?

(She holds up the rose.)

A rose, no less.

ALEX: White, for virginity.

MARSHALL: I doubt he's a virgin.

ALEX: I doubt he has a long history of screwing around.

MARSHALL: I doubt he has a long anything.

(ALEX smiles, smells the rose.)

ALEX: He's sweet. Immature, but sweet.

(She sees the suitcase.)

What's all this?

MARSHALL: I got the call.

ALEX: The call?

MARSHALL: Colorado. They want me.

ALEX: I take it you're taking it.

MARSHALL: I start next week, first summer session.

ALEX: Congratulations.

MARSHALL: Thought I'd drive cross-country, get a first-hand look at the Midwest.

ALEX: It's flat. Until Boulder.

MARSHALL: Maybe you can come out at Christmas, learn to ski.

ALEX: I tried once. My face froze.

MARSHALL: You don't ski on your face.

ALEX: I do.

(Pause.)

MARSHALL: You know what I need?

(She looks hopeful.)

Shaving cream.

ALEX: I've got some in the bathroom.

(She goes. A knock. MARSHALL opens it. DALE stands there with a red rose in his hand.)

DALE: Hi.

MARSHALL: You must be Dale.

DALE: That's me. *(Beat.)* Is Miss Saunders around?

MARSHALL: She'll be right out.

(He shuts his suitcase.)

I'll be at the drugstore, if she asks.

(He picks up his suitcase and walks to the door.)

You know the trouble with you undergraduates? You're all in heat.

(He exits. Beat. ALEX enters with the shaving cream.)

DALE: Hi.

ALEX: Hello.

DALE: Mr. Marshall went to the drugstore.

ALEX: Ah.

(Pause.)

DALE: Does he always take his suitcase to the drugstore?

ALEX: No.

(Fights to maintain composure.)

Marshall is constantly surprising me.

(Pause.)

DALE: I, uh, brought this. Sort of an end-of-the-semester thing.

(He hands her the rose.)

And here's my essay, revised. Very ass-hole, but is has a climax, Miss Saunders. You won't believe the climax it has. (Beat.) I didn't write about House of Usher. I wrote about propinquity, what you said the other day in your office, about it being the cause of love. I hate to tell you this, Miss Saunders, because I like and respect you, but that's a crock, a real crock. Except possibly for meaning number three—I looked it up in the *Oxford English Dictionary*—which defines propinquity as an affinity of natures and not simple proximity—

(She takes his face in her hands and kisses him very lightly. Lights down, up on dorm room.)

ROO: Well?

DALE: Then I told her I'd brought my essay on propinquity—

ROO: What's that?

DALE: Proximity of bodies, but also of human nature, which is the catch—

ROO: Given the two . . .

DALE: See, Mr. Marshall holds simple proximity to be the cause of love, which is obviously false—

ROO: It helps.

DALE: —which is what I told her in my essay. Then—get this—she takes my face in her sweet hands and kisses me, very lightly, right on the lips.

(Pause.)

ROO: And?

DALE: And what?

ROO: That's *all*?

DALE: She kissed me. She changed my life! What do you want?

(He grabs a pillow, sits and hugs it.)

Lemme alone. I want to commune with my love.

ROO: If I'd been that close to her, my lips on hers, I'd've flung myself on top of her and made wild passionate love—

(He flings himself on the bed and kisses his pillow passionately. DALE gets up and walks to the door.)

DALE: You know the trouble with you undergraduates? You're all in heat.

(He exits. Blackout.)

Faculty Contributors

Dianne Aprile, a member of Spalding's creative nonfiction faculty, is the author of four books of nonfiction: *Making A Heart For God: A Week Inside a Catholic Monastery* (SkyLight Paths, 2000); *The Eye Is Not Enough: On Seeing and Remembering* (Trout Lily Press, 2000) with printmaker Mary Lou Hess; *The Abbey of Gethsemani: Place of Peace and Paradox* (Trout Lily Press, 1998), and *The Things We Don't Forget: Views from Real Life* (Trout Lily Press, 1994). While a columnist and staff writer for *The Courier-Journal*, she won the National Society of Newspaper Columnists' first-place award in 1996. Aprile also earned more than a dozen first-place regional awards from the Society of Professional Journalists in the areas of criticism, column-writing, and magazine writing. She shared a *Courier-Journal* staff Pulitzer Prize. The recipient of two Kentucky Arts Council fellowships, including the Al Smith Artist's Fellowship, and two Kentucky Foundation for Women grants (for fiction and nonfiction), she has taught creative writing and journalism workshops at Bellarmine University and Midway College. She and her work were featured on NPR's *Morning Edition* with Bob Edwards. Aprile is a 1971 graduate of the University of Louisville, where she earned a BA degree in English. She currently writes a book column, "Reading Matters," for *Louisville Magazine* and teaches writing workshops throughout the region. She is associate editor of the journal, *Monkscript: A Folio of Art, Literature and Spirituality.* Her work has been published in a number of regional anthologies and collections, including "A Kentucky Christmas," "Conversations with Kentucky Authors," and "Savory Memories," all published by University of Kentucky Press. In 2003, her writing was part of a collaborative show of text and visual art, "Silence as Sacred Text." She is the owner, with her husband, of a Louisville jazz club, The Jazz Factory. She is at work on a Louisville memoir.

SUSAN CAMPBELL BARTOLETTI, PhD, a member of Spalding's writing for children faculty, is the author of a dozen books. She holds a PhD in English from Binghamton University-State University of New York, where she won the Excellence in Research award. She has published award-winning nonfiction titles such as *Black Potatoes: The Story of the Great Irish Famine, 1845 to 1850* (Houghton Mifflin, 2005), *Growing Up in Coal Country* (Houghton Mifflin, 1999), and *Kids on Strike* (Houghton Mifflin, 1999); historical novels such as *No Man's Land, A Coal Miner's Bride*, and *The Journal of Finn Reardon, a Newsie* (Scholastic, 2003); and picture books such as *The Christmas Promise*, illustrated by David Christiana (Blue Sky/Scholastic, 2001), *Nobody's Nosier than a Cat*, illustrated by Beppe Giacobbe (Hyperion, 2003), and *The Flag Maker*, illustrated by Claire A. Nivola (Houghton Mifflin, 2004). Her dog is looking forward to *Nobody's Diggier than a Dog*, also illustrated by Beppe Giacobbe (Hyperion, 2004). Bartoletti's awards include the ALA Sibert Award for Most Distinguished Informational Book, the NCTE Orbis Pictus Award for Distinguished Nonfiction, the SCBWI Golden Kite Nonfiction Award, ALA Notable Children's Book, ALA Best Book for Young Adults, School Library Journal Best Book, Booklist Editors' Choice, among others. In 2001, she was named "Outstanding Pennsylvania Author." A former eighth-grade English teacher, she has also published numerous short stories, articles, and educational materials. She lives in Moscow, Pennsylvania, with her family.

JULIE BRICKMAN, a member of Spalding's fiction faculty, holds an MFA in Writing from Vermont College and a PhD in Psychology from the University of Manitoba. Her first novel, *What Birds Can Only Whisper*, was published in 1997 by Turnstone Press. She is currently working on two books: a memoir of her three months in the Yukon as writer-in-residence at Dawson City and a novel called *The Empty Quarter*, set in the Gulf Arabia. Her fiction and nonfiction have appeared in journals as diverse as *Fireweed, International Journal of Women's Studies*, *Kinesis*, *Canadian Psychology*, and *Canadian Dimension*. She has received two grants for fiction from the Canada Council for the Arts, and an early draft of her memoir was a finalist in the San Diego Book Awards. She reviews books for the *San Diego Union-Tribune* and writes full time. She lives in Laguna Beach, California.

Louella Bryant, a member of Spalding's fiction and writing for children faculty, is the author of two young-adult novels, both set in pre-Civil War times. *The Black Bonnet* (New England Press, 1996), about the underground railroad, was a finalist for the Vermont Book Award. *Father By Blood* (New England Press, 1999), which won the Silver Bay Children's Literature Award, depicts, through the eyes of his daughter, John Brown's weeks leading up to the famous raid on Harper's Ferry. Her picture book, *Two Tracks in the Snow*, was released in August 2004. She has won the Ralph Nading Hill Short Fiction Award, the Lyndon Institute Kingdom Award, and an award from Writers in the Park for a short story published in *Fine Print*. A short story recently appeared in *Hunger Mountain*, and an essay is included in the anthology *Far From Home*. Her poems have been published in *Byline*, *Fine Print*, and online magazines. She also has published numerous newspaper and magazine articles. Currently, Bryant has children's and nonfiction books in the works. She teaches creative writing at the University of Vermont, and is a fellow with the National Writing Project of Vermont. She has recently been appointed to the New

England Young Writers Conference at Bread Loaf. She holds a BA degree from George Washington University and an MFA in Writing from Vermont College. She makes frequent school visits to talk to children about writing.

RICHARD CECIL, a member of Spalding's poetry faculty, is the author of four collections of poetry: *Einstein's Brain* (Univ. of Utah Press, 1986); *Alcatraz*, winner of the 1991 Verna Emery Prize (Purdue Univ. Press, 1992); *In Search of the Great Dead* (Southern Illinois University Press, 1999); and *Twenty First Century Blues* (Southern Illinois Univ. Press, 2004). His poems have appeared in *American Poetry Review*, *Poetry*, *North American Review*, *American Scholar*, *Ploughshares*, *Crazyhorse*, *New England Review*, *Carolina Quarterly*, *Georgia Review*, *Virginia Quarterly Review*, *The Louisville Review* and other magazines. He has taught at the University of Louisville, Loch Haven University, Rhodes College, and, since 1989, at Indiana University, where he is Associate Professor in the Honors College. He holds the MFA from Indiana University.

MARY CLYDE, a member of Spalding's fiction faculty, has published a book of short stories, *Survival Rates* (University of Georgia Press, 1999 and Norton, 2001). She won the Flannery O'Connor Award for Short Fiction in 1997. Her stories have appeared in numerous publications including *American Literary Review*, *Boulevard*, *Quarterly West*, *The Georgia Review*, and *American Short Fiction*, and she has received several Pushcart Prize nominations. She is working on a novel, *A Thing So Small*. She lives in Phoenix, Arizona.

DEBRA KANG DEAN, a member of Spalding's poetry faculty, has published three collections of poetry: *Back to Back* (North Carolina Writers' Network, 1997), which won the Harperprints Poetry Chapbook

Competition, judged by Ruth Stone; *News of Home* (BOA, 1998), which was co-winner of the New England Poetry Club's Sheila Margaret Motton Award; and *Precipitates* (BOA, 2003). She is a contributing editor for *Tar River Poetry*. Her work has appeared in many journals and a number of anthologies, including *The Best American Poetry 1999*, *The New American Poets: A Bread Loaf Anthology*, *Urban Nature: Poems about Wildlife in the City*, and *Yobo: Korean American Writing in Hawai'i*.

Kathleen Driskell is Associate Program Director and a member of the Spalding poetry faculty. She has published a full-length book of poems, *Laughing Sickness* (Fleur-de-Lis Press, 1999), and *Place Gives Rise to Spirit: Writers on Louisville* (Fleur-de-Lis Press, 2001), an anthology she edited as a fundraising project for the Kentucky Writers' Coalition, a non-profit statewide writers' organization she helped to found in 1996. KWC, Inc., now has over 2,000 Kentucky writers, colleges and universities, libraries, writers' groups, bookstores and non-profit agencies in its network. Driskell has published poems nationally in literary magazines such as *The American Voice*, *The Louisville Review*, *GulfStream*, *Hayden's Ferry Review*, *New Millennium Writings*, *The Connecticut Review*, *The Greensboro Review*, and *Mid-American Review*. She received her MFA in Creative Writing from the University of North Carolina at Greensboro, where she was Poetry Editor of *The Greensboro Review*. She has won grants for her poetry and fiction from the Kentucky Arts Council and the Kentucky Foundation for Women and prizes from the Associated Writing Programs and Frankfort Arts Foundation. In 1998, Driskell was appointed to the Kentucky Arts Council's Poet Laureate Selection Committee. A past regular contributor to WFPL 89.3 FM, Louisville's NPR affiliate, she also coordinated the Community Journal Project for that radio station from 2002-03. She is Associate Editor of *The Louisville Review* and has taught creative writing and literature at Spalding University, the University of Louisville, Elon College, and the University of North Carolina at Greensboro, as well as for many writers workshops and conferences.

ROBERT FINCH, a member of the Spalding creative nonfiction faculty, holds degrees from Harvard College and Indiana University. He is co-editor of the Norton anthology *Nature Writing: The Tradition in English* and author of *Special Places: Exploring Conserved Landscapes on Cape Cod and the Islands* (Commonwealth Editions, 2003), *Death of a Hornet and Other Cape Cod Essays* (Counterpoint Press, 2001), and *Times They Will Come No More: Post-Historic Journeys Through Newfoundland* (forthcoming), among many other titles. His work has appeared in *Antaeus*, *The Georgia Review*, *National Geographic Traveler*, *ORION: Nature and People*, *Provincetown Arts*, *The New York Times*, *The Washington Post*, and other publications. He has taught at Williams College, Emerson College, Carleton College, Cape Cod Community College, Bread Loaf Writers Conference, and Cape Cod Writers Conference. He received the New England Booksellers Association Award for Nonfiction, 2001. He divides his time between Cape Cod and Newfoundland.

CONNIE MAY FOWLER, a member of Spalding's fiction, creative nonfiction, and screenwriting faculty, has published *Before Women Had Wings*, an Oprah Winfrey Presents Premiere Offering (for which Fowler wrote the screenplay) and winner of the 1996 Southern Book Critics Award (Putnam, 1996; Ballantine Paperback, 1997); *River of Hidden Dreams* (Putnam, 1994; Ballantine Paperback, 1995); *Sugar Cage* (Putnam, 1992; Washington Square Press Paperback, 1993); *Remembering Blue* (Doubleday, 2000; Ballantine Paperback, 2001); and *When Katie Wakes: A Memoir*, a Book of the Month Club featured selection (Doubleday, 2002). Her essays and stories have appeared in numerous places including *The New York Times Book Review*, *Southern Living*, *The Oxford American*, *Story*, *Southern Exposure*, and *Journal of Florida Literature*. She also wrote the songs for a musical adaptation of *Remembering Blue*. Her graduate degree in writing is from the University of Kansas. She holds the 2003 Bachelor Chair in Creative Writing at Rollins College (Florida). She has taught at the Seaside Writers Conference of Florida International University and the Suncoast Writers Conference of the University of South Florida.

Charles Gaines, a member of Spalding's creative nonfiction, fiction, and screenwriting faculty, is a professional journalist, novelist, essayist, and screenwriter and the author of twenty-three books, three of which were made into movies. His books include the bestselling novel *Stay Hungry*, finalist for the National Book Award (Doubleday, 1972); international bestseller *Pumping Iron* (Simon & Schuster, 1974); the biography *Yours in Perfect Manhood: Charles Atlas* (Simon & Schuster, 1982); and the creative nonfiction books *A Family Place: A Man Returns to the Center of His Life* (Grove/Atlantic Books, 1994) and *The Next Valley Over* (Crown, 1999). He has written for ABC's *American Sportsman* and is a founding member of the U.S. Fly Fishing Team. He has written a series of books for children and youth with Arnold Schwarzenegger called *Arnold's Fitness for Kids*. He has won two Cine Gold Eagle Awards and three Emmys for televison writing. His work has appeared in *Town and Country*, *Sports Illustrated*, *Harpers*, *Esquire*, *Architectural Digest*, *Men's Journal*, *GEO*, *Audubon*, *Sports Afield*, and many other magazines. He previously taught creative writing at New England College in New Hampshire and holds the MFA in Writing from the University of Iowa.

Kirby Gann, a member of Spalding's fiction faculty, is a native of Louisville, Kentucky. He is the author of *The Barbarian Parade* (Hill

Street Press, 2004) and *Our Napoleon in Rags* (Ig Publishing, 2005). With poet Kristin Herbert, he co-edited the anthology *A Fine Excess: Contemporary Literature at Play* (Sarabande Books, 2001), which was a finalist for the Book of the Year Award by *ForeWord Magazine*. He received his BA in English at Transylvania University in 1990 and his MFA in Writing from Vermont College at Norwich University in 1994. His fiction has received a Special Mention in the Pushcart Prize anthology and has appeared in *American Writing*, *Bananafish: Short Fiction*, *The Crescent Review*, *Morning Calm*, *Reveille*, *The Southern Indiana Review*, *Sun Dog: The Southeast Review*, *Witness*, and the *Best of Witness*. He has been awarded a residency fellowship from the Mary Anderson Center for the Arts and an Individual Artist grant from the Kentucky Arts Council. Gann is Managing Editor at Sarabande Books.

RICHARD GOODMAN, a member of Spalding's creative nonfiction faculty, is the author of *French Dirt: The Story of a Garden in the South of France* (Algonquin Books, 1991). He has written on a variety of subjects for many national publications, including *The New York Times*, *Creative Nonfiction*, *Commonweal*, *Vanity Fair*, *Garden Design*, *Grand Tour*, *salon.com*, *National Gardening*, *Saveur*, *Ascent*, *The New York Amsterdam News*, *OP Magazine*, and *The Michigan Quarterly Review*. He has twice been awarded a fellowship at the MacDowell Colony. He was awarded a fellowship at the Virginia Center for the Creative Arts in 2003. He created, wrote, and narrated a six-part series about New York City for Public Radio in Virginia. He contributed extensively to *The Mavens' Word of the Day Collection*, a book on words and word derivations published by Random House. He has taught creative writing in New York City for a number of years where he also works as a landscape gardener. Recently, he wrote the introduction for *Travelers' Tales Provence*, and his essay about Paris appears in the collection, *The Best Travelers' Tales 2004*.

ROY HOFFMAN, a member of Spalding's fiction and creative nonfiction faculty, is a novelist and journalist who has worked as a professional writer for over twenty-five years. He is the author of two novels: *Chicken Dreaming Corn* (University of Georgia Press, 2004) and *Almost Family* (Dial, 1983; University of Alabama Press reprint, 2000), winner of the Lillian Smith Award for fiction. *His Back Home: Journeys Through Mobile* (University of Alabama Press, 2001) is a collection of essays and narrative nonfiction published in *The New York Times*, *Newsday*, *Southern Living*, *Preservation*, and *The Mobile Register*. A native of Mobile who now resides in Fairhope, Alabama, he lived in New York City for twenty years where he wrote articles and reviews for numerous publications, penned speeches for the president of NYU and the governor and first lady of New York, and taught workshops at NYU's School of Professional Studies. Now an award-winning staff writer for his hometown paper, *The Mobile Register*, with a special interest in the diverse cultures of the South, He also continues to contribute elsewhere. His *New York Times* essay, "My Own Private New York," was a notable essay of the year in *Best American Essays 2003*. He appeared on CNN's *Moneyline* to discuss a photo-essay he created and wrote the text for in 2000 for *Fortune* magazine: "Working Past 90," about ninety-year olds in the workforce. His essay "On Keeping a Journal," a "My Turn" column for *Newsweek on Campus*, is in the *Prentice-Hall Handbook for College Writers*. His essay from *Preservation* magazine, "On the Dock of the Bay," is anthologized in *A Certain Somewhere: Writers On the Places They Remember* (Random House, 2002). His young adult story, "Ice Cream Man," is in *Working Days: Short Stories About Teenagers at Work* (Persea, 1997). A portrait of Hoffman on a Mobile Bay dock is in Bill Aron's photo book, *Shalom Y'all: Images of American Life in the Jewish South* (Algonquin, 2002).

SILAS HOUSE, a member of Spalding's fiction faculty, is the author of *Clay's Quilt* (Algonquin, 2001; Random House, 2002), the national bestseller *A Parchment of Leaves* (Algonquin, 2002; Random House, 2003), and *The Coal Tattoo* (Algonquin, 2004). His work has been honored by the Fellowship of Southern Writers and the National Society of Arts and Letters. He is the winner of the Kentucky Literary Award for Best Novel, the Chaffin Award for Literature, two ForeWord Magazine Bronze Awards for best literary novel, and many other prizes, including nominations for the Southern Book Critics Circle Prize and the William Sayoran International Prize for Literature. His work has been widely anthologized in such collections as *New Stories from the South, The Year's Best: 2004*, and *Stories From the Blue Moon Café*, as well as in publications such as *Newsday*, *Night Train*, *Bayou*, *The Southeast Review*, and *The Beloit Fiction Journal*. In 2004 he was nominated for two Pushcart Prizes. He serves as a contributing editor for *No Depression* magazine where he has written features on such artists as Delbert McClinton, Kelly Willis, Hank Williams III, and others. He is also one of Nashville's most in-demand press kit writers, having written the publicity bios for such singers as Lee Ann Womack, Lucinda Williams, and Tim O'Brien. His short fiction is frequently featured on NPR's *All Things Considered* where he is a contributor. A graduate of the MFA program at Spalding, House also serves as Associate Professor in Creative Writing at Eastern Kentucky University.

CLAUDIA JOHNSON, a member of Spalding's playwriting and acreen-writing faculty, is the author of numerous plays, including the one-act comedy, *Propinquity,* commissioned by Actors Theatre of Louisville and produced in its Humana Festival of New American Plays. *Propinquity* and a second one-act, *Paternity*, were produced by the Source Theater in Washington, D.C., and the Provincetown Playhouse in New York. A short drama, *Corsage*, was a finalist in the Actors

Theatre of Louisville's National Ten-Minute Play Contest. Her full-length plays include *Hard Up*, which received the Lorraine Hansberry Playwriting Award and the American National Theater and Academy West Award; *Aspirations*, which received the Warner Brothers Screenwriting Award; and *Y* (originally commissioned as a one-act by Actors Theatre of Louisville), which won the Maud Adams Playwriting Award and was widely produced and staged as a reading by the W.P.A. Theater in New York. Two of her screenplays, *Obscenity* and *Psycho Bitch* (written with Matt Stevens), were finalists for the Sundance Screenwriters Lab, and *Winterfort* (written with Pam Ball) won the Florida Screenwriters Award. She is the author of two screenwriting books, *Crafting Short Screenplays That Connect* (Focal Press, 2000; 2nd edition, January 2005), adopted by film schools nationwide, and the first book about collaborative screenwriting, *Script Partners: What Makes Film and TV Writing Teams Work* (co-written with Stevens; Michael Wiese Productions, 2003). Her memoir, *Stifled Laughter: One Woman's Story About Fighting Censorship* (Fulcrum Publishing, 1994), was nominated for the Pulitzer Prize and optioned for film. For her "ongoing and extraordinary efforts" to restore literary classics to the classrooms of rural North Florida, she received the inaugural P.E.N./Newman's Own First Amendment Award. A literary advisor for the *Exxon/Mobil Masterpiece Theater: The American Collection,* she was a member of the founding faculty of Florida State University's School of Motion Picture, Television and Recording Arts, where she taught for more than a decade. She is currently writing a stage adaptation of her new memoir, *Taking Ross to Texas: A Mother-Son Road Trip.*

ROBIN LIPPINCOTT, a member of Spalding's fiction faculty, has published *Our Arcadia*, a novel (Viking, 2001; Penguin, 2002), *Mr. Dalloway*, a novella (Sarabande Books, 1999—now in its third printing), and *The Real, True Angel*, a collection of short stories (Fleur-de-Lis Press, 1996). His fiction has received nominations for the Pushcart Prize, the IMPAC Dublin Literary Award, the American Library Association Roundtable Award, the Independent Book Award, and the Lambda Literary Award. He has won six fellowships to Yaddo and a fellowship to the MacDowell Colony. His fiction and nonfiction have also appeared in *The Paris Review, Fence, The New York Times Book Review, The Literary Review, The American Voice, Provincetown Arts, The Louisville Review, The Bloomsbury Review,* and many other journals as well as several anthologies. In addition to teaching in Spalding's brief-residency MFA Writing Program, he also teaches at Harvard's Extension School. He lives in Cambridge, Massachusetts.

MAUREEN MOREHEAD, a member of Spalding's poetry faculty, has published three books of poetry: *In a Yellow Room* (Sulgrave Press, 1990), *Our Brothers' War* (Sulgrave Press, 1993), and *A Sense of Time Left* (Larkspur Press, 2003). Her poems have appeared in *America*, *The American Poetry Review*, *The American Voice*, *Black Warrior Review*, *The California Quarterly*, *The Greensboro Review*, *The Iowa Review, The Louisville Review*, *Poet and Critic*, *Poetry*, and other literary magazines. She is featured in *Conversations with Kentucky Writers II* and *Kentucky Voices: A Bicentennial Celebration of Writing*. She has won fellowships for her poetry from the Kentucky Arts Council and the Kentucky Foundation for Women. Early in her career, she was selected to the Bluegrass Poetry Circuit, a competition judged by Robert Penn Warren. She has taught at Western Kentucky University, the University of Louisville, and for the Jefferson County Public Schools in Louisville. For several years, she served on the faculty of the Kentucky Institute for the Arts in Education, a program designed to help educators integrate the arts into their curricula. She earned a PhD in English, with creative thesis, from the University of Louisville in 1986.

Sena Jeter Naslund is Program Director of Spalding University's brief-residency Master of Fine Arts in Writing Program. She is the author of four novels, T*he Animal Way to Love* (Ampersand, 1993), *Sherlock in Love* (Godine, 1993 and Harper Perennial, 2001), *Ahab's Wife; Or, the Star-Gazer* (Morrow, 1999 and Harper Perennial, 2000), and *Four Spirits* (Morrow-HarperCollins, September 2003 and Harper Perennial, 2004) and two short story collections, *Ice Skating at the North Pole* (Ampersand, 1989) and *The Disobedience of Water* (Godine, 1999 and Harper Perennial, 2000). *Ahab's Wife*, a Book-of-the-Month Club Main Selection and national bestseller, was selected by *Time* magazine as one of the five best novels of 1999 and was shortlisted for the United Kingdom's Orange Prize. *Ahab's Wife* appeared on the notable book lists of the *New York Review of Books* and of *Publishers Weekly*. *Four Spirits*, a national bestseller, appeared on the notable book lists of *The New York Review of Books*, the *Los Angeles Times*, *The Seattle Times*, and the Louisville *Courier-Journal*. Sena holds the MA and PhD from the University of Iowa and has taught in the MFA programs of the University of Montana, Indiana University, and Vermont College. She is currently Distinguished Teaching Professor at the University of Louisville. Her short fiction has appeared in *The Paris Review, The Georgia Review, The Iowa Review, The American Voice, The Michigan Quarterly Review*, and other journals. She has received grants from the NEA, the Kentucky Arts Council, and the Kentucky Foundation for Women, as well as the Lawrence Fiction Prize, the Heasley Prize, and the Hall-Waters Award.

Elaine Neil Orr, a member of Spalding's creative nonfiction faculty, is the author of the memoir *Gods of Noonday: A White Girl's African Life* (University of Virginia Press, 2003), which was distinguished as one of the top ten university press books of 2003. As a literary critic, she has also published *Subject to Negotiation: Reading Feminist*

Criticism and American Women's Fictions (University of Virginia Press, 1997) and *Tillie Olsen and a Feminist Spiritual Vision* (University of Mississippi Press, 1987). She has won grants and awards from the National Endowment for the Humanities, the North Carolina Arts Council, and the Virginia Center for the Creative Arts. Her poems and essays have appeared in *The Missouri Review*, *Southern Cultures*, *American Literature*, *Journal of Narrative Technique*, *Kalliope*, *Cold Mountain Review*, *Signs*, *Modern Language Quarterly*, and *South Atlantic Review*. She holds a PhD in Literature and Theology from Emory University and is an award-winning Professor of Literature at North Carolina State University in Raleigh. The daughter of Baptist medical missionaries, she was born and spent her youth in Nigeria. She is at work on *Searching for Lurana*, a mixed-genre book about the life of a nineteenth-century missionary in that country.

GREG PAPE, a member of Spalding's poetry faculty, is the author of eight books of poetry: *Little America* (Maguey Press, 1976); *The Morning Horse* (Confluence Press, 1991); *Border Crossings* (University of Pittsburgh Press, 1978; Carnegie Mellon Classics Contemporary Series, 2005); *Black Branches* (University of Pittsburgh Press, 1984); *Storm Pattern* (University of Pittsburgh Press, 1992); *Sunflower Facing the Sun: Poems* (University of Iowa, 1992), winner of the Edwin Ford Piper Poetry Award; *Small Pleasures* (Lagniappe Press, 1994), and *American Flamingo* (Southern Illinois University Press, spring 2005), winner of the Crab Orchard Award Series in Poetry. He holds the MFA from the University of Arizona and was the Bingham Poet-in-Residence at the University of Louisville. Pape has also taught at Hollins College, Northern Arizona University, Florida International University, University of Alabama, and University of Missouri-Columbia; he is currently on the faculty of the MFA program of the University of Montana. He has been awarded two NEA fellowships, the

YMHA/The Nation Discovery Award, the Robert Frost Fellowship at Bread Loaf, two Fine Arts Work Center fellowships at Provincetown, the Richard Hugo Memorial Award from *Cutbank* and was included in *Pushcart Prize XIII.*

MOLLY PEACOCK, a member of Spalding's poetry and creative nonfiction faculty, is Poet-in-Residence at the Cathedral of St. John the Divine and one of the creators of Poetry in Motion™ on New York City's subways and buses. Her most recent book is *Cornucopia: New and Collected Poems* (Norton, 2002). Molly's other books include *How To Read A Poem & Start A Poetry Circle* (Riverhead, 2000), four other collections of poems, and a memoir, *Paradise, Piece By Piece* (Riverhead, 1998). She is also the editor of *The Private I: Privacy in a Public Age* (Graywolf, 2001) and co-editor of *Poetry in Motion: 100 Poems from the Subways and Buses*. Her articles have appeared in *Elle*, *O the Oprah Magazine*, *Mirabella*, *New York Magazine*, and *House & Garden*. She has been visiting poet at numerous colleges and universities, including Bennington and Bucknell. Peacock has been a Danforth, Ingram Merrill, and Woodrow Wilson Foundation Fellow. Her poems have appeared in *The New Yorker*, *The Nation*, *The New Republic*, *The Paris Review*, and other leading literary journals. She is a former president of the Poetry Society of America.

MELISSA PRITCHARD, a member of Spalding's fiction faculty, is Professor of English and Women's Studies at Arizona State University. Previous publications include three collections of stories: *Spirit Seizures* (The University of Georgia Press, 1987 and Collier Macmillan, 1989), *The Instinct for Bliss* (Zoland Books, 1995, 1997), and *Disappearing Ingenue* (Doubleday/Vintage, 2002), and three novels, *Late Bloomer* (Doubleday, 2004), *Phoenix* (Cane Hill Press, 1991), and *Selene of the Spirits* (Ontario Review Press, 1998). Her work has appeared in over sixty journals, including *The Paris Review, The Southern Review, Story, Open City,* and *Boulevard.* Stories have been reprinted in numerous college textbooks and anthologies, including *Prize Stories: the O. Henry Awards*, *Pushcart Prize*, *Best of the West*, and *American Gothic Tales*. She received a BA in Comparative Religions from the University of California at Santa Barbara and the MFA in Writing from Vermont College. She has won the Flannery O'Connor Award, the Carl Sandburg Award, the James Phelan Award, the Janet Heidinger Kafka Prize, and an honorary citation from the PEN/Nelson Algren Award. She has also been awarded a National Endowment for the Arts Fellowship, a Howard Foundation Fellowship from Brown University, a YMCA Writer-in-Residence Fellowship, and the Ortese Memorial Lecture Prize in North American Literature from the University of Florence, Italy.

JEANIE THOMPSON, a member of Spalding's poetry faculty, has published three collections of poetry: *White for Harvest: New and Selected Poems* (River City Publishing, 2001), *Witness* (Black Belt Press, 1995), and *How To Enter the River* (Holy Cow! Press, 1985) and three chapbooks. *Witness* won a Benjamin Franklin Award from the Publishers Marketing Association in 1996. Her poems, interviews with writers, and critical articles have appeared in numerous literary journals including *Antaeus, Crazyhorse, Ironwood, North American Review, New England Review,* and *Southern Review*. She holds the MFA from the University of Alabama, where she was founding editor of the literary journal *Black Warrior Review.* She has taught at the University of New Orleans, the New Orleans Center for the Creative Arts, and St. Martin's Protestant Episcopal School, as well as in the poetry-in-the-schools program in New Orleans and in Alabama. Thompson has received Individual Artist Fellowships in Literature from the Louisiana State Arts Council and the Alabama State Council on the Arts, and was a

Walter Dakin Fellow at the Sewanee Writers Conference 2000. Thompson and co-editor Jay Lamar edited a collection of essays, *The Remembered Gate: Memoirs by Alabama Writers* (University of Alabama Press, 2002). Since 1994, she has directed the Alabama Writers' Forum, a statewide literary arts organization in Montgomery, Alabama.

Neela Vaswani, a member of Spalding's fiction faculty, is the author of *Where the Long Grass Bends*, a collection of stories published by Sarabande Books in 2004. Her fiction has appeared in numerous journals—among them *Prairie Schooner, Shenandoah, Epoch,* and *American Literary Review*—and has been nominated for Pushcart, Best New American Voices in Fiction, and Scribner prizes. In 1999, she was awarded the Italo Calvino Prize for Emerging Writers. She has taught fiction and creative nonfiction workshops, and studied poetry at the New York State Summer Writer's Institute. She is a doctoral candidate in Cultural Studies at the University of Maryland; her self-reflexive ethnographic research on biracial identity has been highlighted at academic conferences and panels; in 2002, she received a CHASA prize for her scholarly work.

Luke Wallin, a member of Spalding's fiction, creative nonfiction, and writing for children faculty, is Professor of English at the University of Massachusetts Dartmouth, where he teaches in the MA in Professional Writing program. He holds an MFA in Fiction Writing from the University of Iowa, as well as graduate degrees in philosophy and regional planning. His award-winning young-adult novels include *Ceremony of the Panther* (Bradbury Press, 1987), recorded for the blind by the Library of Congress, *In the Shadow of the Wind* (Bradbury Press, 1987), recommended by the Committee on U.S. History Standards for the period 1800-1850, and chosen a Best Book by the New York Public

Library, *The Redneck Poacher's Son* (Bradbury Press, 1981), an American Library Association Best Book, *The Slavery Ghosts* (Bradbury Press, 1983), and *Blue Wings* (Bradbury Press, 1982). His science fiction, *The Bestiary Trilogy* (Bradbury Pressm 1985-1988), under the pseudonym of John Forrester, was translated into Danish. In 1999 Kluwer published a nonfiction anthology, *Nature and Identity in Cross-cultural Perspective*, co-edited with Irish geographer Ann Buttimer. In 1997, he won a Fulbright Fellowship to teach at University College Dublin. Wallin's CD of folk/blues music, his CDs of songs for children, and his memoir CD, *Confessions of a Teenage Bobcat Trapper*, are available at CDBABY.com.

MARY YUKARI WATERS, a member of Spalding's fiction faculty, has been anthologized in *The Best American Short Stories 2002, 2003,* and *2004; The O. Henry Prize Stories; The Pushcart Prize*; Francis Ford Coppola's *Zoetrope Anthology 2*; and *The Pushcart Book of Short Stories: The Best Stories from a Quarter-Century of the Pushcart Prize.* She is the recipient of a grant from the National Endowment for the Arts, and her fiction has aired in NPR's *Selected Shorts*. Her debut collection, *The Laws of Evening* (Scribner, 2003), was a Booksense 76 selection and a selection for Barnes & Noble's Discover Great New Writers program. It was also selected as a Kiriyama Prize Notable Book. *Newsday* and *The San Francisco Chronicle* chose *The Laws of Evening* as one of the Best Books of 2003. She received her MFA from the University of California at Irvine and lives in Los Angeles.

BRAD WATSON, a member of Spalding's fiction faculty, is the author of *The Heaven of Mercury* (Norton, 2002, 2003), which won the Mississippi Institute of Arts and Letters Award in Fiction, the Southern Book Award in Fiction from the Southern Critics Books Circle, and was a top ten pick in the BookSense 76 list, was a finalist for the

National Book Award. *The Heaven of Mercury* was an alternate selection of the Book of the Month Club, and on the BookSense bestseller list as a paperback. His first book, *Last Days of the Dog-Men* (Norton, 1996; Dell Paperback, 1997; Norton Paperback, 2003), won the Sue Kaufman Prize for First Fiction from the American Academy of Arts and Letters, the Great Lakes Colleges Association New Writers Award and was selected as a *New York Times Book Review* Notable Book. His stories and essays have been published in *The Norton Introduction to Literature, Story Magazine, The Oxford American, The Black Warrior Review, Greensboro Review,* and *Best American Mystery Stories*. Watson served as Briggs-Copeland Lecturer in Fiction at Harvard University, and was Director of Creative Writing at Harvard from 1999 to 2002. He has also taught at the University of Alabama, and was Writer-in-Residence at the University of West Florida.

Crystal Wilkinson, a member of Spalding's fiction faculty, is the author of *Water Street* (Toby Press, 2002), which was a long list nomination for the Orange Prize and a finalist for the Zora Neal Hurston/Richard Wright Foundation's Legacy Award in Fiction, and *Blackberries, Blackberries* (Toby Press, 2000), which was named Best Debut Fiction by *Today's Librarian Magazine*. Wilkinson is an assistant professor at Indiana University-Bloomington. She is the 2002 recipient of the Chaffin Award for Appalachian Literature and is a member of a Lexington-based writing collective, The Affrilachian Poets. She has presented workshops and readings throughout the country including the Sixth International Conference on the Short Story in English at the University of Iowa and the African American Women Writers Conference at the University of the District of Columbia. She has been published in the following anthologies *Confronting Appalachian Stereotypes: Back Talk from an American Region* (University of Kentucky Press, 1999); *Gifts From Our Grandmothers*

(Crown Publishers, a Division of Random House, May 2000); *Eclipsing A Nappy New Millennium* (Purdue University, 1998); *Home and Beyond: A Half-Century of Short Stories by Kentucky Writers* (University of Kentucky Press, 2001); and *Gumbo: A Celebration of African American Writing* (Harlem Moon Press, 2002). Her work has also appeared in various literary journals including: *Obsidian II: Black Literature in Review, Southern Exposure, The Briar Cliff Review, LIT, Calyx, African Voices,* and the *Indiana Review.* She is the former creative writing chair of the Kentucky Governor's School for the Arts and former assistant director of The Carnegie Center for Literacy and Learning. She has recently served as Writer-in-Residence at several Appalachian colleges. Wilkinson is a graduate of Spalding's MFA Program.

SAM ZALUTSKY, a member of Spalding's screenwriting faculty, is an award-winning writer/director whose short films "Smear" and "Stefan's Silver Bell" have screened at numerous American and international festivals. "Smear" aired on the Independent Film Channel from 2000 until 2003 and is currently distributed on the DVD/Video collection, "Boys Briefs"; "Stefan's Silver Bell" was nominated for New York University's highest award, the Wasserman, and won awards for cinematography, producing, and acting (twice), as well as several production grants. It recently aired on New York Channel Thirteen's *Reel New York* showcase of independent film. His feature screenplay, "Mama's Boy," is currently in development, and he recently completed a new short, "SuperStore," starring Clea Lewis (ABC's *Ellen*; Woody Allen's "Writer's Block") and Miryam Coppersmith (*The Sopranos*—Fifth Season). He also teaches a weekly screenwriting workshop at the Makor/Steinhardt Center of the 92 Street Y in New York and previously has taught English in the People's Republic of China and Mexico. He is the co-creator/co-star of the hit cable access show, "Holding

Court," about women's professional tennis. He received his BA in studio art from Yale University and his MFA in film from New York University's Tisch School of the Arts.

Permissions

POETRY

"Lament for the Makers," by Richard Cecil. First published in *American Poetry Review*. Reprinted by permission of the author.

"Twenty First Century Blues," by Richard Cecil. First published in *Crazy Horse*. Reprinted by permission of the author.

"Beads," "Peeling an Onion," and "Lights, Please" by Debra Kang Dean. Copyright © 2005 by Debra Kang Dean. Used by permission of the author.

"Nativity," by Kathleen Driskell. First published in *The Licking River Review*. Reprinted from *Laughing Sickness*. Copyright © 1999 by Kathleen Driskell. Used by permission of Fleur-de-Lis Press and the author.

"Leaving the Argument," by Kathleen Driskell. First published in *Mid-American Review*. Copyright © 1999 by Kathleen Driskell. Reprinted from *Laughing Sickness* with permission by Fleur-de-Lis Press and the author.

"Why I Mother You the Way I Do," by Kathleen Driskell. First published in *New Millennium Writings*. Copyright © 2004 by Kathleen Driskell. Reprinted with permission of the author.

"To the Outdoor Wedding," by Kathleen Driskell. First published in *The Southern Review*. Copyright © 2005 by Kathleen Driskell Reprinted by permission of the author.

"Fog," by Greg Pape. First published in *The Atlantic Monthly*. Reprinted by permission of the author.

"Some Guardian Spirit," by Greg Pape. First published in *Black Warrior Review* and *Mid-American Review*. Reprinted by permission of the author.

"Celtic Lady Sex Gargoyle on Medieval Lintel" by Molly Peacock. First published in *Black Warrior Review*. Reprinted by permission of the author.

"Of Night," by Molly Peacock. First published in *Boulevard*. Reprinted by permission of the author.

"Artichoke Hearts," by Molly Peacock. First published in *Black Warrior Review*. Reprinted by permission of the author.

"The Flaw," by Molly Peacock. Copyright © 2005 by Molly Peacock. Used by permission of the author.

"How to Enter the River," by Jeanie Thompson. First published in *White for Harvest: New and Selected Poems* by River City Publishing. Copyright © 2000. Reprinted by permission of the author.

"The Lyrical Trees," by Jeanie Thompson. First published in *White for Harvest: New and Selected Poems* by River City Publishing. Copyright © 2000. Reprinted by permission of the author.

"True Course" and "Poem at Fifty" originally appeared in the online journal *thicket* (www.athicket.com), a publication of the Alabama Center for the Literary Arts at Alabama Southern Community College. Reprinted by permission of the author.

"Fire," "What Makes Things Move," "The Window," and "The Interview" by Maureen Morehead. Used by permission of the author and Larkspur Press.

FICTION

"Uncharted Territory," by Louella Bryant. First published in *Fine Print*. Copyright © 1999 by Louella Bryant. Reprinted by permission of the author.

"Krista Had a Treble Clef Rose" by Mary Clyde. First published in *Boulevard*. Copyright ©1999 by Mary Clyde. Reprinted from the collection *Survival Rates* by permission of the author.

"The Problem with Murmur Lee" by Connie May Fowler. Copyright © 2005 by Connie May Fowler. Reprinted by permission of the author.

"Saints" by Silas House. First appeared in *Journal of Kentucky Studies* (Northern Kentucky University). Copyright © 2003 by Silas House.

"The Land of Cotton" by Roy Hoffman. Reprinted from the novel *Chicken Dreaming Corn*. Copyright © 2004 by Roy Hoffman. Used by permission of University of Georgia Press.

"The 'I' Rejected" by Robin Lippincott. First published in *Crosscurrents*. Copyright ©1996 by Robin Lippincott. Reprinted from the collection *The Real, True Angel* by permission of the author.

"Helicon, September 15, 1963" by Sena Jeter Naslund. From the novel *Four Spirits*. Copyright © 2002 by Sena Jeter Naslund. Used by permission of William Morrow, an imprint of HarperCollins Publishers.

"Port de Bras" by Melissa Pritchard. Reprinted from the collection *Disappearing Ingenue* by Melissa Pritchard, copyright © 2002 by Melissa Pritchard. Used by permission of Doubleday, a division of Random House, Inc.

"The Pelvis Series" by Neela Vaswani. Reprinted from *Where the Long Grass Bends* by Neela Vaswani, published by Sarabande Books, Inc. Copyright © 2004 by Neela Vaswani. Reprinted by permission of Sarabande Books and the author.

"Collecting Butterfish" by Luke Wallin. First published in *The Louisville Review*. Copyright © 1996 by Luke Wallin. Reprinted by permission of the author.

"The Way Love Works" by Mary Yukari Waters. Copyright © by Mary Yukari Waters. Reprinted from the collection *The Laws of Evening* by permission of Simon and Schuster, Inc.

"Bill," from *Last Days of the Dog-Men: Stories* by Brad Watson. Copyright © 1996 by Brad Watson. Used by permission of W.W. Norton & Company, Inc.

"The Fight" by Crystal Wilkinson. © 2005 by Crystal Wilkinson. Used by permission of the author.

Creative Nonfiction

"The Eye is Not Enough," by Dianne Aprile. First published in *The Eye is Not Enough: On Seeing and Remembering* by Trout Lily Press. Copyright © 2000 by Dianne Aprile. Reprinted by permission of the author.

"Sometimes I Live in Town," by Robert Finch. First published in the collection *Death of a Hornet* by Counterpoint. Copyright © 2000 by Robert Finch. Reprinted by permission of the Perseus Book Group.

"Wendell Berry Profile & Interview," by Charles Gaines. Copyright © 2005 by Charles Gaines. Used by permission of the author.

“Witness to Change,” by Roy Hoffman. Courtesy of *The Mobile Register* 2001 ©. All rights reserved. Reprinted with permission.

“Green Like the Green Mamba,” by Elaine Orr. *The Gods of Noonday: A White Girl’s African Life* reprinted by permission of the University of Virginia Press. Copyright © 2003 by the Rector and Visitors of the University of Virginia.

Excerpts from “Piece by Piece” by Molly Peacock. First published in *Black Warrior Review*. Reprinted in the memoir *Paradise Piece by Piece* by Riverhead Books. Copyright © 1998 by Molly Peacock. Reprinted by permission of the author.

“River of Silence,” by Luke Wallin. First published in *Baile*, University College Dublin. Copyright © 1998 by Luke Wallin. Reprinted by permission of the author.

WRITING FOR CHILDREN

Chapter One of Susan Campbell Bartoletti’s novel *No Man’s Land*, was published by Blue Sky Press. Copyright © Reprinted by permission of Susan Campbell Bartoletti.

“Great Gobs of Goose Grease” by Louella Bryant. Copright © 2005 by Louella Bryant. Used by permission of author.

“Grandfather Rattlesnake,” by Luke Wallin. First published in *Ceremony of the Panther* by iUniverse.com, Inc. Copyright © 1987, 2001 by Luke Wallin. Reprinted by permission of the author.

PLAYWRITING & SCREENWRITING

“Superstore,” by Sam Zalutsky. Copyright © 2003 by Sam Zalutsky. Reprinted by permission of Sam Zalutsky.

"Propinquity," by Claudia Johnson was first commissioned and produced by Actor's Theatre of Louisville. Reprinted by permission of Claudia Johnson.